RACE OVER EMPIRE

286 4457

ERIC T. L. LOVE

Race over Empire

RACISM AND U.S. IMPERIALISM, 1865–1900

The University of North Carolina Press

Chapel Hill and London

© 2004 The University of North Carolina Press

All rights reserved

Manufactured in the United States of America

Designed by C. H. Westmoreland

Set in Minion by Keystone Typesetting, Inc.

The paper in this book meets the guidelines for
permanence and durability of the Committee on
Production Guidelines for Book Longevity of the
Council on Library Resources.

Library of Congress Cataloging-in-Publication Data

Love, Eric Tyrone Lowery, 1965–

Race over empire : racism and U.S. imperialism,

1865–1900 / Eric T.L. Love.

p. cm.

Includes bibliographical references and index.

ISBN 0-8078-2900-5 (alk. paper)

ISBN 0-8078-5565-0 (pbk. : alk. paper)

1. United States—Foreign relations—1865–1898.

2. United States—Territorial expansion.

3. Imperialism—History—19th century. 4. Racism—

Political aspects—United States—History—

19th century. I. Title.

E661.7.L685 2004

325′.32′097309034—dc22

2004009096

cloth   08 07 06 05 04   5 4 3 2 1

paper   08 07 06 05 04   5 4 3 2 1

To William Love (1905–1984)

the hero of my life

Contents

Preface xi

CHAPTER ONE American Imperialism
and the Racial Mountain 1

CHAPTER TWO Santo Domingo 27

CHAPTER THREE The Policy of Last Resort 73

CHAPTER FOUR Hawaii Annexed 115

CHAPTER FIVE The Philippines 159

Epilogue 196

Notes 201

Bibliography 219

Index 241

Illustrations

President Ulysses S. Grant 34

Senator Charles Sumner 51

Carl Schurz 54

Queen Liliuokalani 77

Uncle Sam defends Hawaii from imperial Britain 91

Sanford Dole 117

President William McKinley 163

Senator Henry Cabot Lodge 173

President McKinley ponders the fate of the Philippines 180

Preface

This book is about race, racism, and U.S. imperialism from 1865 to 1900, from the end of the Civil War to the annexations that followed the Spanish-American War. It was originally conceived as a critical reinterpretation, as a challenge to the prevailing narratives on race and American imperialism which insist that racial ideologies, ascendant in the last years of the nineteenth century—Anglo Saxonism, social Darwinism, benevolent assimilation, manifest destiny, and the "white man's burden"—worked most significantly to advance empire.

Past accounts have claimed that white supremacy—elaborated in history, culture, tradition, custom, law, and language—armed the imperialists of 1898 with a nearly impenetrable rationale for seizing Cuba from Spain; annexing Hawaii, Guam, Puerto Rico, and the Philippines; and taking in the millions of people who inhabited these places: peoples whom the vast majority of Americans considered biologically and culturally inferior, alien, and unassimilable. The chapters that follow challenge this convention. They demonstrate that racism had nearly the opposite effect: that the relationship between the imperialists of the late nineteenth century and the racist structures and convictions of their time was antagonistic, not harmonious (and no class understood this more acutely than the foreign policy establishment itself); that imperialists, contained by the expectations and demands of the racial social order, neither spoke nor acted in the manner usually presented in the historical literature; that they did not overwhelm the racist invective of the anti-imperialists with more potent racial rhetoric (fighting fire with fire); that, instead, they reacted with silences, disingenuous evasions, and denials that race had anything to do with their expansionist projects. In short, imperialists knew what most historians in recent years have overlooked: that in an era marked by as much racial fear, hatred, reaction, and violence as the last decades of the nineteenth century—by the collapse of Reconstruction; the reversal of civil rights and equal protections, condoned by the U.S. Supreme Court; by the final suppression of Native Americans; by the defeat of the Federal Elections Bill of 1890 (called the "Force Bill" by its enemies); by segregation, disfranchisement, and the lynching of thousands of African Americans; by immigration restriction and other reactions against the so-called new immigrant groups, such as the founding of the American Protective Association and the Immigration Restriction League; by Chinese exclusion and gentlemen's agreements—no pragmatic politician or party would fix nonwhites at the center of its imperial policies. Yet that is precisely what the rhetoric of "benevolent assimilation" and the "white man's burden" would have done and what the dominant narrative insists the student of history believe.

In this book, *racism* is defined generally as exclusionary relations of power based on race. It can be understood more specifically as the sum of culturally sanctioned beliefs, practices, and institutions that establish and maintain a racial social order. In the period of history considered here, racism upheld social hierarchies and systems of privilege and oppression based on the conviction that whites were, by every measure, superior to all nonwhite people. In short, the principal goal of the late-nineteenth-century racial social order was the exclusion of those racial and ethnic groups cast as "nonwhite" from equal access to and participation in America's economic, political, social, and cultural mainstream.

This pattern was not unique to the late nineteenth century. It was, in fact, a defining characteristic of the United States from the time of its founding, when the "master passion of the age," in the words of one historian, "was erecting republics for whites," to the middle of the twentieth century, when the civil rights movement began to dismantle the most gratuitous and brutal elements of the old racial social order.[1] No one can doubt that the United States was originally conceived as a white nation or deny that the deliberate and systematic exclusion of nonwhites was a vital part of American nation building throughout the nineteenth century. The conviction that nations—in particular, great nations—should be racially and culturally homogeneous preceded the founding of the United States and contributed powerfully to its formation (Benjamin Franklin's faith in this, embedded in his "Observations on the Increase of Mankind," was, as we will see, representative in his time as well as the century that followed). The Naturalization Act of 1790, the first definition of citizenship established by Congress, granted that status to whites exclusively. Early antislavery sentiment was also informed by these precedents. The movements and organizations that arose from them worked in relation to the common prejudice that bi- or multiracial democracy was inconceivable, that it was the formula for an irrepressible social, political, and racial catastrophe. Colonizing free blacks outside the United States became, then, the necessary amendment to their emancipation schemes.

Where, during the early national and antebellum periods, free African Americans congregated, segregation and disfranchisement dogged their communities. History shows discrimination in labor, enforced informally and often violently, by whites fiercely determined to guard work as a species of racial privilege. It also reveals patterns of formal discrimination where, on one side, the legislatures of slave states passed laws forcing emancipated blacks to leave and, on the other, politicians of free states prohibited (or heavily taxed) blacks who would migrate in, where they could compete with white citizens for land, employment, resources, and sundry opportunities.

More instances where white predominance (often based on a narrow, peculiar, exclusionary understanding of *whiteness*) was the "master passion" rise out of the historical landscape like jagged massifs: General George Washington's order to forbid the enlistment of black troops during the Revolution (and its ratification by the Continental Congress); the Alien and Sedition Acts; the government's refusal to extend recognition of independent Haiti, the "black republic"; the Indian wars, followed by federal removal and containment policies; at midcentury, the anti-Irish, anti-Catholic paranoia and the popular fear of creeping "popery"; the grave "threats" to Anglo-Saxonism which gave birth to the nativist Know-Nothing Party; the failure of the "all Mexico" movement following the Mexican War; and the policies of exclusion and oppression—based on race, ethnicity, nationality, religion, and ideology—seen after 1877, cited above. The impenetrable and largely (though never completely) unquestioned conviction that the United States was a white nation and that every advance, domestic and foreign, should be pursued for the exclusive benefit of white citizens insinuated itself into and shaped every important expansionist project of the nineteenth century, and all constituted formations of a racial—and racist—social order.

By using *racism* as the book's central analytic concept, I had two intentions. First, I wanted to set aside the terms favored by much of the historical literature on race and the American empire. There can be no doubt that *race ideas*, *racialism*, and *race ideology* have deepened, widened, raised, and complicated our understanding of United States imperialism. My quarrel is not with the words or the concepts themselves but rather with the way historians have applied them in analyzing the past. Too often these terms have been used in ways that obfuscate, that create serious teleological problems; in ways that suggest conclusions which cannot be reconciled with the extant evidence; and in ways that either arrive at or suggest conclusions which are misleading or ahistorical. The problems that these terms create, as well as the ways I believe *racism* removes them, are discussed in the first chapter. My second purpose was to provoke controversy—a predictable reaction when one calls a thing (*racism* in this instance) by its proper name and challenges a familiar, long-standing historical assumption—while presenting a compelling narrative.

This book focuses mainly on the thoughts, words, and actions of policymakers. At a time when the discipline has turned so much of its attention to recovering the histories of women, minorities, workers, and other marginalized groups, has embraced the methods of cultural and literary theory, and in certain quarters has shown a decided preference to transnational and comparative research, some readers may consider this approach as retrograde or too traditional to produce new or significant results. However it is regarded, the logic behind this strategy is simple, direct, and, I think, incontrovertible: to understand how race and racism affected the formation of imperial policies, we must focus our efforts, first, on the makers of those policies.

While recovering the stories of these policymakers from the published sources and the archives, I kept in mind certain criticisms that have been aimed at traditional diplomatic history, two in particular: the suggestion that it has, in the past, concentrated too much and too narrowly on a few elites who appear in many accounts to have lived, worked, and directed the nation's foreign relations from a place where they were untouched by the social forces of their time; and the assertion that it has in the main ignored, to its detriment, methods drawn from the social sciences as well as the intricacies of gender, culture, class, environment, and so on. Considering this, I recalled Karl Marx's *Eighteenth Brumaire of Louis Bonaparte* (1852), in which he observed: "Men make their own history, but they do not make it as they please; they do not make it under circumstances chosen by themselves, but under circumstances directly found, given, and transmitted from the past." British historian J. M. Roberts elaborated: human beings, he wrote, "make history and sometimes do so consciously," but they are limited because they can only do so "with materials they find on hand, the ideas that they and others have confidence in, their notions of what is possible, and what impossible—in short, within conditions set by circumstances and the past."[2]

Recovering for myself the ideas and knowledge that policymakers inherited and embraced (largely without question) helped me to decipher and translate into narrative most of what I found during the research phase of this project. Discovering what was history to these policymakers and what the past meant to them—the powers it conferred as well as the burdens and limitations it imposed—explained only a fraction of their thoughts and actions. The influence, the weight, and inertia of the past—which was the essence of Marx's observation—explained *the past*, but it did not necessarily account for what Roberts called the "conditions set by circumstances," which I interpreted to mean, for purposes of analysis, the immediate social, political, and economic context in which politicians imagined, formed, and executed their policies. The pulls of the past and the present, then, were sometimes but not always the same. The distinction was often significant.

These insights I applied to how I thought about the subjects at the center of this book. All were tethered to their world, to the people, institutions, and ideas all around them, in ways that were both obvious and unseen. Further along, while writing, I kept in mind a lesson drawn from astronomers who have in the most ingenious way discovered planets orbiting very distant stars: not by direct observation—despite their titanic mass, the distances are far too great, even for the most powerful telescopes—but indirectly. The gravity of those giant, unseen worlds tug on the stars, causing them to move, to change appearance, or, in astronomical terms, to "wobble." As I worked through the archives I found something analogous. I saw my policymakers wobble.

The wobble had multiple sources originating from the past and contemporary times, from ideas the policymakers inherited and internalized as well as the weight and inertia of history, all of which told them (following Roberts) what was and was not possible. Race and racism loomed large in their reckonings. The extant evidence demonstrates clearly that these men were guided—though their actions were never dictated—by racist sentiments and prejudices, by precedents and expectations forged in the past: among them, that territorial expansion had been circumscribed, historically, by the con-

[handwritten margin notes: "racism, white supremacy"; "Condition, set by"; "Circumstance"; "not good"; "for expansion"]

victions that the United States was a white nation, by ideas about whiteness and a constellation of beliefs regarding the alleged inferiority of nonwhite peoples. Private and public writings reveal that most policymakers confronted the demands of the racial social order not with a sense of celebration or liberation but with resignation, often with regret and frustration, and acceptance of the limits they imposed.

The balance of evidence contains tantalizing indications that the racism arising from the white labor class and public leaders who exploited the fears of white workers—a constituency of millions of voters spread across the nation—had the greater influence over imperial policy formation than the writings of several social Darwinist intellectuals and propagandists: a group of men who, besides being minuscule in number, could not even agree among themselves whether their pseudoscientific faith required them to uplift so-called inferior races, Catholics, and new immigrant groups, or quarantine them.

This study is organized around four attempts by American policymakers, made between 1865 and 1900, to annex territories away from the continent that were occupied by significant numbers of nonwhite people. The cases selected are, the reader will discover, conventional and, although lesser cases have been omitted, representative. Chapter 1 provides an introduction and background. Borrowing Langston Hughes's grand metaphor, I argue that a racial mountain has stood in the way of a full and accurate account of how race and racism moved, shaped, advanced, and constrained American imperialism in the decades after the Civil War.

Chapter 2 is a treatment of President Ulysses S. Grant's effort in 1870 to annex Santo Domingo, now the Dominican Republic. Privately, Grant acknowledged the racial elements of his policy and in private wrote about them in considerable detail. He believed that if the island-nation was annexed it would serve as a refuge for the former slaves, part of a postbellum colonization scheme that Grant hoped would quicken the advance of sectional reconciliation and restore peace to the South. This chapter demonstrates that so long as the treaty was alive, in the Senate and before the public, the president kept this element of his policy—the part that placed African Americans at the center, positioning them as its main beneficiaries—deliberately hidden. Grant was certain that racism would quash ratification. His apprehensions were well founded. Opponents of expansion into the tropics turned racism and the racist ideology of the Reconstruction era against the treaty and defeated it, soundly. Only when the treaty was dead and Grant was desperate to vindicate his failed policy, his administration, and himself, did he reveal, in a series of explanations that shifted dramatically over time, the racial elements of his annexation scheme. To the eve of his death, Grant would insist that his policy of racial separation through annexation was just and correct.

Chapters 3 and 4 describe the nation's attempts to annex Hawaii in 1893 and again in 1897 and 1898. Although the 1893 initiative failed for many reasons, pillars of the racial social order, both old and newly raised, in particular the Chinese Exclusion Act (passed by Congress in 1882 and renewed in 1892) blocked its way. Chapter 4 puts forth the argument that the annexationists succeeded in 1898 not because they exploited concepts of racial uplift and the "white man's burden" but because, in the ferocious racial climate of those years, they rejected them. Anti-imperialists cast Hawaii as a distant, exotic island chain dominated by degenerate races, by indolent natives and tens of thousands of unassimilable Chinese, Japanese, and Portuguese workers. In response the imperialists rationalized annexation by insisting that these groups did not matter, that the islands should be taken not for their sake and not to uplift them, but despite them. They insisted that Hawaii should be annexed because it was, in fact, a *white* nation. The racial justification that prevailed in this case privileged white racial brotherhood, not white supremacy, not benevolent assimilation.

The final chapter demonstrates that the imperialists succeeded in annexing the Philippines not by exploiting race as the dominant narrative portrays but because they were able to cover it over with distracting appeals to war fervor, jingo patriotism, and politics. President William McKinley largely ignored race while making his decision to annex the Philippine Islands as a condition of peace (to the extent he acknowledged race, it was, in his mind, a discouragement). When the treaty came to the Senate, however, racism showed itself again to be a formidable obstacle to expansion. The imperialists worked with no small amount of ingenuity to disconnect racism from the annexation policy. First, they proposed to take only enough of the archipelago to build a naval base, a course that would have absolved the United States of any responsibility for the ten million inhabitants. When this plan was exposed as impracticable, policymakers considered taking only the island of Luzon and leaving the remaining seven thousand (of which approximately four hundred were inhabited) to the mercy of the other great powers. When, finally, on the advice of military strategists McKinley determined that America must take the entire chain, the annexationists hid the race issue behind the rhetoric of duty and national honor.

Race was an imperfect crusading ideology: far too volatile a thing, politically, for the imperialists to place at the center of their furiously contested campaign. By the end of the nineteenth century, policymakers had learned to accommodate and compromise with the demands of the domestic racial social order. Their success in 1898 was the result of compromise as well as clever backroom bargaining, favor trading, bribery, and other kinds of political chicanery, all necessary to disarm skeptics and opponents of the treaty and maintain discipline among its supporters. Even with all these maneuvers, the treaty passed by a single vote. No reading of the poems of Rudyard Kipling or appeals to the Mississippi Plan could have done this. Race would serve the imperialists well after annexation was a fact, but what was fine as ex post facto rationalization was, in the course of policy formation, bad politics.

This book can be understood in part by briefly taking account of what it is not. It is not a general history of U.S. foreign relations or imperialism, nor does it attempt to articulate a new theory of empire. It is not intended to be a retelling of the battle between imperialists and anti-imperialists. Though by necessity it mentions pivotal moments in the war of 1898, this book is not a military history. Several episodes found in this book reveal that racism did occasionally undermine initiatives that would have opened new markets, but I do not (intentionally) challenge interpretations that have placed economic and commercial motives at the center of imperial policy formation. For example, in the 1870s and 1880s, trade with China was jeopardized by virulent anti-Chinese sentiment, much of it concentrated in California, the state that might have gained the most from improved commercial relations with East Asia. Local, racialized confrontations in that state's labor market between Chinese immigrants and native whites competing for work eclipsed foreign markets in importance. The lessons to be drawn from this episode are telling, and their significance—both in the context of the pages that follow and in their broader implications—should not be underestimated: first, we see that local, state, and regional agendas could frustrate, and even trump, national designs; second, when expansionism collided with the demands of the domestic racial social order, the latter—white privilege, manifested in this instance in the labor market and union activism—demanded, unequivocally, and almost always received priority. In foreign policy, then,

just as at home, Joel Williamson has observed, white Americans were willing
to foot the bill for their racism.[3]

A final word. This book is based on the premise that in the long history of
the United States, racism has always been destructive toward innovation and
progressive change. The findings presented throughout this book only reaffirm that belief in my mind. Racism is not simply a burden borne by its
most obvious victims: it was a problem of power as well. The dominant narrative's insistence that racism effectively loosened the restraints on policymakers, allowing them to advance outward and extend their domination
over territories and peoples at will, strikes me as disturbing, and not simply
because this presumption—if my argument is correct—is for the most part
historically inaccurate. Convictions of American exceptionalism, in those
instances where it has been corrupted by white supremacy, deformed the
nation's capacity to engage with much of the world on a just, moral, equal,
and democratic basis consistent with its creed. Certainly, without the re-
straint of racism, our interactions with peoples of color around the world
over more than two centuries might have been more constructive, materially
and morally, than they have been.

Debts are owed to many people who helped with the research and writing of
this book. Thanking them is a great pleasure. James M. McPherson, Daniel
T. Rodgers, Kevin K. Gaines, and the late Richard D. Challener provided the
intellectual inspiration, guidance, direction, and indispensable criticism that
shaped this project from its conception. Along the way other scholars I have
had the privilege to know shared their considerable knowledge and wisdom.
I thank Reid Mitchell, Sean Wilentz, Christine Stansell, Fred Greenstein, and
especially William Chester Jordan and John Murrin.

Generous financial support was provided by the American Historical Association, the Center for Domestic and Comparative Policy Studies at
Princeton University, the Ford Foundation, the Andrew J. Mellon Foundation, the Society of Fellows of the Woodrow Wilson Foundation, and the
University of Colorado at Boulder. In 1999–2000 the Princeton University
History Department welcomed me as a visiting research fellow, a crucial
year in the history of this book. Sincere thanks go to Judith Hanson for her
assistance and support.

My research was facilitated by the holdings and staff of many fine research
libraries and archives. I wish to express my gratitude to the Firestone Library

at Princeton University, the John Hay Library at Brown University, the Houghton Library at Harvard University, the Sterling Library and Beineke Rare Book Library at Yale University, the Library of Congress, the Massachusetts Historical Society, the Joseph Regenstein Library at the University of Chicago, the Norlin Library at the University of Colorado at Boulder, and the Hawaii State Archives. While at the Hawaiian Historical Society I benefited greatly from the courteous, expert assistance of Barbara Dunn.

Many scholars and friends read the manuscript in its various stages, talked points through with me, and listened patiently while I sorted through it all. Each provided intellectual, spiritual, and occasionally material sustenance. I thank Benjamin Alpers, Steven Aron, Kathy Baima, Julie Barnett, Susan Basalla, Alistair Bellamy, Lisa Bitel, Sharon Block, Jennifer Delton, Vince DiGirolamo, Janice Earle, Jonathan Earle, Logan Fox, John Giggie, Brad Gregory, Jennifer Jasa, Walter Johnson, Steve Kantrowitz, Josh Landy, Adam Leffert, Pamela Main, Peter Mancall, Michael Millender, Darryl Peterkin, Geoff Plank, Chris Rasmussen, Peggy Reilly, Daniel Seidman, Kim Spaulding, Leslie Tuttle, and Henry Yu.

Warm thanks are extended to my colleagues at the University of Colorado at Boulder for their close, incisive readings and suggestions: Fred Anderson, Abigail Dyer, Steven Epstein, Padraic Kenney, Patricia Nelson Limerick, and Ken Orona.

It has been a great pleasure to work with the University of North Carolina Press, especially with Chuck Grench, Amanda McMillan, and Paula Wald. I would also like to thank Lew Bateman of Cambridge University Press.

The deepest thanks I reserve for my mother, Rosalyn Byrd, and grandmother, Ruth Castleberry. Eddie Castleberry supported me with bootstraps when I needed them most. Mary Flynn has been my lifeline, a true friend in countless ways. Bill Doonan remains the best and most constant influence on my life. To my great-grandparents, William and Lula Love, I owe everything.

RACE OVER EMPIRE

CHAPTER ONE

American Imperialism
and the Racial Mountain

Race is and will remain a vital part of the story of American imperialism. That it loomed large in the minds of policymakers, that it was a potent force in nation building, policy formation, and expansionism, has been demonstrated repeatedly and convincingly in the historical literature. In answer to the question at the center of this book—how did race move, shape, and even perhaps inspire late-nineteenth-century U.S. imperialism?—there is a remarkable level of consensus among historians, who assert that racial ideologies rooted in white supremacy gave expansionists a grand and compelling rational for empire. Anglo-Saxonism, social Darwinism, benevolent assimilation, and the "white man's burden"—almost unassailable elaborations of white supremacy—justified the annexations that followed the war with Spain in 1898, brought millions of people of color under the jurisdiction of the United States, and helped to elevate the nation to the status of a world power. The pages that follow challenge this convention; they begin with a critical review of the literature. While the reigning narrative on race and empire has recovered significant aspects of the past, it has also been fettered by clearly identifiable and long-standing problems. Put another way (borrowing Langston Hughes's most elegant metaphor), it can be said that a racial mountain stands between historians and an accurate accounting of race, racism, and late-nineteenth-century American imperialism.

The conventional narrative can be summarized briefly.[1] In the three decades following the Civil War, an expansionist, market-oriented foreign policy evolved that gave America's global affairs renewed logic, coherence, motive, and direction. The search for markets, for dependable outlets for the nation's massive and growing agricultural and industrial production, advanced with each passing year. It was a restless, aggressive movement, infused with a peculiar urgency by the cycle of economic growth and collapse that occurred in every decade between 1870 and World War I. Leading economic theorists of the era believed the cause of the recurrent booms and busts was "overproduction." American capitalism suffered, they said, because it had become too efficient, too productive. Ironically, it had become too successful for its own good. Inventing, assembling, building, sowing, and reaping more than domestic markets could absorb destabilized the economy, drove tens of thousands of businesses into bankruptcy and millions of workers out of jobs, and fed what was, by the standards of the time, a species of social malaise of the most fearful kind. Farmers and the urban working classes turned to political radicalism: toward insurgent populism, unionism, socialism, public demonstrations, and protests that all too frequently exploded into violent (and occasionally murderous) confrontations with capital. The solution to overproduction and the attendant social chaos, theorists said, was to find and open new markets abroad where the excess production could be sold off, profitably. This would lift the economy, employment, and wages and suppress political and class tensions. It was a beguiling stratagem embraced by a mass of followers: agrarians and industrialists, social theorists and economists, public intellectuals, missionaries, military men, and others, all of whom subscribed to a common vision of natural greatness whose prerequisite was empire. As this outward advance brought the United States into contact with nations thickly populated with polymorphous, dark-skinned peoples—literally millions of individuals consigned by science, theology, sentiment, prejudice, history and tradition to a class of inferior races—these accounts maintain that at home white supremacist ideas saturated the culture, dissolved the class, sectional, religious, and ethnic divisions among whites, and unified that race.

In this interpretation, white supremacy became an indispensable feature of the imperial project. Nell Irvin Painter, for example, wrote that "[i]n justification for empire, Anglo-Saxonism combined variously with arguments for Anglo-American identity, the white man's burden, manifest and ordinary destiny, and duty." Painter went on to say that imperialism "rose above politics and laws because within the unity that was human history, Americans [believed that they] were playing a pre-ordained role. Imperialism," she insisted, "was elemental, racial, predestined." Alan Dawley stated that racial nationalism fueled the outward thrust and cited as evidence statements by the Reverend Josiah Strong ("Strong expanded Manifest Destiny from continental to global dimensions, writing of 'the final competition of races'") and Senator Albert Beveridge regarding the duty of English-speaking nations to govern "savages and senile peoples."[2]

Though Michael H. Hunt maintained that race "served equally as a reason for a cautious self-limiting policy and as justification for a bold, assertive one," he concluded that in the final account, race ideology favored imperialism. "Had the issue of [annexing Hawaii and the Philippines] been resolved on the basis of racial arguments alone," Hunt wrote, "the opposition might well have stymied the McKinley administration." Annexation triumphed in 1898 in large part, he said, because the imperialists "could play more directly on Anglo-Saxon pride" than those who opposed expansionist policies on racial grounds. Charles S. Campbell agreed that race ideology's effect on imperial policy was ambiguous: "it led to a belief in the righteousness of annexing supposedly inferior people," he observed, "but it led also to a disinclination to annex them, out of fear that the superior [racial] stock would be depreciated." Like Hunt, Campbell, in the final account, set his ambivalence aside and declared: "whereas racism was a deterrent [to territorial imperialism] in the 1870s, it was not in the 1890s. On balance," he concluded, "the belief in Anglo-Saxon supremacy encouraged territorial expansion at the end of the century."[3]

Within this body of work, historians drew a direct connection between empire and the rise of a rigid, often brutal domestic racial social order: what Rayford Logan famously called "the nadir" of the African American experience and American race relations. According to Joseph Fry, in the years after the Civil War, social Darwinism "provided an ostensibly scientific rationale" for racial oppression at home and imperialist aggression abroad. Emily Rosenberg concurred. In the 1890s, she wrote, "[c]oncepts of racial mission, so well rehearsed at home, were easily transferred overseas." Many scholars were persuaded. Especially influential were observations that historian C. Vann Woodward put forth in both *Origins of the New South* and *The Strange Career of Jim Crow*, where he explained that by 1898 "[t]he North had taken up the White Man's Burden" and "was looking to southern racial policy for national guidance in the new problems of imperialism resulting from the Spanish war." Woodward pushed his assertion further, declaring that the imperialists modeled their policies not just on ideas borrowed from the old

Confederacy but also on the actual framework and structures of the South's antiblack social order. "The Mississippi Plan," he explained, "had become the American way."[4]

Though they pursue a diversity of subjects, some of the most important recent works on the cultures of U.S. imperialism have embraced the prevailing narrative on race and empire and have taken its conclusions and implications as points of departure, reference, and authority. In *Black Americans and the White Man's Burden*, for example, Willard Gatewood conscripts Woodward's observation ("the nation's embrace of an imperialistic policy played an important role in transforming the 'Mississippi plan' of race relations into the American Way") as a framework for his study of African Americans' responses to and role in the quest for empire. In *All the World's a Fair*, Robert Rydell proceeds from this interpretation when he states that the "vision of the New South manifested at the southern fairs was . . . a powerful explanatory ideology that shaped the national and world outlook of untold numbers of . . . Americans." Expositions that took place in 1898 and after, spectacles "concomitant to empire," argues Rydell, served mainly to reaffirm familiar racial prejudices and justify what were, after the war with Spain, established policies: the "white man's burden" transformed into "knowledge" and entertainment.[5] In *Barbarian Virtues*, a study of the United States and its encounters with foreign peoples at home and abroad in the age of empire, Matthew Frye Jacobson uses a diversity of cultural sources to retell, in new but essentially familiar terms, the standard narrative of an imperial process, including the interactions between the domestic racial social order and expansion abroad. In this account, empire is still justified by convictions of white supremacy and rationalized by the "white man's burden."[6] Kevin K. Gaines used the dominant narrative as a point of departure in his study of the African American intellectual Pauline Hopkins, who, he argues persuasively, used the new imperialism to invent subversive antiracist discourses.[7] Besides the fact that still more scholars—Rubin Weston in *Racism in U.S. Imperialism* and Kristen Hoganson in *Fighting for American Manhood*, to give two more examples—have cited this narrative in perfunctory ways in their books, popular and highly regarded college textbooks continue to disseminate the narrative, a clear yet peculiar indication of the great authority the prevailing interpretation of race and empire retains through continued (yet largely uncritical) repetition and manipulation.[8]

Over time, then, a consensus has hardened around this interpretation. Evidence that it has shaped the critical dimensions of more recent scholarship indicates not only that it remains viable and popular but also that it might become part of a renewal of the study of late-nineteenth-century American foreign relations. In an essay on the state of the field, Edward Crapol wrote that diplomatic history could be revitalized if historians conquered their fear of the word "imperialism" and engaged the period using a conceptual framework "comparative in design and free of [the] ethnocentric and exceptional bias" that fettered past works. Such an approach, he explained, would integrate the methods of social history as well as findings drawn from newer works on racism and colonialism. This would begin the work of advancing the history of American foreign relations and rescue it from critics who have dismissed it as "a languishing intellectual backwater." Significantly, Crapol gave race only a passing mention in his essay (on the last page of a twenty-four-page article) and cited scholarship at the center of the conventional narrative as a model for future research.[9] For its general observations on imperial history, this essay deserves close attention, but on the specific matter of race and empire it suggests that the next stage of scholarship follow a model that is highly problematic.

Several aspects of the literature on race and late-nineteenth-century imperialism deserve reconsideration. Let us begin with the problems that arise from the analytic concept most favored by the conventional narrative: _racial ideology_. The term refers to the ascendance of white supremacist ideas—the conviction that people of European descent were inherently different from and universally superior to Native Americans, Mexicans, African Americans, Asians, and even certain European groups (in particular the so-called new immigrants, arrivals from the southern and eastern regions of the Continent who poured into the United States in this period). White supremacy benefited from the rise of pseudosciences that were alleged to provide both objective and quantifiable proof of the Anglo-Saxon's moral and intellectual superiority.

The first problem with racial ideology, already mentioned, is its ambivalence. However powerful and ubiquitous, the dominant racial ideas of the period provided no clear direction in foreign affairs, nor did they propose a program of action toward empire. Campbell, Hunt, Walter LaFeber, and others understood this. They conceded the point that white supremacist ideas could be mobilized equally well both for and against imperialism.[10] Therefore, the conclusion that they share, that race ideology facilitated the annexations of 1898, appears to be based less on argument and evidence than on a teleological assumption: that since the fierce resurgence of political and economic disfranchisement and lynching based on race coincided with the United States extending its domination over millions of people of color, the two must be connected—connected specifically in such a way that the former advanced the latter.

On the surface this is a compelling thesis, but it quickly comes up against serious difficulty. Historians who support this version of events have relied too much on generalization—Fry, Rosenberg, and Woodward, for example —and a small number of favored, often-repeated, and ambiguous sources and quotes. Josiah Strong, who had no direct say in policy formation and questionable influence on the larger culture, is one example. A second would be nearly every statement found in the conventional narrative that is attributed to Senator Albert Beveridge. Beveridge did not enter the Senate until 1899, weeks after that body ratified the treaty that brought the Philippines to the United States and months after Hawaii's annexation. Beveridge's words, then, are best understood yet almost never presented as ex post facto justifications, not as statements that had any substantive bearing on the making of imperial policy. Rudyard Kipling, author of the poem "The White Man's Burden," a third example, is perhaps the most misused. Many who call the poem into evidence, citing it as a classic exhortation to empire, ignore the fact that it appeared in McClure's Magazine in February 1899—after, not before, the United States seized its empire. Most also ignore the poem's churning irony and cynicism; its references to the contradictions of this crusade ("Take up the White Man's burden / The savage wars for peace / Fill full the mouth of Famine / and bid the sickness cease"), the Four Horsemen of the Apocalypse (war, famine, pestilence, and, by implication, death), and the seven deadly sins. The poem ends with a dark prophecy of the fate of imperialists, who would to Kipling's reckoning be reduced to servility, exile, and the cold judgment of their countrymen. This was hardly an appeal to the glories of empire.

The second problem of racial ideology as an analytic concept has to do with historical explanation. In Manifest Destiny and Mission in American History, Frederick Merk observed that until the late 1890s, race had acted as a powerful barrier to territorial acquisition.[11] There is little dispute over this point: it helps explain, for example, why the United States did not seize even more of Mexico in 1848; why it limited its acquisitions to Texas, an independent republic governed by whites, and the northern provinces where few native Mexicans lived; and why it stayed away from the more torrid and densely populated southern regions. No study so far, however, has presented a persuasive, evidence-based account demonstrating what factor or combination of factors reversed this pattern so suddenly and dramatically in 1898. The literature cites missionary impulses, market demands, and strategic necessity, but no one has shown how these parallel movements uprooted racist laws, structures, and institutions and overturned centuries of accumulated racial thought, then redirected them at the point where they intersected with the nation's expansionist traditions. The social Darwinists, whose literary and intellectual output is supposed to have turned the public mind and ushered in this change, on reexamination, hardly seem capable of such a feat.[12] Nor were the missionaries, whose labors in this regard were ambiguous, at best. Many did feel a strong and perhaps overwhelming sense of Christian duty and charity toward the races that had come into the American fold in 1898, especially the inhabitants of its Pacific acquisitions. But the Philippines were already an outpost of Christianity in East Asia; most of the Filipinos were Catholic, having been converted by the Spanish three hundred years earlier.[13] American missionaries had been active in Hawaii only since 1820, but as later chapters will show, their various writings —books, articles, pamphlets, and letters—probably did more to damage than support the expansionist cause, particularly on matters of and contiguous to race.

With regard to historical explanation, racial ideology fails to describe the course of policy formation as well as the behavior of the imperialists. Between 1865 and 1900 the United States tried to acquire Alaska, the Midway Islands, the Dominican Republic, Hawaii, the Philippines, Guam, and Puerto Rico. Until 1898, even though the prerequisite racial ideology existed, every attempt it made to purchase or annex territories populated by significant numbers of nonwhite peoples failed.[14] Race was central to each incident: the vital optic for nearly every participant and witness. Though both sides in the debates over empire shared an unshakable faith in white supremacy in each episode race ideas were used most openly, aggressively, and effectively by the enemies of imperialism. (Both pro- and anti-imperialists, Christopher Lasch explained, "saw the world from a pseudo-Darwinian point of view. They accepted the inequality of man—or, to be more precise, of races—as an established fact of life. They did not question the idea that Anglo-Saxons were superior to other people, and some of them would even have agreed that they were destined eventually to conquer the world.")[15] More significant, in each instance, while policies were being formulated and treaties were in Congress and before the public, the imperialists worked deliberately to avoid race. Put simply, references to social Darwinism, Anglo-Saxonism, benevolent assimilation, and the "white man's burden"— language on which the dominant narrative depends—do not appear at the center of the expansionists' discourse. As later chapters show, their silences were conspicuous and revealing, and the reasons for them can be easily discerned.

Specific issues of race trouble the prevailing interpretation. One rises out of its treatment of African Americans, who are typically portrayed as the archetypal victim of resurgent racism both at home and abroad. At a time when the term was appropriate, John Hope Franklin called the annexations of 1898 "America's Negro Empire." It was a profound insight at the time it was written and remains so, I think, because of, not despite, the dated racial reference.[16] Franklin accomplished two things here: he captured the *mentalité* of the majority of Americans who, to comprehend the awesome consequences of the war and its aftermath, lumped the inhabitants of the new possessions living in two oceans and set thousands of miles apart into categories of "Negro" and "black," a species of humanity they believed they knew well and understood thoroughly. Franklin also anticipated a narrative strategy, embraced by many historians, in which African Americans act as the conceptual bridge connecting domestic racial oppression and the domination of millions of people of color abroad. Franklin and Woodward had made much the same point with slightly different language: that the South's antiblack social order was, in theory and praxis, the model for the imperialism of the 1890s. The North, Woodward claimed, looked "to southern racial policy for national guidance" in 1898. Several difficulties emerge from this scheme. It suggests either that the North had no racist legacies of its own to turn to for instruction or that its racial strategies were considered but were judged to be insufficient to the task of empire building. Neither implication can stand under close scrutiny.

In *North of Slavery*, Leon Litwack correctly observed that the Mason-Dixon Line was "a convenient but often misleading geographical division" frequently used by scholars to "contrast southern racial inhumanity with northern benevolence and liberality."[17] He is correct. The North knew racism intimately. It knew slavery; compromised with the institution's demands; sympathized with its supporters; persecuted its enemies; and even while abolishing it gradually in its own states in the late 1700s and early 1800s, profited handsomely from its expansion in the South and the West.

Even though the northern states initiated gradual emancipation, African Americans—both former slaves and blacks who had never known slavery—living in them were systematically denied citizenship rights: the vote, access to work and education, and equal protection under the law. Alexis de Tocqueville wrote in *Democracy in America* that "the prejudice which repels the Negroes seems to increase in proportion as they are emancipated": that it was in the North that "the white . . . shuns the Negro with the more pertinacity," that the "prejudice of race appears stronger in the states that have abolished slavery than in those where it still exists." Since the time that Tocqueville wrote in the 1830s, historians have only confirmed his observations regarding the North:

> The electoral franchise has been conferred upon the Negroes in almost all the states in which slavery has been abolished, but if they come forward to vote, their lives are in danger. If oppressed, they may bring action at law, but they will find none but whites among their judges; and although they may serve legally as jurors, prejudice repels them from that office. The same schools do not receive the children of the black and of the European. In the theaters gold cannot procure a seat for the servile race beside their former masters; in the hospitals they lie apart; and although they are allowed to invoke the same God as the whites they must be at a different altar and in their own churches, with their own clergy. The gates of heaven are not closed against them, but their inferiority is continued to the very confines of the other world. When the Negro dies, his bones are cast aside, and the distinction of condition prevails even in the equality of death. Thus the Negro is free [in the North,] but he can share neither the rights, nor the pleasures, nor the labor, nor the afflictions, nor the tomb of him whose equal he has been declared to be; and he cannot meet him upon fair terms in life or in death.[18]

Over the length and breadth of the nineteenth century the North's institutions—state and local governments, public and private organizations, factories, churches, schools, and workers' unions—raised daunting barriers against African Americans as well as millions of immigrants from Ireland, Germany, Asia, and southern and eastern Europe. By 1898, then, the North had a long history and tradition of ethnic and racial repression to refer to for guidance in solving the problems of the new empire. It had no need to take lessons from the South. And a persuasive body of evidence shows that it did not.

The leading imperialists, a formidable group dominated by northerners, turned to the history of their section for direction; they took cues from its institutions and from the sentiments and prejudices of its people, not the South's, when forming their strategies of expansion. It cannot be coincidence that by 1899 the language and structure of American empire reflected northern priorities, culture, and sensibilities; that it acted in accordance to the paternalistic and accommodationist racism that prevailed in the North, not the racial extremism that had taken hold of the South.[19] The rhetoric of mission, duty, assimilation, and uplift conformed more closely with intellectual currents found in the North: in northern reform movements from abolition to temperance, reforms in education, prisons, and asylums, to the progressivism of the late nineteenth and early twentieth centuries. The symbols conjured up by the press and propagandists and exploited by the imperialists building up a rationale for empire—the schoolhouse, Uncle Sam as the stern teacher and headmaster over the "children" or wards of empire, the spreading of civilization through commerce and trade in industrial products, and even the emphasis on soap as a metaphor for the crusade against pollution and disease—stand as further evidence of a distinct northern bias that coursed through these policies.

Another problem connected with this narrative scheme is that it fixes analysis into a rigid, narrow North-South binary that diminishes (when it does not outright ignore) the role of the West, whose peculiar interests and prejudices affected, demonstrably, the course of American imperialism. On the matter of race, anti-Asian prejudice in the West—specifically the anti-Chinese movement of the 1870s, 1880s, and 1890s—takes on extraordinary significance, especially as we approach discussions of the annexations of Hawaii and the Philippines (where the African American example is neither particularly useful nor appropriate). In the decade before the Civil War, spurred by the gold rush, California's admission into the Union, the expansion of mining, agriculture, and railroad construction, contract labor was imported from China. The Burlingame Treaty of 1868 quickened the pace of this immigration (330,000 Chinese migrants entered the United States between 1850 and 1882). It recognized the "free migration and emigration" of Chinese visitors, traders, and "impermanent residents," as well as their right, while in the United States, to "enjoy the same privileges, immunities, and exemptions in respect to travel or residence . . . as the citizens or subjects of the most favored nation."[20] This meant, of course, that Chinese labor, though concentrated in California and the other Pacific states, was not necessarily bound to that region. It could go anywhere, and that, in the minds of many Americans, was the problem.

Wherever the Chinese went, sentiment against them soon followed, catalyzed by the fears of native white workers who reacted mostly with suspicion to their strange and unfamiliar culture, language, and "heathen" religion, but with hostility to their low standard of living and minuscule wages. Whites' fears of the Chinese "coolie" were exacerbated by men such as Dennis Kearney, a charismatic and violent nativist (even though he was, himself, an immigrant), who rose to lead California's Workingman's Party on the crest of this sinophobic wave, and Henry George, who, in his most famous and influential work, *Progress and Poverty*, railed against the "unassimilable" Asian hordes. While exclusion stemmed from the economic fears of the white working class in the far West, the movement had the support and sympathy of most Americans, who shared their blatant anti-Asian racism.[21]

By 1871, California's Republicans and Democrats were in a rough competition to appear and behave in a manner more anti-Chinese than their rival. By the middle of the 1870s, both parties had fixed exclusion planks into their national platforms. A cruel, cold logic could have easily predicted what next occurred. Congress put an end to the importation of contract labor in 1875. Five years after that, the Burlingame Treaty was revised so that the United States could regulate Chinese immigration however it saw fit, short of prohibiting it. The final measure came in 1882, when Congress passed the first Chinese Exclusion Act: the coup de grâce that for ten years formally barred Chinese nationals from entering the United States, denying them citizenship as well. In 1892, practically on the eve of the first attempt to annex Hawaii, the act was extended for ten more years. Chinese exclusion would become one of the most formidable obstacles in the path to empire.

To get beyond these problems, a new optic is needed. That optic might contain any number of elements, but if future investigations are to progress at all, four are essential: first, it must firmly reestablish the role of policy-makers and politics at the center of the imperial process, acknowledging the complexities of the human participants in this story and rejecting the prejudices against so-called white-male and top-down history; second, it should recognize and set aside assumptions, implicit in much recent work, that any past exercise of American imperial power abroad was morally wrong; third, it must employ an analytic concept that is more precise than *racial ideology*,

[margin note: racism as conceptual frame, rather than racial ideology]

one that possesses its interpretive strengths, transcends its pronounced weaknesses, and is historically appropriate (I shall build on statements made in the book's preface and elaborate further my case for *racism*); and fourth, it should interrogate more rigorously the role of *whiteness* in imperial policy formation.

[margin note: lumping complex human beings into categories]

To begin, rather than acknowledge policymakers as individuals and complex human beings, a pronounced tendency exists in the dominant narrative to lump them into a small number of abstract and, many times, biased and emotionally loaded categories. To a point this is appropriate—as when the actors identified themselves as "imperialists" and "anti-imperialists," Democrats, Republicans, and so on—but if the historian is not careful, the result may not be good history. Myth, caricature, and epithet may replace evidence and argumentation. Theodore Roosevelt provides the best example of what I have in mind. Despite many fine works that demonstrate this man's exceptional depth, complexity, and capacity for change and contradiction, he is still introduced in the context of the events of 1898 as "that damned cowboy," following Mark Hanna's braying yet famous comment; as the leading practitioner of an aggressive, quasi-imperial species of Victorian masculinity; as a man uncritically infatuated with war. His racist, expansionist, nationalistic arrogance is often "proven" in reprints of contemporary political cartoons that depict him straddling or wading through the Caribbean swinging a "big stick." Similarly, his imperialist brethren—ancestors such as William Henry Seward and contemporaries like John Hay, Henry Cabot Lodge, and Alfred Thayer Mahan—are called "insatiable," "ardent," "prolific," and "rabid" expansionists, committed social Darwinists and Anglo-Saxonists. Much is sacrificed and lost in this approach.

In a critique of this strategy in which classificatory categories substituted for real human beings, Tim Breen and Stephen Innes noted that while it had some advantages, it typically "leaves one with a sense that one knows a great deal more about an abstract category . . . and not much about the cultural and social interdependencies that gave meaning to people's lives."[22] It is a marvelous observation. The difference in our case is that the prevailing narrative, in most instances, does not even provide the reader with much of a sense of the complexities at the heart of those abstract categories. The evidence demonstrates that the line between imperialist and anti-imperialist was blurry more often than not and that it could shift, wildly and unpredictably, from person to person, incident to incident, and even within the same person during the same incident.

Race was often the motive force, smudging borders and altering allegiances. Charles Sumner and Carl Schurz wanted Alaska but opposed taking the Dominican Republic on racial grounds. Secretary of State Hamilton Fish's racism made him an opponent of African American rights at home and the annexations in the Caribbean, but he worked diligently for the acquisition of the Dominican Republic out of loyalty to President Grant. Senator George Frisbie Hoar of Massachusetts supported the annexation of Hawaii because he believed that the nonwhite element would soon be extinct, making room for white immigration, and opposed the annexation of the Philippines, defying his party's leadership, because he believed it was climatically inhospitable to whites. Senator John McLaurin gave one of the most aggressively racist anti-imperialist speeches delivered during the debates on the Philippines, yet he voted in favor of the acquisition because, off the senate floor, he cut a deal. On the matter of social Darwinism, it is clear that both sides rationalized their position using this theory—while men like Roosevelt appealed to it to justify empire, the Yale sociologist William Graham Sumner, generally acknowledged as the leading social Darwinist thinker of his time, was a staunch anti-imperialist—but how do we account for the divisions we see if not by understanding the idiosyncrasies of these men: the contradictions in their racial beliefs, the tensions between their racial attitudes and competing interests, and the indispensable role played by politics in each episode?

The next matter in need of consideration is put forth mainly as a suspicion, but one that I believe many will recognize: that a critical number of historians writing on 1898 from the vantage point of the postcolonial, post–civil rights, and post-Vietnam era in particular, work from an assumption that the past exercise of American imperial power was in nearly every case calamitous, unjust, and morally wrong. It is not my purpose to engage this position; indeed, there is no small amount of evidence that one could cite, both obscure and infamous and for which objective accounts are available, to support it: the array of treaties the United States government made with Native American tribes, then broke; Indian removal and the forced migration of fifteen thousand, a quarter of whom died from disease, starvation, and exposure en route to present-day Oklahoma; southern filibustering in the Caribbean and Central America; military participation in the overthrow of the leader of a sovereign nation, Hawaii, in 1893 (there were, according to the State Department, 103 interventions in the affairs of other countries between 1785 and 1895); and the bloody three-year war in the Philippines (an intervention some believe foreshadowed Vietnam) from 1899 to 1902. The twentieth century, the most violent in human history so far, provides only more (and more deadly and terrible) examples. At the time I am writing, the doctrine of preventive war, applied in a war on global terrorism, excites both defenders and critics who look to the past to justify their positions.

The issue at hand is not the politics of the moment but how judgments of the moment and good people who bring to their work anti-imperialist and antiracist sentiments might distort their renderings of the past. Here, the best example involves the Philippines. Few accounts of 1898 and America's actions there—annexation, the war to suppress the Filipino nationalists, the decades of occupation that preceded independence—are not critical (here I have in mind those works which explain the events of 1898 as being the result of a conspiracy of a few men, beholden to industrial capitalism and motivated by greed, fear of social revolution at home, and racism), but only a handful acknowledge what in all likelihood would have followed had the United States withdrawn from the islands and granted them full and immediate independence: a general war among several of the great powers and between the great powers and those same Filipino nationals. It is a sobering counterfactual that is supported by the extant evidence. Both Great Britain and Japan urged President McKinley to take and keep the entire archipelago in order to avert a war both nations seemed certain would come if the United States abandoned the islands.

There is no questioning the inhumanity of the Philippine-American war, and no good can come of any attempt to diminish it. But historians must recognize that its catalyst, annexation, was an imperfect decision dictated largely by nearly impossible circumstances created at home by a divided and unpredictable electorate and abroad by a local and geopolitical situation that was volatile long before the Americans plunged the nation, somewhat blindly, into its maw. Regardless of what the United States did, the predatory maneuverings of rivals Germany and France, Britain, Japan, and Russia would have collided with the desires of the Filipinos. Here was an irrepressible conflict. The only thing worse we can imagine than the calamity of the two-sided war that did occur would have been the three-, four-, five-, six-, or seven-sided conflict that annexation almost certainly prevented.

The next essential element of the new optic is an analytic concept that replaces race ideology: one that sustains its benefits and insights but is not choked by its ambiguities. I have chosen to use the term *racism* in this study as deliberately as some historians have avoided it, finding it too loaded or presentist.[23] As an analytic concept, racism can be utilized in ways that extend our knowledge, clarify our understanding of the past, and still be historically accurate and appropriate. Definitions of racism are now available to scholars whose work would be advanced by their use. This book was informed mainly by three. The first describes racism as culturally sanctioned strategies that defend social, economic, and political advantage on the basis of race. According to the second, racism is best understood not as hate speech or episodic acts of violence but as exclusionary relations of power based on race. Most recently, George Fredrickson wrote that racism must be understood as something more than "an attitude or set of beliefs; it also expresses itself in practices, institutions, and structures that a sense of deep difference justifies or validates. Racism," he concluded, "is more than theorizing about human differences or thinking badly of a group over which one has no control. It either directly sustains or proposes to establish a racial order, a permanent group hierarchy that is believed to reflect the laws and decrees of God."[24]

Just as *race* must be studied with respect to how it functioned and was maintained within a specific historical context, so must *racism*.[25] But when speaking of the last decades of the nineteenth century, is it appropriate to use a term that did not come into common usage until the 1930s? We can answer in the positive for two reasons. First, as is the case with many terms historians use, the phenomenon it describes existed before the word we use to describe it was invented.[26] Second, though the definitions of racism just cited draw from theory, they accurately describe the racial social order of the late nineteenth century. We know, for example, that a concept very similar to racism, *prejudice of color*, existed at this time and was a familiar and frequently used phrase in the public discourse. Those who fought with ferocious intensity to suppress the last impulses of resistance by Native American and remove them to reservations for the benefit of white settlers and speculators, to exclude the Chinese from the United States, to keep the African American "in his place" using legal, extralegal, and murderous methods, and put restrictions on the unwanted "new immigrant" groups, practiced "prejudice of color" and put it to use in the creation of a racist social order. They would recognize "racism" as a concept that described significant parts of their world, as would the antiracists of the age. Evidence left to us by the most reliable witnesses from the time confirms this thesis.

On 9 March 1892 three African Americans, Calvin McDowell, Thomas Moss, and Henry Stewart—respectable men: fathers, husbands, leaders of their community, and co-owners of a successful business, the People's Grocery—were lynched on the outskirts of Memphis, Tennessee, by a white mob. Their friend, Ida B. Wells, exposed the monstrous nature of the crime in her newspaper, the *Free Speech*. Wells was a bold and relentless crusader against lynching. She declared that those who justified the lynching of black men as just penalty for the rape of white women were knowing tellers of a "threadbare lie." The murder of her friends was but one tragic example. McDowell's, Moss's, and Stewart's "crime" was not rape but competing with a white-owned business. Lynching was unrivaled in the terror it imposed on black communities: the most brutal weapon in a broad arsenal of repression. It was about sex, but it was also a tool of political and economic oppression. Its purpose was to deny African Americans, through murder and intimidation, free and equal access to areas in public life where they might, through their own efforts, realize progress and power.

A second representative example of racism as exclusion is the prohibition of African Americans from the organizing bodies of the 1893 World's Columbian Exposition in Chicago. Black men and women protested; they agitated for inclusion in the planning committees and exhibits, but to no avail. Ferdinand Barnett called the event "our greatest National enterprise of the century," an event brought to life by "one all absorbing question . . . 'How shall America best present its greatness to the civilized world?' " No part of the answer would allow for a black contribution. Barnett and other protesters discovered that the "unwritten law of discrimination" meant total exclusion on every level, from representation on the National Board of Commissioners to "positions of no more importance than the Columbian Guards." Petitions failed to break the color bar. The final protest took the form of a extraordinary pamphlet coauthored by Barnett, Ida Wells, Irvine Garland Penn, and Frederick Douglass, titled *The Reason Why the Colored American Is Not in the World's Columbian Exposition*. In its final essay, Barnett summarized the black position with respect to both the celebration and the country. "Theoretically open to all Americans," he declared, "the Exposition practically is, literally and figuratively, a 'White City,' in the building of which the Colored American was allowed no helping hand, and in its glorious success he has no share."[27]

Over the last century, countless writers have cited from *The Souls of Black Folk*, W. E. B. Du Bois's penetrating account of the racist exclusions of this era: his prophecy that the problem of the twentieth century would be that of the color line, and the metaphor of "the veil." Though it is cited less frequently, a far more startling vision of racism's true nature appears only a few lines later. Du Bois was confident that he could "live above" the obstacles represented by the veil, but the mass of African Americans, not as fortunate as he, he wrote, "wasted itself in the bitter cry, Why did God make me an outcast and a stranger in mine own house?" Here, the veil gives way to a far more grim vision of racism and exclusion. "The shades of the prison-house closed round about us all," said Du Bois, "walls straight and stubborn to the whitest, but relentlessly narrow, tall, and unscalable to sons of night who must plod darkly on in resignation, or beat unavailing palms against the stone, or steadily, half hopelessly, watch the streaks of blue above."[28] Taken together, these testimonies indicate that African Americans would recognize the experience we call racism through language and violence but that in the final account they understood, felt, and described it on the level of everyday experience as exclusionary relations of power based on race. I have attempted to take full advantage of these definitions and interpretations in this book.

Revising the history of racism and empire must include rethinking that place which whiteness occupied in imperial policy formation: not just the idea of whiteness but also how multiple understandings of this race concept intersected with territorial expansion throughout the period in question. The first point to acknowledge is that whiteness was not fixed. White racial formation was a continuous process, catalyzed and altered by the individual and combined forces of industrialization, urbanization, mobility and advances in communication, the shifting dynamics of class and gender, immigration, the expansion and contraction of rights for racial and ethnic minorities, and imperialism. Also, as the chapters that follow demonstrate, divisions within the racial group called "white," along the lines of nationality, ethnicity, religion, class, section, and politics, mattered significantly in relation to how the acquisition of distant territories was negotiated and debated. Despite some of the assertions contained in the dominant narrative, Anglo-Saxonism, imperialism, and extending dominion over millions of nonwhites were poor solvents with respect to ending these divisions. While it facilitated an Anglo-American rapprochement, the effectiveness of this narrative at home in uniting white Americans behind an aggressive and controversial expansionist foreign policy—especially when they were divided, sometimes violently so, over countless other issues—was negligible.

Rethinking whiteness in the context of American imperialism would reveal, next, that white supremacy was an imperfect crusading ideology, flawed and enfolded in more contradiction and irony than is usually accounted for.[29] At present the historical literature does acknowledge one example of this contradiction: the battle between the imperialists and anti-imperialists, two separate and monolithic camps who shared a similar faith in white supremacy, we are told, but who turned it toward opposite ends. This account is only superficially correct. Ultimately it is misleading, because it can explain neither the defections that took place back and forth between the imperialists and anti-imperialists nor the reasons why imperialists conspicuously muted their racial rhetoric over the course of three decades, to cite just two examples.

A way through this problem comes into focus when one notes that even though both imperialists and anti-imperialists embraced the same white supremacist ideas, both were also beholden to them: sometimes vaguely, sometimes acutely, and for the imperialists no more oppressively and perilously than when their policies took them to the borders of distant and alien places dominated by nonwhites. The reasons for this are complex, but they began with three basic assumptions: first, that the United States was a white nation and, second, that great nations were homogeneous.

These ideas took shape before independence and were, therefore, present at the creation. In "Observations concerning the Increase of Mankind and the Peopling of Countries," Benjamin Franklin expressed his regrets that "the number of purely white people in the world" was "proportionately very small" and that the constant importation of Africans went on, displacing the white Englishmen he favored. He wanted more "Saxons" to come to America. "And while we are . . . scouring our planet, by clearing America of woods," Franklin asked, "why should we . . . darken its people? Why increase the sons of Africa, by planting them in America, where we have so fair an opportunity, by excluding the blacks and tawneys, of increasing the lovely white[?]"[30] The statement is representative: indicative of how race burrowed into the minds of the nation's founders. Slavery and the fate of the new African arrivals and free blacks loomed largest. Washington, Jefferson, Madison, and others pondered and wrestled with questions regarding the ultimate fate of Native Americans. The details of the founders' deliberations need not detain us long when their conclusions regarding the place that Africans, African Americans, and Native Americans would occupy can be summarized in a few words: they would exist—if they did not first stagger and tumble into extinction—in a place that was separate, unequal, and subordinate.

Throughout the early national and antebellum periods, the sentiments and prejudices articulated by Franklin in 1751—that he was "partial to the complexsion [sic] of my country" and that "such kind of partiality is natural to mankind"—were fashioned into national policy. The Naturalization Act of 1790, the first act of Congress to define American citizenship, declared that only free white immigrants could become naturalized citizens of the United States. In *Notes on the State of Virginia*, Jefferson, building on his 1777 proposal to the Virginia legislature to remove free blacks from the state, described a separation of the races in which whites remained and blacks were deported. To his mind this was necessary to avoid a race war, but closely related to this was Jefferson's vision of an "Empire of Liberty," populated almost entirely by his ideal citizen, the self-governing and virtuous yeoman farmer, who was most certainly white.

These foundational notions only gained strength over generations. The Society for the Colonization of Free People of Color and other groups that linked emancipation with colonizing former slaves abroad acted from the same impulse: a vision of a nation free of racial contrasts. In 1857, Chief Justice Roger Taney, in the majority opinion of the Dred Scott case, was speaking from a commonly held belief when he wrote that slaves and their descendants "had for more than a century . . . been regarded as beings of an inferior order, and altogether unfit to associate with the white race, either in social or political relations," that they were considered "so far inferior that they had no rights which the white man was bound to respect." To Taney's reckoning as well as the court's majority, this was the founders' intention: blacks were not men, much less citizens of the United States. The Declaration of Independence and the Constitution applied to whites exclusively. The following year from a stage in Galesburg, Illinois, Senator Stephen Douglas declared that "this Government was made by our fathers on the white basis . . . made by white men for the benefit of white men and their posterity forever." Thinking ahead to the postwar social order, President Lincoln plotted with Congress and the State Department to revive the old colonization scheme. In 1862, he told a delegation of black leaders that it was for their own good if they separated from whites and allowed themselves to be removed to another country, "in congenial climes, and with people of their own blood and race."[31] We see here that at least until the middle years of the Civil War, Lincoln's vision was of a white nation. This idea remained a powerful force through the remainder of the century.

The conviction that the United States was a white nation folded naturally into its expansion. Herein lies the third assumption: the overwhelming majority of Americans believed that territorial expansion should be for the principal if not exclusive benefit of whites. Whiteness served as perhaps the most compelling rationale and justification for all species of territorial aggression. It acted as a kind of shorthand for expansion: the unanswerable response to almost any question regarding who had the superior claim to the land. The belief that whites possessed the ultimate entitlement to the West was cast in both secular and religious terms. The principle at work was simple and direct: the people, the nation, the race that could draw the greatest production from the land had the superior right to possess it. Such a belief could only work in favor of white desires. In their eyes, history, technology, every objective measure of comparative productivity, and race science—from murky speculations that linked skin color to superior morality and intelligence, to the measuring of heads—provided self-evident proof of white superiority over the "savage" races. Indian removal, both before and after the Civil War, can be understood in this light. Frequently, the racial arrogance this begot was cast as the expression of divine will. "The white race [are] a land-loving people," Senator Thomas Hart Benton said in 1843. Whites had the right to conquer new space "and possess it," he declared, "because they used it according to the intentions of the Creator." This racial impulse was "founded in their nature and in God's command," he said, "and it will continue to be obeyed."[32]

Just beneath these examples of racial arrogance, entitlement, and bold declarations such as Benton's, we can begin to glimpse, ironically, sentiments and convictions that would circumscribe American territorial expansion. First, the land that was taken had to be put to good use: taken, in other words, with the purpose of working and developing it, drawing wealth from it. Acquiring new territories also had political consequences. Because of its anti-imperial, anticolonial roots and the requirements of its Constitution (as well as its silences), the majority conviction was that the United States could not hold land or govern its inhabitants in a colonial relationship. Therefore any land the nation annexed had to be incorporated into the Union.

Race informed these assumptions at every stage. According to popular belief, tradition, and history, expansion assumed a predictable course: new, contiguous territories would be occupied, settled, and improved by whites, most likely Protestant and northern European stock. In a period of time, the new territories would organize politically, and after achieving a prerequisite stage of self-government, they would approach the United States voluntarily and request admission into the Union. Once accepted into the Union, the new state's white occupants would be granted full citizenship. They would enjoy equal rights, protections, and privileges under the law. They would have two senators and proportionate representation in Congress. This assumption, grounded in race, would frame debates over empire throughout the nineteenth century; as noted before, there was never a time when race was not a source of uncertainty, a daunting massif in the way of the imperialists.

Jefferson's biographer Dumas Malone noted the hesitation that some felt over the purchase of the Louisiana Territory, engendered by doubts about the capacities of its inhabitants, who were described at the time as a mass of "Creole ignorance" as "incapable of self government as children."[33] A critic of Jefferson's, in the *Boston Columbian Sentinel* under the name Fabricus, condemned Louisiana as "a great waste, a wilderness unpeopled with any beings except wolves and wandering Indians." He grieved over the prospect that this vast territory would be "cut up into States without number, but each with *two votes in the Senate*."[34]   *Concern over LA. territory, Creoles*

These sentiments and concerns emerged again, only far more aggressively, during the Mexican War. Debates erupted over how significant a fraction of Mexico the United States might keep, an argument that turned on the issue of race. Some called for the annexation of the whole, but most were less land hungry, less predatory, and based their stand largely on racial and ideological grounds. The *Richmond (Va.) Whig* declared that it wanted neither Mexican soil or the "wretched population" that occupied it.[35] Senator John C. Calhoun, an expansionist with respect to Texas, an independent republic governed by whites, raged against the annexationist tide because he believed that conquering Mexico, holding it as a province, or incorporating it into the Union would rend the nation and inflict on it a violent "departure from the settled policy of the Government." Mexico's acquisition would be in "conflict with its character and genius," an act that would prove to be "subversive to our free and popular institutions." The discontinuity was clear in Calhoun's mind: it involved not the territory, not the land, but the Mexican people. Although the United States had taken territory before, Calhoun said, and "conquered many of the neighboring tribes of Indians," the nation "never thought of holding them in subjection, or of incorporating them into our Union."[36]   *land good, inhabitant bad*

The United States, Calhoun observed, had never "incorporated into the Union any but the Caucasian race." Absorbing Mexico would overthrow history, tradition, and assumptions of white nationalism. "[F]or more than half of [Mexico's] population are pure Indians," Calhoun declared, "and by far the larger proportion of the residue is mixed blood." Their inclusion would be akin to embracing corruption or introducing some awful infection into the United States. "Ours is the government of the white man. The great misfortune of what was formerly Spanish America," he said, "is to be traced to the fatal error of placing the colored race on an equality with the white."[37] He denounced "those . . . who talk about erecting these Mexicans into territorial governments, and placing them on equality" with American citizens. This, the senator argued, would be the worst of mistakes as no people of color had ever established and maintained a free government. "Are we to overlook this great fact?" he asked. "Are we to associate with ourselves, as equals, companions and fellow citizens, the Indians and the mixed races of Mexico?" Such a relationship, he predicted, would bring calamity to the nation, disasters that would be "fatal to our institutions."[38]

Senator William Henry Seward responded to the calls for annexing "all Mexico" with dismal warnings for his reckless colleagues. "Those states cannot govern themselves now," he said, asking rhetorically, "can they govern themselves better after they are annexed to the United States?" The answer to Seward's mind was no. He challenged his opponents to state clearly how they planned to govern the Mexican people. "Pray, tell me how. By admitting them as equals, or by proconsular power?" Neither option was acceptable to the senator. Seward wanted the territories but did not believe in acquiring territory by conquest. Nor did he want to allow more territory into the Union that could be carved up into slave states. He argued that Mexico would come to the United States in time.

To those senators anxious for more territory immediately, he said: "Have you not more passages already across your domain to open than you can open in fifty years? Have you not more gold and silver that you can dig in a hundred years?" Exigencies aside, Seward looked forward to the day when the western territories were occupied, organized, and securely integrated into the Union. Seward's vision, representative of his time, was also highly racialized. The West and eventually Mexico would be dominated by white Americans, men like himself. "Time," he said, "will speedily fill the regions which you already possess with a homogeneous population and homogeneous States; yet even long before that event . . . shall have come, this nation will have acquired such magnitude, such consistency, such strength, such unity, such empire, that Mexico, with her one million of whites, her two millions of mixed races, and her five millions of Aztecs and other aborigines, can be received and absorbed without disturbing the national harmony, impairing the national vigor, or even checking, for a day, the national progress." Biographer Frederic Bancroft concluded that Seward favored expansion not rabidly or recklessly but "merely in proportion to our capacity for absorption."[39] In other words, as a senator and later as secretary of state, Seward wanted more territory only when he believed the inclusion of non-whites would have no discernible impact on the prevailing social order.

What troubled Seward prior to 1870 weighed heavily on later imperialists. Questions of race, expansion, statehood, and citizenship were hardly abstractions in the imperial era. In the half century following the Civil War, twelve states joined the Union: Nebraska (1867); Colorado (1876); Montana, North Dakota, South Dakota, and Washington (1889); Wyoming and Idaho (1890); Utah (1896); Oklahoma (1907); and Arizona and New Mexico (1912). White supremacy never stood alone; on the critical issue of expansion and nation building, it was inseparable from politics and its characteristic entanglements and contradictions.

Two more ways in which race placed hard limits on American expansion deserve attention. The first, alluded to already, involves the nation's tradition of avoiding territories that were too densely occupied by "alien" races that could not be assimilated into the country under the standards mentioned above. The Mexico example demonstrates this best. Once the war commenced, distinctions were quickly made regarding which sections of Mexico could be annexed and which could not. California seemed preeminently satisfactory in part because of the smallness of its Mexican population. After declaring to his Senate colleagues in a February 1847 speech that the nation did not want any "deplorable amalgamation" with the people of Mexico either as subjects or citizens, Lewis Cass spoke of what Americans did desire: "All we want is a portion of territory, which they nominally hold, generally uninhabited, or, where inhabited at all, sparsely so, and with a population which would soon recede, or identify itself with ours."[40] Events following the end of hostilities closely followed Cass's vision. The Treaty of Guadalupe Hidalgo provided for citizenship to Mexicans living within the acquired territories, but California's state constitution, ratified in 1849, by limiting the right to vote to whites alone, obliterated this promise. And naturalization for the Mexicans living under American jurisdiction was still prohibited by the act of 1790. Even manifest destiny abided by the limits imposed by race and racism.

Finally, any new account of the history of whiteness and the imperial process must consider the belief in *white racial limitations* that held great sway in the nineteenth century: boundaries dictated by climate that, for anti-imperialists and imperialists alike—including Seward, Charles Sumner, Carl Schurz, James Blaine, and Henry Cabot Lodge—marked the limits of territorial expansion. These were hot and tropical places, points beyond which it was believed that members of the white race could not occupy, settle, develop, or transplant their institutions without suffering some moral or physical calamity.

The idea that whites were bound by the dictates of nature within a specific climatic zone can be traced back to the ancient Greeks. Hippocrates and Aristotle speculated that both the physical and temperamental differences between the races were caused by geography and climate, in particular heat and cold. To their reckoning, people with the finer virtues congregated in the temperate zone. Between the frigid regions and the torrid zone, Aristotle said, lived "the Hellenic race, which is . . . high spirited and also intelligent. Hence it continues free, and is the best governed of any nation, and if it could be formed into one state, would be able to rule the world."[41] In the first century A.D. the Roman geographer Pomponius Mela divided the earth into five zones: northern frigid, northern temperate, torrid, southern temperate, and southern frigid. According to Mela's *De situ orbis* (A description of the world), only the temperate zones were habitable to the people of his race. Occupants of the northern temperate zone were cut off from its southern counterpart by the interloping torrid region. Some of the particulars of these theories disappeared over the centuries, but others evolved and survived into the nineteenth century.

In the essay "Fate," Ralph Waldo Emerson spoke of "the sword of climate in the west of Africa, at Cayenne, at Panama, at New Orleans, cut[ting] off men like a massacre." Further along he quoted the Scottish anatomist and ethnologist Robert Knox, citing the list of "pungent and unforgettable truths" that Knox had catalogued in his treatise on science-based racism, *The Races of Men, a Fragment*, among them: "Every race has its own *habitat*," and "Detach a colony from the race, and it deteriorates." Alexis de Tocqueville embraced the same "truth" in his descriptions of the United States, its institutions and belief systems. "The geographical position of the

British race in the New World," he wrote, set between "the icy regions of the Pole" and "the burning climate of the Equator," is peculiarly favorable to its rapid increase." The Anglo-American was "therefore placed in the most temperate and habitable zone of the continent."[42]

As Tocqueville considered the matter further, his writings anticipated the problems the expansionists would face when the doctrine of useful occupation and convictions about race and climate collided. When policies looked to take men and women of European origin into regions outside the tropical zone, those policies were deprived of a powerful and compelling traditional rationale. As Tocqueville wrote: "[I]t is well known that, in proportion as Europeans approach the tropics, labor becomes more difficult for them. Many of the Americans even assert that within a certain latitude it is fatal to them." Though this belief was contradicted by experience—"I cannot believe," he said, "that nature has prohibited the Europeans in Georgia and the Floridas, under pain of death, from raising the means of subsistence from the soil"—in the last account Tocqueville conceded that white labor "would unquestionably be more irksome and less productive" in the hotter places.[43] As the following chapters demonstrate, these ideas were a leitmotif of the debates on empire in the late nineteenth century. In the minds of the imperialists, they aroused doubt and hesitation; for the anti-imperialists, the weight of history and tradition, the argument that the annexation of tropical places was dangerous and undesirable because their acquisition could never benefit whites, was a potent weapon.

It is the thesis of this book that in the last decades of the nineteenth century, the weight and inertia of all this history placed a range of formidable racial obstacles in the way of imperialists. I argue that as old obstacles were fortified by many new ones in an age marked by intense, ferocious, even murderous racism—the final suppression of Native Americans, the Chinese Exclusion Acts of 1882 and 1892, Jim Crow, the Mississippi Plan, *Plessy v. Ferguson*, countless race riots and lynchings—policymakers would not, and indeed did not, behave as the dominant narrative insists. They did not use the language of social Darwinism, benevolent assimilation, and the "white man's burden" when taking their arguments to the people: to do so would have had the effect of placing hated groups at the center of their policies, disfiguring them, guaranteeing their defeat. What follows, then, is a story of how the imperialists struggled against the obstacles thrown in front of them by a racial social order and how, in 1898, they overcame them. This book is not about how the imperialists manipulated racism to secure their empire (in actuality it reaffirms Thomas Holt's observation that while men create race, they cannot always make it do as they wish). Instead, it presents racism as a problem of power.

CHAPTER TWO

Santo Domingo

Lecturing in the spring of 1880, the writer John Fiske recalled from the legends of the Civil War a story of expatriate Americans living in Paris and a dinner party "at which were propounded sundry toasts concerning not so much the past and present as the *expected* glories of the great American Nation." Each celebrant praised "the unprecedented bigness of our country," and at the same time all looked forward to the end of the war, expecting the peace would breathe new life into and restore the nation's expansionist traditions. The vast borders of 1865, commended by the first guest, were, said the next, "far too limited a view of the subject." The key was to look forward, "to the great and glorious future which is prescribed for us by Manifest Destiny and the Anglo-Saxon race. Here's to the United States," he said, "bounded on the north by the North Pole, on the [s]outh by the South Pole, on the east by the rising and on the west by the setting sun." The party responded with a shout of jubilant, emphatic applause.[1]

The next guest to speak, "a very serious man form the Far West," insisted that if manifest destiny was the issue and not the historic past or present, then all the old, narrow limits—even the earthly ones—must be cast off entirely. He raised his glass to a vision of a United States "bounded on the north by the Aurora Borealis, on the south by the procession of equinoxes, on the east by primeval chaos, and on the west by the Day of Judgment!"

The historical record contains countless examples of bold declarations of national destiny similar to the ones Fiske cited, yet caution should be used when repeating them. Rarely do they take into account the powerful obstacles, counterforces, and opponents with which they would collide. More important, even a casual glance at the history of expansion in the postbellum era uncovers a great disparity between imperial rhetoric and real accomplishment.[2]

After Alaska, all of Secretary of State William Henry Seward's attempts to acquire distant territories failed, but one. The single exception was the Midway Islands, a congregation of specks on the nautical map representing roughly two square miles of sand and rock near the center of the Pacific Ocean. When Seward took them in 1867 they were occupied by plants, birds, and very little else. The islands were uninhabited, and no no other nation held a claim to them, so the transaction cost the United States nothing. Congress found the price agreeable. There was nothing offensive morally or financially in the acquisition and no politics in opposing it, so the Midway Islands were taken without much ruckus or controversy.

Seward's treaty with Denmark for the Caribbean island of St. Thomas was not as fortunate. It made its way to the Senate but died there from partisan hostility and deliberate, calculated neglect. By turning its back on the St. Thomas treaty and smothering several more imperialist schemes, Congress, in effect, had established its own policy regarding empire, "the principle of which," Henry Adams observed, "was soon to find utterance in a concise formula: 'No annexation in the tropics.'" To Adams's reckoning Seward failed because his expansionist projects had moved "too far and too fast for the public."[3] By "too far," Adams may have simply meant that Seward wanted too much: in other words, far more territory than the public thought was either wise or proper to take, much less pay millions of dollars to acquire. But more likely, given what he said about the peculiar prejudices affecting Congress at the time, Adams was thinking not about land area but about direction and climate: "No annexation *in the tropics.*" The significance of this distinction will be made clear shortly.

On the matter of whether Seward moved too fast for the public, it is important to remember—indeed, it is an inescapable point—that while the secretary of state chased every opportunity to snatch up new territories, the country was still struggling in the furious wake of the Civil War, the most destructive war in U.S. history. Six hundred and twenty thousand men had been killed. Tens of thousands more who survived their battlefield wounds lived out their lives as wreckage: broken, scarred, disfigured, many crippled for life. The South was destitute and in ruins, its economy crushed and much of its infrastructure laid to waste. Emancipation had released the

South's principal labor force, four million slaves, and liquidated, without compensation, property valued in the billions of dollars. Refugees scattered over the whole of the region in search of work, shelter, and sustenance. As controversial, divisive, costly, and (for a time) radical as it was, no one could predict when the work of reconstruction would be finished. Given even this partial accounting of the nation's condition in the days and years immediately after Lee surrendered at Appomattox, one can hardly doubt that for the vast majority of Americans, empire could wait.

Those who believed that Seward's failures—to purchase the Danish West Indies and land in the Dominican Republic for a naval base, to annex Hawaii—were his alone, that they held no implications or lessons for the policymakers who succeeded him, were mistaken. At the very least they proved that Congress could, if it wished, stop such schemes cold, a truth that would loom over Seward's imperialist descendants and embolden their opponents.

Ironically, even Seward's victories contained negative lessons for expansionists. He made enemies unnecessarily by negotiating with foreign nations in secret, provoking Congress and challenging its authority. He pushed ahead with his territorial ambitions, apparently unconcerned with the strain that their fulfillment would place on the treasury. At times, his methods appeared to violate the rules of ethics and statesmanship. He appeared reckless (Charles Francis Adams declared that Seward's "thirst for new land seems insatiable") and radical, in particular when he tried to attach noncontiguous lands to the United States: islands in the "tropical" zone inhabited by inferior, uncivilized, dark-skinned races.

Seward is often cast as the architect of the imperialist project that achieved its height in 1898.[4] Writing in the *North American Review* that year, Frederic Bancroft called him "by far the best type of those who favored expansion in the last generation."[5] Historians have called him a "prophet" of territorial expansion, "the foremost proponent of expansion" of his era, and "the prince of players" in the new empire's unfolding.[6] More-critical assessments of Seward have argued that neither his grand visions of expansion nor the glittering rhetoric he attached to them dictated a specific program, that his schemes were nourished by impulses that flowed out of greed rather than reason, from "a politician's desire for public acclaim, an intellectual's yen for historic reputation, and a craving personality's undifferentiated need for power."[7] But however historians decide to interpret Seward, for the men who followed him the ruins of his projects represented a daunting and perilous political terrain to cross. The first to understand this was the secretary of state himself.

In July 1868, after another of his schemes had come to nothing (a reciprocity treaty with Hawaii that included a passing gesture toward annexation) and approaching the last days of his political life, Seward admitted defeat. The demands of reconstruction, the determination of his enemies, the accumulation of social, political, and economic obstacles, accusations that he had abandoned both his party and the cause of the former slaves were too much for him to overcome. The result, Seward confided to a friend, was a kind of hostile disinterest to the kind of expansionism he pursued. The public mind, he observed, "sensibly continues to be fastened upon the domestic questions which have grown out of the late civil war," and being so fixed, he said, it "refuses to dismiss these questions even so far as to entertain the higher, but more remote, questions of national extension and aggrandizement." Politics—the national and presidential elections were just four months away—tangled matters further. Democrats and Republicans had become more timid and conservative. Both parties, Seward wrote, "suppose that economy and retrenchment will be the prevailing considerations," so their leaders "shrink from every suggestion which may involve any new territorial enterprise, especially a foreign one." Seward concluded that as a nation the United States had "already come to value dollars more and dominion less. How long sentiments of this sort may control the proceedings of the Government is uncertain."[8] Despite these constraints and obstacles, expansionism endured.

In *Manifest Destiny*, historian Albert K. Weinberg likened the postbellum resurgence of expansionism to "a convalescent's impulse to leap from a bed of nearly mortal sickness." The urge, almost irresistible, he said, took hold of some "with a vigor greater than any of the past."[9] Expansion was a vital part of the nation's mythology. Movement across space, the peopling of open and supposedly unoccupied lands, was its manifest destiny. For citizens it signified progress, it was essential to their democracy. Expansionism survived the Civil War and at the same time was transformed by it. After Lincoln's election and the attack on Fort Sumter, southern legislators abandoned the capital, leaving federal governance in the hands of nationalistic Republicans and northern Democrats. The Thirty-seventh Congress then proceeded to enact a body of legislation that has been called "the blueprint for modern America."[10] It established a national system of banking and taxation; raised tariffs to protect home industries from foreign competition; passed the Homestead Act, the Morrill Land-Grant College Act, and the Pacific Railroad Act. Each law quickened the peopling and development of the West. More profound than all this was the destruction of slavery. The ratification of the Thirteenth Amendment laid to rest the awful and divisive question that had dogged the nation for generations: would the western territories be dominated by slave labor or free, by black workers or white? After abolition, newly occupied lands would be organized and enter the Union uncorrupted by antebellum sectionalism and the South's "peculiar institution." After 1865, the story of American expansionism begins again.[11]

Here Fiske's story speaks to us again. Although this movement had reached its continental limits long before Appomattox, many believed that there were still frontiers to conquer. The Pacific held irresistible attractions: deepwater harbors and raw materials of all kinds—plentiful, practical, exotic, and rare—that American genius and industry would transform into spectacular wealth. There was the bewitching lure of the legendary China market. Along a less materialistic arch, the Pacific contained islands and continents thick with heathen races waiting to be led out of their spiritual darkness, scrubbed clean, clothed, civilized, and Christianized.

A separate hive of expansionists looked to the north, guided by tradition, history, an unquestioned faith in manifest destiny, and commonplace assumptions regarding race and natural law. Proximity and familiarity returned tremendous advantages. Those who kept their expansionism bound to the continent had little explaining to do to a citizenry thoroughly familiar with and invested in the act and discourses of landed expansion. Contiguous expansion needed only to be praised and pursued, rarely justified. Just beneath the surface of these discourses—"contiguous expansion," "landed expansion," "manifest destiny"—lay the ancient conviction that the temperate zone was the one proper field on which to raise an empire of Anglo-Saxon peoples. Louis Agassiz, the Swiss-born biologist, ensconced behind the red brick walls of Harvard, labored over his theories of race and climate. According to Agassiz, God, in his awesome genius, made the races as separate species of humanity and set each down in the place that it was best suited to exist. When displaced or free to choose its destiny, a race would gravitate instinctively toward the climate of its original homeland. In this scheme the Anglo-Saxon race's domain was the earth's temperate northern zones, its God-given domain. The darker races, lackadaisical and uncivilized by nature, were, to this scientist, created specifically for the torrid zone. They would not find the temperate band any more congenial than whites would the world's tropical places.[12]

Agassiz wrote and lectured prodigiously, spreading his conviction that the races were different species. Stephen Jay Gould tells us that for his work Agassiz was lionized in social and intellectual circles from Boston to Charleston.[13] He also won the respect of at least one very powerful man in politics. In 1867 Charles Sumner, the brilliant but hyperthermic senator from Massachusetts and chairman of the Senate Foreign Relations Committee, was wavering over the Alaska treaty when Agassiz wrote to persuade him to support the purchase. Climate made Alaska a desirable acquisition, he told Sumner, because it was perfectly suited to the Anglo-Saxon temperament and because it was largely unpopulated. These facts would carry "great weight" with the public, he said, because they would allow for "settlement by our race."[14] Here, Agassiz's influence on Sumner is difficult to measure; this is not the case when the senator stood against the annexation of the Dominican Republic. His attacks on that treaty, described later, clearly echo Agassiz's theories of race, climate, and geography.

As Ernest May observed, everyone at this time accepted the rightness and inevitability of America's engrossing the upper portion of North America, yet even this movement was never entirely free from controversy.[15] Alaska provides the most obvious example. By itself, an army of critics and skeptics ridiculed the purchase, calling the land, among other things, a "white elephant, a costly keepsake."[16] To lawyer and diarist George Templeton Strong it was a wasteland, a "desolate, dreary, starved region" where "otters and seals and so forth are yearly persecuted toward extermination."[17] To the *New York Herald*'s reckoning it was "utterly worthless and good for nothing . . . a land of snow, icebergs, Esquimaux men and dogs."[18] Horace Greeley, the spectacled, round-faced editor of the *New York Tribune*, denounced the treaty as a craven, transparent attempt by Andrew Johnson's administration to "cover up its failures at home by a stroke of foreign policy." If by some miscarriage of good judgment the Senate ratified the treaty, Greeley urged the House of Representatives to "think twice before it flings away the public money on this Quixotic land hunt."[19] *The Nation* condemned what it called "Mr. Seward's chimerical project of saddling us with a frozen desert of a colony." Its editor, E. L. Godkin, believed that he spoke for the entire country when he declared: "We do not want far-distant, detached colonies, nor ice and snow territories, nor Esquimaux fellow citizens."[20]

Though strongly, even fiercely worded, these condemnations proved to be quite alterable once more ambitious possibilities were realized. For the *New York Herald* the change occurred with the revelation that "Mr. Seward has always had a weakness for Canada." In this light the Alaska purchase ceased to be a "folly." Suddenly it became visionary, a brilliant act of statesmanship, "a flank movement for this great object [the annexation of Canada], a step gained, a foothold [secured] for closer and more decisive operations."[21] This helped turn Charles Sumner from Seward's enemy into the Alaska treaty's indispensable friend. He set aside his quarrels with the secretary of state in hope of fulfilling a dream he held for decades: to tug Canada "into the wide orbit of her neighbor."[22] Horace Greeley, who had said that "[o]ur country has already an ample area for the next century at least," also had a weakness for Canada. To his mind the United States had a solemn obligation to annex it, to "form at last one great, free nation."[23] Godkin's reversal, affected by the same impulse, was just as dramatic. To his reckoning, the union of the only two Anglo-Saxon nations in the Western Hemisphere was a wise and imperative goal, endorsed by the country's most informed men.[24]

Expansion to the south, into the Caribbean and beyond, was another matter entirely, complicated by history, tradition, ancient beliefs about European "blood" withering in hot climates, and the presence there of millions of nonwhite people. Yet the pull still seemed irresistible. Some—not just Congress—confronted the prospect of an American empire in the tropics with extreme vigilance. The same E. L. Godkin who purred at the suggestion of taking Canada breathed fire when policymakers ambled too far into the tropical zone in search of territories to annex. Others faced this issue with a strain of fatalism. Sumner believed that *want* of an empire in the Caribbean hardly mattered: "Sooner or later we shall have one," he told a correspondent.[25] Others embraced the prospect with reckless anticipation. Congressman Nathaniel Banks, elected to chair the House Committee on Foreign Affairs in the spring of 1869, represented this type. "Chairman of foreign affairs is the best position I could have," he told his patient and indulging wife, Mary Theodosia Banks. "I want to identify my name and that of our children with the acquisition of the Gulf of Mexico as a Sea of the United States. *That*," he declared, "will be the event of the new [Ulysses S. Grant] administration."[26]

On 4 March 1869, direction of the nation's foreign policy passed into President Grant's inexperienced hands. At first his attitude toward expansion seemed to reflect the dominant mood of Congress. Grant rejected outright half of the expansionist project he inherited from the Johnson

President Ulysses S. Grant
(Library of Congress, Prints and Photographs Division
[LC-DIG-cwpbh-05120])

administration. He refused to reopen negotiations for St. Thomas, dismissing it as "a scheme of Seward's" and insisting that he would have "nothing to
do with it."[27] This was enough to satisfy the president's mind in this case, but
it makes his extraordinary campaign to annex the Dominican Republic, the
subject of this chapter, all the more curious. It, too, was part of Seward's
expansionist legacy, but Grant seems to have been unaffected by this inconsistency.

What allowed Grant to think that he could succeed where Seward—by far
the more canny and masterful politician—had failed so recently and several
times over? He may have believed the Senate's stance against territorial
expansion had nothing to do with economics, politics, or the tropics: that it

was personally motivated and pointed specifically against Seward. Grant may have believed that since the new project would come from his administration, not that of the hated Andrew Johnson; since the land to be annexed was the Dominican Republic, not St. Thomas; and since his party controlled Congress as well as the Committees of Foreign Affairs in both houses, the outcome would be different. He was wrong.

Santo Domingo, the modern Dominican Republic, fills roughly the eastern two-thirds of the island of Hispaniola. In the long arch of islands that mark the boundary between the Caribbean Sea and the Atlantic Ocean it is part of the second largest, separated from Cuba on the east by the Windward Passage and from Puerto Rico on the west by the Mona Passage. The republic is also distinguished by its physical characteristics: mountains rising ten thousand feet above sea level are complemented by lush, prolific valleys, serpentine rivers, and thick tropical forests rooted in dark, fertile soil. Columbus cast his eyes over all of it in the fall of 1492 and pronounced Hispaniola "a miracle."

Three and a half centuries later, many Americans, projecting their desires onto the island, would have agreed with the Genoan. Years before Seward and Grant made their attempts to annex the republic, U.S. army engineers walked the peninsula overlooking the Bay of Samaná in search of the best sight on which to build a naval base. The survey, conducted in 1854, gathered dust while a small class of entrepreneurs established themselves on the island. They were drawn there by the potential of its natural resources, its mineral wealth, the potential of its agricultural regions, and its geographic position along the busiest trade routes in the Atlantic and the Caribbean. Under these circumstances ambitious, determined, and talented men could build great fortunes.

William Cazneau and Joseph Fabens were such men. Cazneau arrived in Santo Domingo in the 1850s, bought a plantation near Samaná Bay, then spent the next two decades inventing and pursuing various moneymaking schemes. Fabens was a speculator, Cazneau's friend and closest business partner. Their cooperative projects were, at their best, interesting, and occasionally silly, as when they imported camels from North Africa to serve as vehicles in a transportation and carrying trade, linking the island's interior to its coastal cities, and, at their worst, deadly, as when they sponsored the immigration of several dozen families from New York and New England, many of whom, being poorly provisioned, died from disease shortly after their arrival. More often than not their schemes turned out to be highly profitable.[28]

While chasing wealth by every means they could devise, Cazneau and Fabens were able to insinuate themselves into Dominican politics. In the summer of 1868 the Dominican government commissioned Fabens to conduct a geologic survey to map and catalogue the island's mineral resources. He was well compensated for his labors, receiving one-fifth of the land he surveyed. The partners' landholdings grew considerably from this arrangement, so much that within a short period, Fabens and Cazneau stood to own one-tenth of the Dominican Republic, the richest fraction that their geologists could identify. They were just as aggressive in matters involving trade, commerce, and finance. The two forged partnerships with a confederation of American shippers and manufacturers and by 1869 had in their hands a charter for what would become the National Bank of Santo Domingo.[29]

By the time Grant entered the presidency, Cazneau and Fabens had built an impressive empire for themselves. Despite being very profitable, it was never secure, a fact that could only have been a source of profound and relentless anxiety for the two men. Threats came from both outside the republic and within. Haiti, which occupied the western third of Hispaniola, threatened once again to invade, which had occurred under Toussaint L'Ouverture and again in 1822 (Haiti occupied the republic until a revolt expelled its forces in 1844). Internally, Dominican politics were in almost constant turmoil, the detailed history of which need not detain us except to cite them as the prologue, the backdrop, and the catalyst for what follows. The motives of Fabens, Cazneau, and their partners for luring the United States back to the island were framed entirely by self-interest. American intervention in the Dominican Republic on whatever basis—whether it be building a naval base or, on the other extreme, annexation—would, they believed, secure their investments by bringing an end to all the violence and factionalism. The Haitian threat would end, and peace and order could be restored once and for all. Stability, political and economic, would beget new investment and continue to feed Fabens and Cazneau's ambitions.[30]

Their most willing and powerful ally in this stratagem was the Dominican president, Buenaventura Báez, who was himself ambitious and extremely generous and accommodating when it came to supporting the schemes of the two Americans. More than this, Báez was in desperate need of friends. He was encircled by enemies who were clearly prepared to end his regime and, if possible, to kill Báez. Báez held onto power, and his life, because he pursued it with utter ruthlessness and, in at least one instance, murderous resolve. On 18 June 1868, little more than a month after holding fake elections that would give his regime the appearance of legitimacy, Báez ordered the execution of every armed opponent of his government.[31] But even this did not give the president the sense of security he wanted. Here his desire to rule and survive aligned with Fabens and Cazneau's motive to grow more wealthy. An alliance with the United States would provide what all three men wanted most. So it was in 1868 that Báez approached Seward with a proposal to sell both the bay and peninsula of Samaná for one million dollars in gold and an additional one hundred thousand dollars in arms and munitions. When he heard simultaneous rumors of a coup and an invasion from Haiti, Báez asked the United States to send three of its battleships to Santo Domingo, hoping that this show of force would cow his enemies and keep him in power until his negotiations with Seward were complete.[32]

In the meantime, Fabens had traveled to Washington, D.C., to corner key congressmen and persuade them to support the acquisition of Samaná and hopefully the entire Dominican Republic. Seward was interested, of course, but Fabens needed others to make his scheme work. From the House of Representatives he recruited Nathaniel Banks by appealing to his ambition, and Benjamin Butler by appealing to his greed, bribing him with a valuable tract of land overlooking Samaná Bay. On 12 January 1869, the two congressmen introduced a resolution that "authorized the President . . . to extend to the Government and people of the republics of Hayti and San Domingo the protection of the United States for the purpose of assisting them to establish permanent republican institutions." Congress voted down the resolution, 126–36, the very next day.[33]

The defeat was serious but not final. Fabens, Cazneau, Banks, and Butler carried on and pressed ahead with the annexation scheme after Seward's retirement. They would provide the continuity between the Johnson and Grant administrations. Within a month of Grant's inauguration, Fabens was back in the capital, beguiling the new president with breathless accounts of the island's superior harbors, and fertile river valleys and its prospects as a field for American investment. Grant was convinced of annexation's benefits and in July 1869 sent one of his most trusted men, General Orville Babcock, to Santo Domingo to start negotiations with President Báez.

Babcock, like the president, was a West Point graduate and a veteran of the Civil War. He joined Grant's military staff in 1864, and there he earned his reputation as a man who handled his duties, even sensitive ones, effectively and with discretion. The president placed a very high value on these qualities, which, alongside others, accounts for the intense loyalty he felt toward his aide. By most accounts, Babcock was intelligent and charismatic, well liked and respected by the influential men whom he orbited—men as different from each other as the prickly William Tecumseh Sherman and the refined and conservative Hamilton Fish.

Otherwise, and in nearly every respect, Babcock was wholly unsuited for the job he was sent to do. He had no experience in the conduct of foreign affairs. His driving ambition and weakness for quick money schemes, as well as his reckless opportunism—which would lead to his downfall in the "whiskey ring" scandal of 1875—made him vulnerable to manipulation and corruption. Though he was motivated by a sense of duty and feelings of genuine loyalty to the president, Babcock's enthusiasm for annexation most likely arose because he, too, had purchased land in the Dominican Republic, an investment that was certain to return a fortune if the United States annexed it.[34] Like the president, Babcock was seduced by the visions of wealth and luxury conjured up by Cazneau and Fabens. Later, when the negotiations fell under the scrutiny of hostile and suspicious senators, Babcock's association with these speculators would give the annexation scheme the appearance of a corrupt bargain.

Before Babcock departed on his mission, the secretary of state gave the president's "special agent" a set of detailed instructions that he was to follow strictly. Babcock was to report—nothing more—on the republic's agricultural and mineral wealth, its commerce and the state of its economy, "the disposition of the government and the people toward the United States," the activities of other foreign powers that might have representatives there, and sundry related matters.

Hamilton Fish was especially concerned with the people, specifically with the races that occupied the island. He told Babcock to collect information and statistics on "the number of whites, of pure Africans, of mulattoes, and of other mixtures of the African and Caucasian races; of Indians, and of the crosses between them and whites and Africans respectively."[35] This intense concern with race is significant, so it is useful to pause briefly and consider the racial attitudes that Fish brought to policymaking.

Hamilton Fish was the scion of New York aristocracy. His father, Nicholas Fish, had been an officer during the American Revolution and later a leading Federalist and wealthy landholder. The more impressive line of genealogy, however, descends from his mother. It includes the Livingstons, a prominent clan, and archs back to the middle of the seventeenth century, to Peter Stuyvesant, the last Dutch governor of New Amsterdam. Fish's aristocratic character and temperament, his sense of privilege and worldview, rose out of this inheritance, as did his ideas about what constituted a proper social order. Here, race and class loomed large. For men of his time and background, the inherent inferiority and crude ways of nonwhite peoples were taken for granted. Rarely were these prejudices questioned. Fish did not like the thought of vulgar people impinging on his world, particularly if they were of an inappropriate color.[36] As a conservative Republican in the early days of Reconstruction, Fish opposed the Freedman's Bureau and showed little sympathy for the former slaves in their struggle for equality and citizenship rights. The reason for this, one historian suggests, is that Fish did not want such a vital portion of the country, the South, governed by a people with whom he would have been uncomfortable dining. Certainly, Fish believed that African Americans should have no role in governing *him*, and it did not matter whether they came from Mississippi or the Caribbean.[37]

Fish knew something of the Caribbean first hand, enough to make the strong, mixed, but lasting impressions that he carried with him into the State Department. As a private citizen he had visited Cuba in 1855. Afterward he confessed to having been "charmed" by "the climate, the scenery, and the natural productions of the island 'where only man is vile.'" The last part, that regarding the people, was to Fish reason enough to reject any plot to annex Cuba. "With its present population," he said, "the island of Cuba will be anything else than a desirable acquisition to the Untied States, and" he continued, "I can see no means of getting rid of a population of some 450,000 called *white* but really [of] every shade and mixture of color, who own all of the land on the island."[38]

Fourteen years later, with Seward making his last push for empire and expansionism, "again agitating our country," Fish observed, he shared with his friend Charles Sumner some candid impressions of St. Thomas. "It is one of the most God-forsaken islands I ever saw," Fish wrote. Besides the harbors, which "would require [a] large expenditure of money to make . . . safe," and occasional earthquakes ("There was an earthquake the morning I arrived there," Fish recalled, musing that "if a Committee from Congress could visit the Island and get a good shake it would have a beneficial effect"), it was the population that made Seward's scheme most abhorrent. "The island contains about fifteen thousand inhabitants and the great majority of them," he said, "are filthy looking negroes." This made him "very much

If the racism of anti-imperialists is so significant a deterrent, why isn't the racism of imperialists a stimulant?

doubt the propriety of . . . accepting [St. Thomas] as a gift" and hope that "the thought of purchasing it will not be entertained for one moment."[39] Three months after writing this, Fish was the secretary of state. In office, at the president's right hand, with policies to support and defend, Fish was compelled to set aside some of these apprehensions, but not all. Writing in his diary on the Santo Domingo policy, Fish said that he "might have paused before entering upon it." But he was affected by Grant's determination to have the island and resolved to support the policy as best he could.[40] His dedication was severely tested from the start.

Babcock completed his mission in early September 1869 and returned to Washington, D.C., to deliver a draft of an annexation treaty he had not been officially instructed to pursue or empowered to negotiate. Fish was incensed and grumbled to another cabinet member, "Babcock is back and has actually made a treaty for the cessation of Santo Domingo, yet I pledge you my word that he had no more diplomatic authority than any other casual visitor to that island!"[41] The secretary of state had not been told about the true purpose of Babcock's errand and interpreted its result as an affront to him and his office. Faced with the threat of Fish resigning from the cabinet, the president rushed to apologize and assured the secretary of state that he had meant no offense. Grant had barely avoided a great and unnecessary public embarrassment.

Throughout this episode the president remained strangely unaware of how his naïve and eccentric methods appeared to outsiders looking in on his annexation scheme: to political rivals, the press, the public, the Senate, and even to members of his own cabinet. Secretary of the Interior Jacob Cox recalled how Grant explained his choice of a "special agent" to the cabinet: "The Navy people seemed so anxious to have the Bay of Samaná as a coaling station that [Grant said] he though he would send General Babcock down to examine it and report upon it as an engineer."[42] When the president presented the annexation treaty to his surprised cabinet—they had been left in the dark along with Secretary Fish—his demeanor was blithe, even as he acknowledged its irregularities. "I suppose that it is not formal as [Babcock] had no diplomatic powers," Grant admitted, speaking of the treaty, "but we can easily cure that."[43]

The treaty was not so easily cured. Under its main provisions the United States could take Samaná Bay alone for $2 million or have the whole of the Dominican Republic simply by paying the public debt, which was $1.5 million less. The draft obligated "his Excellency President Grant" to remit

$150,000 in cash and munitions and "guarantee the safety of the country against every foreign aggression and machination." Finally, Babcock had committed the president to "privately use all his influence" on Congress to secure the treaty's ratification. Here Grant's representative had gone far beyond the usual formalities of diplomacy. Allan Nevins has left us a cogent summary of these excesses: "In short, Babcock, had not only agreed that the United States would make a treaty providing for alternatives of annexation or the Samaná Bay purchase; he had tried to commit the executive power to political, financial, and military acts that are usually regarded as requiring the consent of Congress. He apparently thought that Grant might furnish $150,000 in cash and arms to the Dominican Government, and might engage in hostilities with the Haitians, without consulting any other branch of government! Truly, the cocksure young officer had taken a great deal upon himself."[44]

Fish reworked the strange draft into a formal treaty. Under the new terms, the Dominican Republic would give up its rights as a sovereign nation in exchange for $1.5 million and the repayment of the public debt. In the event that the Senate vetoed annexation—not unlikely given its recent hostility toward expansionism and given the present state of the country—a pair of articles would let the United States purchase Samaná Bay alone. Article 4 created the framework for a plebiscite on the island to show that annexation had the support of the people and, to a lesser extent perhaps, to demonstrate that the Dominican people were capable of democratic self-government.

In the context of the debate that followed, the most significant elements of the new treaty were contained in article 2. It stated that the "citizens of the Dominican Republic shall be incorporated into the United States as citizens thereof," that they "shall be maintained and protected . . . as citizens," and that the republic "may be admitted into the Union as a State."[45] The most severe and devastating objections to the treaty—the racist objections—would focus on this article and would assume two forms. The first was environmentalist, exploiting popular beliefs about climate, fixed racial distinctions, and the lowly and irreversible nature of the peoples who inhabited the tropical zone. The second line of objection—a natural extension of the first—sought to conjure up fear among both politicians and the American people: fear based on the promise that (although the time was not specified) annexation would eventually make the republic a state of the Union and the Dominicans citizens of the United States, the political and social equals of white males. How intolerable this prospect proved to be to the treaty's opponents as well as to many of its supporters, both reluctant and enthusiastic, will soon be made clear.

The treaty was presented to the Senate on 10 January 1870 and immediately turned over to the Foreign Relations Committee, where it sat ignored for eight days. Sumner wanted to let the treaty die using the same technique that had smothered the St. Thomas accord. Delay was a very practical strategy given the circumstances. All but one of the committee's members was opposed to annexation. Also, its Republican majority wanted to avoid an open confrontation with Grant: such a fight would have been foolish, destructive to the party, unnecessary, and wholly avoidable. Recent experience had proven neglect and evasion were reliable means of killing treaties that involved controversial acquisitions in the Caribbean.

Days, then weeks passed after the treaty became public, but aside from the White House and the Navy Department, almost no one demonstrated in its favor. "Wall Street was full of the subject," said the *New York Herald*, yet annexation had failed to win any support from the leading commercial and financial interests.[46] The public's reception was so cold and indifferent that the *Nation* noted its appearance with sarcasm rather than with its usual anti-imperialistic invective. Ratification was very unlikely, the journal said, but if it did by chance occur, the Dominicans were bound to suffer the worse for it. They "have hardly any taxes, and will consequently incur some heavy and novel burdens in casting their lot with us, but in return [they] will get a quiet life, under the rule of some of our finest politicians."[47]

This mass indifference left Grant grim and agitated. Fish noted in his diary that the treaty had "not attracted as much attention or excitement as he [the president] anticipated," that the "sentiment in its favor is not as strong as he expected."[48] What was at risk politically for Grant was clear to nearly every observer. The failure of such an audacious policy initiative would be an embarrassment; it would lay a serious blow to his administration, still in its first year. And the Republican Party would suffer from this humiliation, not just the president. Less apparent at the beginning was Grant's deep emotional attachment to this treaty, an investment of feeling and determination more intense than anyone could have expected.

At different times during his life, President Grant spoke and acted like a man whose experience and principles made him an enemy of empire. In his *Personal Memoirs*, Grant called the war with Mexico "one of the most unjust ever waged by a stronger against a weaker nation." He condemned it as a shameful episode in which the United States abandoned its finer principles and instead followed "the bad example of European monarchies in not considering justice in their desire to acquire additional territory." In his first days in office, Grant condemned Seward's expansionist program. How, then, should we understand his transformation?

The Civil War played a part. The weakness that the Union navy showed against Confederate blockade runners convinced American strategists that in the event of a future war, the nation needed a base in the Caribbean. Also, the opportunity to acquire a station, and perhaps more, presented itself. The Dominican Republic was available, the price reasonable (or at least negotiable), and its people apparently willing to attach their country to the United States. The last point carried considerable weight with Grant, for whom expansion had to be honorable and consistent with democratic principles. Fabens's and Babcock's lobbying and trusting assurances influenced him greatly (time would show that the president had a peculiar weakness for speculators like these). And was there not also reason to believe that the nation might be prepared to recommence its expansionist traditions? When Grant took office the war had been over nearly four years. The slaveholders and their motives were relics of the past. Andrew Johnson and his men were gone, discredited, retired, and the new administration's policies would be unlike those of its predecessors. They would not be fettered by Johnson's intemperance, by Seward's apostasy, or by the corruption and rumors of corruption that had tainted the latter.

Sometime in 1869 Grant wrote in his own hand a private memorandum on the acquisition question and titled it "Reasons Why Santo Domingo Should Be Annexed to the United States."[49] Very likely this was the president's first attempt to put his motives into words and explain why, to his mind, annexation was necessary, beneficial, and consistent with the nation's interests. The "Reasons Why" memorandum is a rather homely document; marked by vagaries and hyperbole, it lacks the decisiveness and clear-mindedness of Grant's more famous writings, that is, his battlefield orders and *Personal Memoirs*. The fine, simple, and direct prose style that drew praise from Mark Twain, Gertrude Stein, Edmund Wilson, and Gore Vidal failed him here, suggesting that there were perhaps circumstances in which Grant's mind worked with exceptional clarity and power—during war, when he made decisions that meant life or death for thousands of men, and years later, in his last days, when he rushed to complete his memoirs while cancer ravaged his body—and other places, in the thick of politics and policymaking, where it struggled to find purpose and order.

The content of this memorandum can be arranged into four categories. The first involved the material benefits of annexation. Grant noted this island's "unequaled fertility" and reports that nearly half of Hispaniola was teeming with "the most valuable timbers known to commerce." Once the land was "cleared of its native forrest [sic]," he wrote, the island could provide every American household with "all the exports of the equatorial region." Dyes and tropical fruits would stream into American markets, along with "the two great necessities of every family, sugar and Coffee," which the president added, "would be cheapened by nearly one half."[50]

The military and strategic benefits of annexation began, according to Grant, with the fact that the Dominican Republic was "the gate of the Carib[b]ean Sea, and in the line of transit to the Isthmus of Darien," a place "destined at no distant day to be the line of transit for half the commerce of the world." Grant predicted that rival powers might someday swarm the Caribbean, challenge American commercial supremacy, and threaten both the nation's security and the Monroe Doctrine. England, the most powerful of the nation's rivals, already possessed "a cordon of islands extending from southern Florida to . . . the main land of Central America," thus commanding "the entrance to the Gulf of Mexico . . . which border[s] upon so large a part of the territory of the United States." To Grant's reckoning, this made the Caribbean "foreign waters," and in the event of a war with England, "New York and New Orleans would be as much severed as would be New York and Calais, France."[51] A Dominican Republic controlled by the United States would counter this, the president said. "Its acquisition is carrying out our Manifest Destiny. It is a step toward [clearing] Europe [and] all European flags from this Continent." Logically, Grant asked, "[c]an anyone favor rejecting so valuable a gift who voted $7,200,000 for the icebergs of [Alaska]?"[52]

Grant cited humanitarian and abolitionist motives. He cast a picture of a Dominican lamb in a den of wolves. The republic was internally weak, yet it struggled bravely to hold off an invasion from Haiti. The European powers coveted the islands for its natural resources and strategic position and would surely intervene at the first opportunity. To let the republic seek protection from another country would be "to abandon our oft repeated 'Monroe doctrine,' " he wrote. Furthermore, Grant argued, annexation would deal a powerful blow to slavery in those places where it still existed in the hemisphere. The United States, he said, consumed 70 percent of Cuba's exports and "a large percentage of the exports of Brazil," both slaveholding nations. This made the United States "the largest supporter of that institution." If the Dominican Republic were acquired, he insisted, slave labor would become unprofitable and "that hated system of enforced labor" would quickly wither and die.[53]

The last category is, for the purposes of this book, the most significant. Two remarkable passages reveal the very large role that race occupied in the president's mind, how it shaped his motives, and the extraordinary effects it had on imperial policy formation. The first passage speaks to the Dominican people, their numbers and collective character. The republic, Grant said, had only "a sparse population and that in entire sympathy with our institutions." They were "anxious to join their fortunes with ours; industrious, if made to feel that the products of their industry is [sic] to be protected; tollrent [sic] as to the religious, or political views of their neighbors."[54] As we shall see, no one else would speak so well—in public—of the Dominican people, praise their work ethic, or refer to their assimilability in such positive terms.

The second passage on race is more important still. In it, Grant revealed layers of motive beneath his pursuit of annexation, each of them tangled up in contemporary problems of race and racism. Grant argued that taking Santo Domingo would quicken sectional reconciliation, restore peace and order to the South, and solve the vexing "Negro question." The "present difficulty in bringing all parts of the United States to a happy unity and love of country grows out of prejudice of color," he wrote. "The prejudice is a senseless one, but it exists." Grant imagined that annexation would provide a safety valve for the country and a safe haven for African Americans. The island, the president said, was "capable of supporting the entire colored population of the United States, should it choose to emigrate." He continued: "The colored man cannot be spared until his place is supplied, but with a refuge like Santo Domingo his worth here would soon be discovered, and he would soon receive such recognition as to induce him to stay: or if Providence designed that the two races should not live together he would find a home in the Antillas."[55]

Several points emerge from this passage which require our consideration. First, Grant states that racism—or, as he put it, "prejudice of color"—was both the root cause of sectional discord and the main obstacle to sectional reconciliation. The president was not the only one at the time who believed this, but by any measure it was and is a poor summary of the problems of reconstruction and the complicated past that led to it. Grant's unfortunate solution to what was, in effect, a problem of white racism rather than a "Negro question" was to resurrect an old and discredited scheme: colonization.

Plots to colonize emancipated African Americans, returning them to Africa or disposing of them elsewhere, had been considered since the late eighteenth century. Jefferson outlined such a plan in *Notes on the State of Virginia* in 1781, complete with motive. Colonization not only would rid the United States of the barbarism of slavery but would also be a means of avoiding the catastrophes of race war and miscegenation, of "the slave staining the blood of his master."[56] This conviction—that the only solution to the race problem was the mass evacuation of blacks out of the country—became the founding principle of the American Colonization Society in 1817. That organization and the movement it represented ultimately failed because of the staggering costs of transporting millions of men, women, and children across the sea; because the slaveholders refused to cooperate by freeing their slaves; and because most African Americans refused to go, insisting fiercely (along with a minuscule band of whites) that they were cocreators of the nation, deserving citizenship rights, due process, and equal protection under the law. Lincoln, who sympathized with both the plight of the slaves and the colonization movement, resurrected the idea during his presidency, despite having expressed serious and reasonable doubts about its workability years before. (In 1854 Lincoln announced that he would like "to free all the slaves, and send them to Liberia—their own native land. But," he continued, "a moment's reflection would convince me, that whatever high hope . . . there may be in this, in the long run, its sudden execution is impossible. . . . there are not surplus shipping and surplus money enough in the world to carry them there . . .").[57] But according to Gideon Welles, his navy secretary, Lincoln talked of the possibility of deporting African Americans "almost from the commencement of his administration" and was "very earnest in the matter." Lincoln ultimately chose a different course. (It is interesting to note that during his meeting with the delegation of black leaders on 14 August 1862, Lincoln justified colonizing African Americans in central America, in part, by using Agassizan reasoning: "The country is a very excellent one for any people . . . and especially because of the similarity of climate with your native land—thus being suited to your physical condition.") Andrew Johnson toyed with colonization but had neither the force of will nor the political power to make it a reality.[58]

Grant, then, was not offering a new solution to the problems of sectionalism or American racism. Indeed, instead of working to devise one and

Jefferson

perhaps exploit a moment of unprecedented racial liberalism, he chose instead to exhume a desiccated old plot that far more gifted and imaginative politicians failed to make work. Grant's empathy for the former slaves was genuine, and it would have been commendable had it been attached to policy more admirable and just than colonization.

Two points must be made regarding "Reasons Why Santo Domingo Should Be Annexed to the United States." This first bears repeating: the memorandum clearly reveals that race figured most prominently in the president's mind when he formulated his annexation plan. It gave reason, logic, motive force, and justification to the policy. The second point is far more significant. So long as annexation was alive and before the public, Grant would never use the racial justifications he outlined in "Reasons Why" to support the policy. The absence of any reference to race from all the public statements he made regarding the treaty is a glaring and conspicuous silence: remarkable because each of these pronouncements—from the messages the president sent to Congress urging the treaty's ratification to the last words he ever wrote on the subject in his *Personal Memoirs* seventeen years later—repeat, without significant alteration or amendment, every other point first mentioned in the "Reasons Why" memorandum. Each reaffirmed his commercial and strategic reasons, the appeals to anti-British prejudice, the Monroe Doctrine, and humanitarianism, but not one mentioned race, colonization, or annexation as a solution to the problems of sectional discord. Race was not simply forgotten, as evidence I present at the end of this chapter will demonstrate. It was deliberately erased.

The reasons for Grant's silence on race are easily explained. For a very brief period following the war, the very worst manifestations of antiblack prejudice, while never quite gone, seemed to be in momentary retreat. The Freedmen's Bureau assisted the former slaves in making the transition to free labor and citizenship. Congress passed a historic civil rights act to protect their liberties. Successive constitutional amendments had abolished slavery, granted African Americans citizenship rights and equal protection of the laws, and gave voting rights to black men. But by the time the last of these amendments was ratified in 1870, the few economic opportunities open to blacks in the South were disappearing, and a resurgent southern Democratic Party was undoing social and political advances, assisted by terrors meted out by the Ku Klux Klan. By this time Grant's party was tethered to the "Negro" in the public mind: black suffrage had become, according to the *New York World*, "the hinge of the whole Republican [reconstruction] policy" and "the vital breath of the party."[59] Many in the party had come to resent the association, convinced that African Americans were to blame for its dramatic electoral reverses.

Race and reconstruction dominated the elections of 1867. That year, for the first time, Eric Foner tells us, Republicans went before the voters united in support of black suffrage (at least for the South), and Democrats, sensing their opportunity, exploited antiblack prejudice with a vengeance.[60] Black suffrage referendums were on the ballot in several northern states including Pennsylvania, New York, New Jersey, Minnesota, and Kansas. They failed in each state. In Ohio the initiative was defeated by calls to save the state from "the thrall of Niggerdom." In the aftermath of the elections, *The Nation* declared: "It would be vain to deny that the fidelity of the Republican party to the cause of equal rights . . . has been one of the chief causes of its heavy losses." The *New York Herald* proclaimed that white voters were in revolt because the prospect of "Southern negro political supremacy and . . . a negro balance of power in our national affairs, have startled the public mind of the North."[61] So chastised were the Republicans that the national platform Grant ran on in 1868 avoided the race and suffrage issue entirely. Direct confrontations with antiblack prejudice must have made deep impressions on Grant's mind. During his campaign for the presidency, out among the people, Grant had personally faced accusations that he was a "nigger lover," thus he learned to avoid the dangerous currency of equality.[62]

By the time the treaty went public in the winter of 1869–70, then, Grant and his party knew all too well the volatility of racism and the importance of avoiding the "Negro question" at all costs. Certainly any such connection, made explicit, would have damaged the treaty's chances with conservative and moderate Republicans as well as with the mass of northern whites, a class that had expressed the intensity of its white supremacist, antiblack sentiments at the polls.[63] The Democrats, already committed to the politics of white supremacy, would naturally oppose anything that gave solace to blacks.

Cast in this light, the president's silence on race and colonization appears to have been pragmatic and deliberate. Racism would be a formidable obstacle in the path to ratification. Grant knew it. Fish knew it, felt it, and sensed it among politicians both within and outside of the administration. On 9 February 1870 the secretary of state bluntly told his friend George Bancroft that the treaty would "not be approved" and cited several reasons. Very important was the political climate of the time. After the war and its battles with Andrew Johnson, Congress was intent on asserting its power over the executive branch. The senate, Fish observed, was prepared "to antagonize every proposition emanating from the Executive." Before this, however, Fish cited the force that racial prejudice had on politics. Opponents would be motivated to defeat annexation, he wrote, by "doubts honestly entertained by many of the policy of acquiring insular possessions, and . . . the effect of the tropical climate upon the race who inhabit them."[64] Three months later Fish spoke again of these apprehensions. In May 1870 the British Foreign Office contacted its minister to the United States, Sir Edward Thornton, requesting information on the treaty and Grant's intentions toward the Dominican Republic. Thornton spoke to the secretary of state, who told him that "certain persons in high position" wanted the island-nation annexed and brought into the union as a state. Thornton told his superiors in London that Fish opposed this based on his personal conviction "that however possible it might be for the United States to annex countries inhabited by the Anglo-Saxon race and accustomed to self-government, the incorporation of . . . the Latin race would be but the beginning of years of conflict and anarchy."[65]

The *London Spectator* predicted a short career for American imperialism in the tropical zone. Annexation, it said, would be too expensive in a time when so many politicians demanded that the government practice more tightfisted economy. It would necessitate building and maintaining a large standing navy and army, which would offend the nation's antimilitarist traditions. Worse still, the publication declared, taking the republic would break open Pandora's box. Taking Santo Domingo would inevitably lead to the annexation of the black republic Haiti, "in order to stop the frequent disruptions" that were certain to come. Furthermore, the Senate was "not likely . . . to forget that the vote of the island, if once annexed and admitted to the system, would cancel that of a million whites in the House of Representatives, that in fact a seventh of the House would be returned by coloured men." Santo Domingo was an expensive present "which nobody particularly wanted . . . and which may draw after it an increase in the dark electorate, an incident," the *Spectator* observed, "the genuine American tolerates, but does not as yet cordially approve." Without the support of the white majority— indeed, given the hostility it had recently shown toward African American citizenship and voting rights in both the North and the South—Congress would never approve the treaty. "[T]he dread of the negro," it concluded, "is on all politicians."[66]

On 15 March 1870 the Senate Foreign Relations Committee announced its decision on the Santo Domingo treaty; it recommended against its ratification. Despite the weeks of anxious waiting, public indifference, and the long, ominous silence that preceded the report, Grant did not expect, nor was he prepared for, this setback. In the days after the committee made its pronouncement, men close to the president stalked the corridors of the Capitol, spreading word of his intense disappointment over the final judgment. Minister Thornton told his superiors in London that Grant was especially angry at the committee's chair, Charles Sumner, "because when he [Grant] spoke with him, he promised to support it."[67]

The meeting that Thornton referred took place in Sumner's home on 2 January 1870. The senator was dining with guests when Grant appeared unexpectedly at his front door, come to persuade Sumner to support the annexation treaty. Before this—despite his position on the Foreign Relations Committee and his personal relationship with the secretary of state—Sumner had been unaware that the administration was pursuing the Dominican Republic, so being confronted in such an unusual way, by President Grant, with a treaty for its annexation could only have come as quite a shock to the senator.

Grant made his case for annexation in the broadest terms, casting only the most flattering light on all the advantages he believed it would bring the United States, promising to have Babcock deliver papers containing all the details of the negotiation the next day so that the senator could peruse them at his leisure. As Grant prepared to leave, one of Sumner's guests asked the senator directly if he would support the treaty. The senator is supposed to have told Grant: "I am an administration man, and whatever you do will always find in me the most careful and candid consideration."[68] Sumner's answer soon became a matter of intense controversy: first between the senator and the president—resulting in a commotion that would divide the Republican Party; the episode, David Donald observed, "was destined to be the turning point in Grant's administration and in Sumner's career as well" —and then later among a small congregation of biographers and historians.[69] The controversy, such as it exists at present, turns on the arranging and rearranging of small details, on recovering Sumner's exact words (which none of the extant testimonies agree on); on divining his intentions; on

Senator Charles Sumner
(Library of Congress, Prints and Photographs Division
[LC-DIG-cwpbh-00477])

determining what Grant heard in relation to what was said; and finally, on discerning the meaning the president placed on those words. Historians may continue to sort through the shards of evidence passed down to them, but the words that were spoken than evening are, in fact, unrecoverable. What we know, and what matters in the context of the events that followed, is this: Grant left Sumner certain that the powerful chairman of the Foreign Relations Committee had promised to support his treaty. Sumner believed—and later on the Senate floor would vehemently insist—that he had done no such thing, that if he had promised Grant anything it was only to give the treaty a fair, if somewhat partisan, reading, and nothing more.

Grant would fight for his treaty with great determination and, at times, utter recklessness, against the antiexpansionist currents. Two days after the Foreign Relations Committee made its announcement, Grant marched to the Capitol, "somewhat in the style of Oliver Cromwell" according to the *New York World*, settled in the President's Room, and sent word that he wanted members of the Senate to come and speak with him. Fifteen answered his call.[70] Grant coaxed and bargained for over two hours and by the end persuaded a few senators over to his side.[71] A second group of senators, men who were more skeptical of the annexation scheme, were called to the Executive Mansion to hear the president's case: onto ground where Grant could put to their best use his own prestige and that of his office.[72] As Grant spoke to the politicians, Secretary of State Fish hovered conspicuously in the background: the president's homely, jowly guardian angel in muttonchops. Fish's presence was staged to impress upon every senator that Grant had the full and unanimous support of his cabinet. Newspapers were reporting that "a portion of the Cabinet" was at the Capitol "using their influence to get the treaty ratified."[73] Fish's attendance was orchestrated for a second reason: to undermine rumors—allegedly started by Sumner—that the secretary of state opposed annexation and the treaty but kept his true feelings in abeyance out of respect for the president.[74] The rumors were true, and it was Fish, in a characteristic moment of indiscretion, who started them, hence the need for this pantomime.

Grant worked aggressively and tirelessly to fulfill the promise made in his name, to use "all his influence" to secure the treaty's ratification. His methods, closely observed, attracted bemused attention and scolding criticism. John C. Hamilton confessed to his friend Secretary Fish: "I regret the active agency of the President as to this Dominican treaty." His "interference, in *advance*, in the treaty power of the Senate" had excited "unpleasant thoughts: It is regarded as unusual at least."[75] Henry Adams, who rarely spent a generous word on Grant's behalf, declared that the president had "condescended to do the work of a lobbyist almost on the very floor of the Senate Chamber, using his personal influence to an extent scarcely ever known in the American experience."[76] Adams exaggerated, but his complaint, like Hamilton's, was perhaps more about the violation of boundaries than the shock that attended these "unprecedented" actions. The sensitivity of these critics was sharpened by their having lived in an era when presidents strictly observed the boundaries that marked the separation of powers, in a time when, rather than delivering the State of the Union message themselves, it was sent to the Capitol and read by a clerk. Grant's transgression was a grave one not because it failed to win votes but because it revealed political weakness, even naïveté. In this instance the great soldier, said Adams, had proven himself to be "a baby politician."[77]

Grant was not swayed by his critics. He had a soldier's discipline and experience, and stern determination had brought him through far greater challenges at Shiloh, Vicksburg, and Chattanooga. Criticism from such men as Hamilton and Adams should have made little impression on ears that had heard far worse: cries of failure, drunkard, butcher. Grant tried to ignore the yelps of political rivals, false party men, and the intelligentsia, his efforts helped along by the impression that his lobbying was working. He saw senators, one or two at a time, pledging to support the treaty. Some had favored expansion from the beginning. Others were loyal party men: if they had doubts about the wisdom of this treaty, they were subordinated to the greater cause, the interests of the Republican Party. Some were probably awed by Grant: the savior of the Union, the leader of the party, the president of the United States, arguably the greatest living American and, in 1870, perhaps the most famous man in the world. It must have been irresistibly appealing to some to play the role of good administration man.

Some senators would not be moved, regardless of the enticements. One was Carl Schurz. Schurz was born in Prussia, embraced radical politics, participated in the revolutions of 1848, and emigrated to the United States four years later. He rose quickly in politics and in 1870 was a Republican senator from Missouri, a member of the Foreign Relations Committee, and, after Sumner, the treaty's most visible and determined opponent. Extant photographs of Schurz show a man with the appearance of a fierce goblin. He possessed a formidable intelligence and, to the fullest degree, Robert Beisner has written, "the mugwump's sense of righteousness and moral superiority."[78] Schurz had opposed the treaty behind the closed doors of his committee, yet Grant hoped that he could change the senator's mind. The effort would be in vain.

Schurz recalled his meeting with the president in his autobiography, *Reminiscences*. After Grant explained the benefits of annexation and asked Schurz to support the treaty, the senator decided to be "entirely frank." He was "happy to act with [the] administration whenever and wherever [he] conscientiously could," he told the president, but not with this annexation scheme because it "would be against the best interests of the Republic." He explained to Grant what he called the "dominant reasons" behind his opposition: "in short, acquisition and possession of such tropical countries

Carl Schurz
(Library of Congress, Prints and Photographs Division
[LC-DIG-cwpbh-04020])

with indigestible, unassimilable populations would be highly obnoxious to the nature of our republican system of government; it would greatly aggravate the racial problems we had already to contend with; those tropical islands would, owing to their climatic conditions, never be predominantly settled by people of Germanic blood." Furthermore, he said, "this federative republic could not without dangerously vitiating its principles, undertake to govern them by force, while the populations inhabiting them could not be trusted with a share of governing our country." Taking the Dominican Republic, he insisted, would only worsen "existing conditions . . . within our Southern States" and give back "absolutely no compensating advantages." Schurz had one more reason for opposing the treaty: conversations with other senators had convinced him that it would never secure enough votes to pass. Schurz warned the president, as he "sincerely regret[ted] to see [the] administration expose itself to a defeat," which he thought was inevitable.[79]

Schurz's recollections are important both for what was said and what was not. First, Schurz's anti-imperialism arose out of his conception of republicanism, loyalty to party, and temperament, but race ideas were clearly at its core. His brief recollection lets us discern the foundational racial ideas that fired his anti-imperialism, which are significant because they represent the assumptions held by many Americans of his time: that racial homogeneity was the prerequisite characteristic of a republic; that white racial limitations, fixed by nature and dictated along the lines of climate separating the temperate and tropical zones, made Santo Domingo unsuitable for settlement by people of "Germanic blood" and therefore a worthless, wasteful acquisition for the United States; and that alien people of color could not be trusted with citizenship. Taking the island-republic could only result in calamity for the administration, the party, and the nation.

As for what was not said, in the face of Schurz's objections, Grant kept utterly silent about the influence that race had also had on his considerations. He failed to respond even to the senator's argument that taking the Dominican Republic would exacerbate the nation's existing racial problems and unstitch old wounds. It is hard to imagine a more opportune or appropriate moment for Grant to have returned to the content of his private memorandum and to have explained how he believed annexation would advance sectional reconciliation, provide a safe refuge for the former slaves, settle the "Negro problem," and restore national unity. His silence in this instance is significant.

The president lost Schurz that evening; he probably never had Sumner, whose support was essential for the treaty's ratification. Grant sensed the precariousness of his situation and tumbled into a dark mood. He blamed Sumner for the treaty's misfortunes, believing that the senator had betrayed him. In a letter to Fish, Grant denounced the senator as "an enemy of the treaty," who "will kill it tomorrow if he can . . . and favors delay probably to better secure its defeat." It was not good policy, he said, "to trust the enemies of the treaty to manage it for . . . its friends." He would thereafter rely only on "devoted friends" to guide it through the Senate.[80]

The Senate debates on the annexation treaty began on 24 March 1870, four months after it was signed and just five days before it was due to expire. Time, meaning the shortness of time, and the prevailing political currents favored the anti-imperialists overwhelmingly. Sensing this, behind the closed doors of executive session Sumner struck the first severe blow against the treaty in his opening speech. The press described it as "very able and exhaustive, covering all points likely to arise in connection with the subject." The *New York Tribune*, impressed by the objections raised regarding the daunting cost of empire building, said that Sumner "showed that the expense to our Government would be enormous before all the obligations which the Government assumed would be discharged."[81]

By most accounts Sumner's colleagues were similarly and deeply impressed by the force of his arguments. Many called the speech "one of the most powerful ever made in the Senate." Democrats, the newspapers announced, "will oppose the treaty in a body," and word circulated in the press that the House Committee on Appropriations had met and "appeared to be unanimous in opposition to recommending an appropriation for the purchase should the Senate ratify the treaty."[82] Caleb Cushing wrote to Sumner the day following his speech: "You must be gratified to find that all the journals commend your speech on Dominica, especially seeing that these opinions are, of course, but an echo of the judgment of the Senators."[83]

What did Sumner say that made such a powerful impression on so many? The speech was delivered in executive session, so no complete record of it exists. Thus its content must be reconstructed from extant sources, in particular from the newspapers that covered the debates. From these sources as well as other, later writings by the senator, we know that race loomed large in his objections.

According to the *New York Herald*, Sumner opposed the acquisition because "the people [of the Dominican Republic] were a turbulent, treacherous race, indolent and not disposed to make themselves useful to their country or to the world at large." It reported that to Sumner's reckoning, the country's continual conflicts with Haiti provided the clearest demonstration that "the character of the people would render acquisition of their country undesirable." On 26 March the *Herald* again said that Sumner's attacks on the treaty made "special reference to the inhabitants of the islands of the American tropics" and that the senator "did not appear to have so high an opinion of the specimens of sable humanity found in these regions as he has of his own [black] countrymen."[84] (In a critical turn the newspaper accused the senator of hypocrisy, stating "Mr. Sumner and some other Senators pretend to oppose any acquisition of territory in the West Indies on the ground that we have enough already and that the negro and foreign populations there would not be desirable citizens." It called this "turning around on the negroes" by the senator "a curious fact." The *Herald* declared that Sumner "wants to have nothing to do with the negro [unless] he can ride him as a political hobby.")[85]

Such statements, attributed to Sumner, will probably surprise those who know the senator's place in history as an abolitionist, a leader in the struggle for African American rights and for the radical Republicans of the postwar era, and as the man Frederick Douglass called "my honored and revered friend."[86] It is possible that his words were twisted by the press, which was accustomed to attacking the man for his controversial politics, occasional extremism, and tendency to sympathize with the former slaves and other unpopular causes. It is important, then, to note that Sumner's biographers, in their discussions of the Santo Domingo controversy, assigned the same motives to his treaty opposition as did the press. Moorefield Storey, who as a young man knew and worked with Sumner, wrote that the senator knew "[t]he country was in no mood for annexing a hot-bed of revolution with a population like that of San Domingo." Edward L. Pierce contended that Sumner took his oppositional stance to annexation because taking the Dominican Republic was "likely to encourage further acquisitions in the same direction, bringing the United States a population difficult to assimilate."[87] It seems, then, that the press accounts, though perhaps exaggerated, cannot be dismissed, particularly where more reliable and moderate accounts, as well as sources left by Sumner himself, echo their basic content.

Race was a critical factor in Sumner's thinking, the theory behind his opposition to the treaty and the arguments he presented on the floor of the Senate. Annexation was impractical, not just wrong, and prohibited by differences in history as well as the laws of nature. He declared in his speech that the United States was "an Anglo-Saxon Republic, and would ever remain so by the preponderance of that race." To his reckoning the West Indies were, in contrast, "colored communities" where the "black race was predominant." Agassiz's theories lie beneath these statements, along with those of the ancient Greeks, Aristotle and Plato, who speculated that the races of humankind were fitted into distinct climatic zones. Thus, Sumner could say without embarrassment, "To the African belongs the equatorial belt and he should enjoy it undisturbed."[88]

This conclusion allowed Sumner to imagine a middle way between formal acquisition, which he believed would violate the rights of the Dominican people (and would be inconsistent with his concern for the rights of African

Americans), and total retreat from the Caribbean, an impractical notion. The senator stated that the United States should establish a policy under which the nations of the Caribbean "remain as independent powers," free to "try for themselves to make the experiment of self-government." The United States, he said, instead of annexation, should create a protectorate for the Dominicans, "giving them moral support and counsel, as well as aid them in establishing a firm and energetic republican government of their own." In time, under this arrangement, Sumner maintained, the islands of the Caribbean would emerge as a "free confederacy, in which the black race should predominate."[89]

After Sumner concluded, Oliver Morton rose to defend the treaty and make the best case he could for annexation. He stressed the humanitarianism that was bound up in the policy, the island's beauty—it "approached nearer an earthly paradise than probably any other portion of the globe"—and the strategic advantages of building a naval base there, as well as making allusions to the Monroe Doctrine. He warned the Senate that if the United States did not take the republic, another power would "and gain a dangerous foothold, while the United States government could not object, having thrown away its opportunity." This, Morton said, made the Dominican Republic worth "ten Alaskas."[90] Morton then produced examples (cordially supplied by Babcock) of the island's fecundity. Among the displays was a chunk of rock salt, "clear as crystal," according to the newspapers, and giving the appearance of "a piece of ice." While a few senators played tug-of-war with a length of Santo Domingan hemp and "gave the fibre a thorough testing," a number of incredulous and curious politicos gathered around the salt. It was an astounding scene, said the *New York Herald*: African American senator Hiram Revels and the negrophobic Garrett Davis on the chamber floor "licking salt together."[91]

Before he closed, Morton challenged Sumner's indictments of the Dominicans. He extolled their finer characteristics, their "docility, integrity, and kindness." They were "in their true natures," he insisted, "a harmless set." The turbulence that Sumner spoke of came not from the Dominicans but from external sources. The violence was unfortunate, according to the senator, but it contained one virtue that should make annexation more palatable to the United States: it had reduced the island's population. "The question in this light," said Morton, "presents a vast territory open to the hand of art and science and industry, *and almost without inhabitants*."[92] This was neither the first time nor the last that an imperialist would try to remove a dark-skinned population and race, the most critical obstacles they would confront, from these debates.

A day before the treaty was set to expire—though it was unlikely that it would come to a vote—Schurz launched his assault. He elaborated many of the objections he had presented to the president. Annexation, he said, would "only bring another element of trouble into our political and social system." The implication was that the United States, in the middle years of Reconstruction, already faced enough troubles. Schurz believed that these could serve his purpose, that they could be piled up and turned into a barrier to annexation. Empire building would require millions out of a treasury depleted by the war and the restoration of the Union: more money thrown into the pit of expansionism, so soon after the controversies that attended the Alaska purchase. Lavish government spending was also bound up with fears of corruption and cronyism; both added fire to Schurz's opposition.[93]

Inevitably, there was the matter of race. Schurz knew that racism, exploiting fear of dark races, alien peoples, from hot places, was his best weapon. The senator could not resist tying annexation and the prospect of adding the Dominicans to the nation to the fierce, divisive, and ongoing controversies over African American citizenship. This was the other "element of trouble" that the nation did not need, particularly when "the problem of what to do with the same race in the South under much more favorable circumstances has taxed the best intellects of our country for years."

The difference in this instance was that the Dominicans were aliens to the American system twice over. Schurz's speech in the Senate simply exploited common prejudices surrounding Dominicans' foreign nature and everyday assumptions directed toward the gumbo of peoples—African, European, French, Spanish, Haitian, and Catholic, all set against a violent and tumultuous history—they supposedly represented. The senator maintained that the Dominicans were strangers to democracy, that "like the people of Mexico and the other Spanish colonies," they had "thoroughly demonstrated their incapacity for self-government." Indeed, he asserted, "their whole history was a history of revolutions." He condemned the Dominicans as "immoral, vicious, and lazy," people who "have no interests in common with us." Worse yet, Schurz warned, "if we must take them it must be as political and social equals," as citizens under the Constitution. The Fifteenth Amendment, which promised that a citizen's right to vote "shall not be denied or abridged . . . on account of race," would be ratified two days after this speech.

Other limitations were there to consider as well, not just the Dominicans' incompatibility with republicanism and the ways of democratic and self-government but also the boundaries that restrained people of European descent. Nature and climate made it so that whites could not benefit from the land at the center of this debate. Republican principles never had and never would prevail in the tropical zone, he said, and the Anglo-Saxon who ventured there would be diminished and separated from his civilized self, "enervated by the climate, demoralized by association, and would, instead of raising the natives to his scale, inevitably sink to their level." That this fundamental law was dictated by nature, that whites could not dominate this new land, removed a powerful, traditional justification for expansion and empire.

The real question, Schurz concluded, was, "Can we bear any further strains upon our institutions by introducing these incongruous people to our nation?" The answer was clearly no. "Certainly there is no inducement to compensate for the danger," he said. "We have no real need for any of these West India Islands." He cautioned, "If we commence with one [Caribbean island], our manifest destiny will compel us to go until we acquire the whole." Days later Schurz boasted that the speech was "the best one I ever made."[94]

Compared with Sumner and Schurz, who had dominated the debate, established its terms, and crippled Grant's treaty, its supporters were weak, colorless, and unpersuasive. Matthew Carpenter of Wisconsin tried to counter Sumner and Schurz's environmentalism, stating that their observations about the withering climate of the Caribbean could be applied just as well to Louisiana and other parts of the South where white men lived quite successfully under republican institutions. Carpenter chided Schurz for attempting to turn manifest destiny against expansionism, and while doing so, he advanced familiar arguments involving race and climate. The compass of manifest destiny also pointed north, into the temperate zone where, the senator declared, "we have a people equally hardy, equally energetic, equally industrious with us, and certainly able to overbalance any tendency to sloth, enervation, or immorality to be infused into us by contact with our tropical possessions."[95]

The treaty expired on 29 March 1870 without coming to a vote. Grant was prepared to fight on but the opposition was clearly in control. John C. Bancroft Davis, the assistant secretary of state, advised Hamilton Fish regarding the goings-on in the Capitol, on the informal conversations and arguments being traded outside the Senate chamber, and the news was not good. The best that the administration could hope for was a bare majority, far short of the two-thirds majority needed for ratification. Other disturbing news came to the surface about this time. Fish learned that men identifying themselves as representatives of the administration were shadowing various senators, offering bribes, favors, and patronage in exchange for votes. Davis repeated Sumner's accusation that an agent of the administration had attempted to bribe James Patterson, a member of the Foreign Relations Committee: "to have [Patterson's] brother appointed third auditor if he would vote for the Treaty—and that a general had said to a Senator that if he would vote for the Treaty he would have whatever patronage he desired." Schurz said that he, too, had been approached by emissaries from the White House who offered him all the patronage he wanted in exchange for his support for the president's annexation scheme. More ominous were rumors that the president himself was directly involved. Grant denied the accusation and ordered Senator Morton to deny them. Schurz listened intently to the president's claims but remained incredulous, believing that all this had been done with Grant's full knowledge and approval.[96]

The public's attitude toward annexation, the treaty, and the debates took on every appearance of indifference. On 12 May 1870 expansionists held a protreaty rally at the Cooper Institute in New York City, a sincere but ineffective attempt to arouse public excitement for empire. The event was advertised aggressively. Joseph Fabens was in attendance, announced as the "Special Embassador from San Domingo." Nathaniel Banks, the staunchest of administration men on the treaty issue, attended so as to make his emphatic appeal. Music "which appeared to please the popular taste" blared, but on the appointed night the meeting hall was only two-thirds full, according to the *New York Herald*, "with an audience composed entirely of men."[97]

Like their Senate counterparts, these men were underwhelming in their advocacy. Many of their words were spent reciting lists of the island's natural bounty, its proximity to the United States, and its strategic value. Banks, full of jingoistic huff, predicted that Europe's final retreat from the hemisphere and Cuba's independence would come soon after "the American flag is raised upon the hights [sic] of San Domingo." The duty of defusing the race question fell on the unready shoulders of John Fitch. "Though the tropic sun may have stained the skins of those who dwell by the gateway of the further Indies," he said, "shall we close our hearts to their human cries for freedom and shut our door against Domingo . . . because there will be a few contributed to a class which is not at present too clear in complexion, or because 500,000 colored people may be added to 4,000,000 which already exist?"[98] As a further sign that the proponents of annexation wanted to diminish the racial obstacle, the resolutions announced at the meeting ignored references to the Dominican people.[99]

The feeble demonstration made almost no impression on the distant Senate. On 14 May, Schurz brought a survey of his colleagues to the secretary of state which counted thirty-two votes against annexation. A second canvass by Senator William Stewart contained similar results. True to his commitment to the president, Fish took this intelligence and set to work on a plan to persuade its opponents to change sides. He would try to remove what he believed were the two principal obstacles standing in the way of ratification. Fish proposed that Grant share the treaty-making power with the Congress and allow it to decide the perilous matters of statehood and citizenship. The secretary of state's recommendations to the president were simple and direct: "instead of making the future admission as a State *imperative*," he said, "reserve to Congress the right *either* to admit [the Dominican Republic as a] State *or* to remit it to a condition of either separate or of confederate independence and nationality, with three of the West Indian Islands." To remove statehood and citizenship was to remove, simultaneously, the race issue: three branches belonging to the same vine. Taking race out of the debate would disarm the treaty's enemies, accommodate the prejudices of many senators, and perhaps win their support. "The proposition," Fish told the president, "would find friends among those who desire the influence of our institutions and our protection to be extended to San Domingo, and to the other islands, but who hesitate upon the question of the absorption of tropical possessions."[100] Grant rejected the proposal at first glance because he believed that it had come from Schurz. Fish assured the president that the suggestions were his, not the senator's, and that it was imperative that Grant consider some form of compromise before it was too late. "[T]he treaty," he argued, "will be rejected unless some of the opponents are gained over by some new feature or principle." Taking out those parts that many senators—and the secretary of state himself—found most objectionable seemed to Fish to be a means "possibly capable of gaining some."[101]

The president was not yet prepared to cede an inch of ground, to settle for a protectorate or anything less than an acquisition settled on his terms. Dismayed by Grant's impolitic stubbornness, Davis told Fish that the president's "mind is evidently made up for annexation pure and simple."[102] Grant resisted for good reason, he thought, mainly because he believed that Schurz's poll was wrong. In early May, he and Fabens conducted their own survey and counted forty senators in favor of annexation; by this calculation they stood just two votes away from ratification. Indeed, Fabens reported back to the Dominican government that Grant "was almost certain of carrying the annexation by two-thirds vote."[103] In truth their math was severely flawed. In 1870 there were seventy-two senators. To ratify a treaty, forty-eight votes were needed, not forty-two.

Whether two votes short or six, Grant still had to persuade more senators to favor ratification. On 31 May he issued his final plea. Grant told the Senate that the treaty's deadline had been extended, then he proposed changes that he hoped would "obviate objections which may be urged against the treaty as it is now worded." The first change was an amendment limiting the amount of the Dominican debt the United States would assume following acquisition. The second concession took the form of a curious and open-ended invitation to "insert such amendments as may suggest themselves to the minds of Senators to carry out in good faith the conditions of the treaty." This suggests that over the space of a few weeks in May 1870, Grant had come down from a position of optimism, confidence, and even stubborn arrogance to a point where he was acutely aware that his treaty was in peril and would attempt to pursue realistic compromises. He needed support and was ready to repair bridges and bargain for votes as well as to persuade. Once again, the president reminded the Senate of the economic, strategic, and humanitarian benefits of annexation. He tried to force the Senate's hand by implying that inaction would threaten the Monroe Doctrine: an unnamed "European power" was supposedly prepared to offer two million dollars "for the possession of Samaná Bay alone."[104] Nowhere did Grant mention race.

Two weeks passed and the president grew only more anxious. On 13 June, "with considerable feeling," according to Fish, Grant complained about the party's galling failure to line up behind the treaty as he believed it should, the cabinet especially. To Grant's reckoning the secretary of the treasury was resistant and the secretary of the interior "never said a word in its favor." To the president's mind the attorney general, Ebenezer Rockwell Hoar, was the worst of them all. He "says nothing . . . but sneers at it," the secretary of state recalled Grant saying. Fish wrote in his diary of how the president spoke passionately "of the San Domingo treaty, [and] his desire for ratification" at the next day's cabinet meeting, and how he expected his "Cabinet and all his friends to use all proper efforts to aid him; that he will not consider those who oppose him 'name Ministers to London.'" Grant's speech received "general approval" from the secretaries who were present, according to Fish, no doubt because they realized that threats lay just beneath the earnest pleas for support. It would turn out that Grant's threats had teeth. His talk of naming "Ministers to London" was a reference to Charles Sumner. The senator had used his influence to win the coveted post at the Court of St. James for his friend John Lothrop Motley.[105] The president was never satisfied with Motley. The animus he felt toward Sumner only worsened this sentiment. The day after the Senate rejected the annexation treaty, Grant had Motley removed, an act that was widely interpreted at the time as an indirect but unmistakable insult directed at Sumner.

Motley was not, however, the first man sacrificed over the treaty. One day after Grant told his cabinet that he expected their full support for annexation, Attorney General Hoar abruptly resigned. There was no forewarning that this was coming, no indication from Hoar that he was dissatisfied with his position, so the news surprised most observers. Hoar's reasons for resigning remain shadowy, but Fish suspected that Grant was behind it.[106] If the secretary of state's suspicions were correct, the president had only made good on the threat he had issued behind closed doors: that no one who opposed his policy—or, in this instance, failed to support it to the president's satisfaction—would hold a position under him. Grant could have interpreted Hoar's reticence to be opposition, and forced him out of the cabinet. Historian Charles Campbell offered a second and far more intriguing possibility: that Hoar, a controversial figure despised by some key senators, was sacrificed in an attempt to win votes for ratification.[107] If this was the case, the effort was in vain.

The Senate resumed its debates on 29 June and voted the following day. The treaty was soundly defeated, 28–28. Nathaniel Banks received the news with disgust. "Had [the treaty] been well managed," he wailed, "it would have [received three-fourths] of the votes of the Senate." He closed ominously: "All confidence in the President is lost on the part of many people."[108] Grant refused to take responsibility. He blamed the Foreign Relations Committee for the treaty's defeat, telling Rutherford Hayes that he thought it "badly constituted." He disparaged Sumner as "a man of very little practical sense, puffed up and unsound." Carl Schurz, said the president, was "an infidel and atheist," a rebel in his home country comparable to Jefferson

Davis. Senator Casserly was "a bigoted Catholic who hated England," a politician whose "prejudices made him unsafe."[109]

The matter of annexation was, for all intents and purposes, dead, but Grant refused to lay the matter to rest. In his annual message in December 1870, the defiant president repeated his belief that the nation's best interests demanded that the treaty be ratified. He requested that Congress, by a joint resolution, appoint a committee to investigate conditions on the island and negotiate "with the authorities of San Domingo for the acquisition of that island."[110] Seven days later Senator Oliver Morton introduced a resolution authorizing the president to appoint three commissioners who would survey the island-republic's social, political, and economic situation and ascertain the population's "desire and disposition to become annexed to and form part of the people of the United States."[111]

The resolution was immediately attacked. Opponents cast it as the administration's furtive attempt to force through a policy that the Senate had already defeated. And authorizing a commission that was empowered to negotiate a treaty of annexation would, they said, amount to giving the project congressional sanction ab initio. Morton declared before a mass of criticism that the resolution neither contained nor implied anything so sinister. The commission, he insisted, would merely "procure information upon the important questions" surrounding acquisition, nothing more. "It commits nobody in favor of annexation."[112] Its opponents were not persuaded, but neither did they have the power to stop the Morton resolution. A motion to send it to the Committee on Foreign Relations, where Sumner and Schurz would have smothered it, failed, and debates over it began on 20 December.

The most significant event of these deliberations came on the second day when Sumner delivered the infamous Naboth's Vineyard speech. The title referred to the biblical story of Naboth, whose vineyard was coveted by Ahab, king of Samaria. Naboth refused to give his land to the king because, he said, God forbid *"that I should give the inheritance of my fathers unto thee."* Sumner declared that the resolution would commit Congress to "a dance of blood" and represented a policy corrupt in every detail, "a new step in a measure of violence" that sought to destroy the independence of both the Dominican Republic and Haiti. But of all the arguments that Sumner put forth against the resolution and annexation, one stood out in his mind as "vast in importance and conclusive in character." The laws of nature, of climate and race, forbade it. The island, "situated in tropical waters, and occupied by another race, of another color," he maintained, "never can become a permanent possession of the United States." Taking them by diplomacy or force would be in vain because "[a]lready by a higher statute is that island set apart to the colored race. It is theirs by right of possession, by their sweat and blood mingling with the soil, by tropical position, by its burning sun, and by unalterable laws of climate. Such is the ordinance of Nature," said Sumner, "which I am not the first to recognize." He suggested that the nation's attitude toward the Dominican Republic follow that of a good neighbor. A duty that "is as plain as the Ten Commandments," he said, demanded that the United States devise a policy that would never threaten the island-republic's sovereignty, not only because "their independence is as precious to them as ours is to us," Sumner remarked, but in addition because their independence was "placed under the safeguard of natural laws which we cannot violate with impunity."[113]

These debates do not require a lengthy analysis, but two points emerge that demand consideration. First, on 22 December the Morton resolution passed in the Senate by a 32–9 vote. The House of Representatives then took up the resolution, to which it attached and passed by a vote of 108 to 76 a strongly worded, restrictive, anti-imperialist amendment. It stated that nothing in the Morton resolution "shall be held, understood, or construed to committing Congress to the policy of annexing the territory of said republic of Dominica." The amended Morton resolution passed the House, 123–63. The Senate followed suit and approved the amendment unanimously, 57–0.[114] The president got his commission but no victory. Most of the votes supporting the Morton resolution came from Republicans who were not motivated by Grant's logic, a change of heart, or a sudden desire to take the Dominican Republic. They wanted, rather, to save the party from internal division and even greater public embarrassment over a failed imperialist policy. "The San Domingo business is a blunder," concluded Rutherford Hayes. "It ought not to have been entered upon . . . and if entered upon it ought not to have been pushed in a way to offend needlessly the men of the party who opposed it." The president, he concluded, "is not a man of policy. . . . He does openly, instantly, without regard to effect or time, what he thinks ought to be done."[115] The commission, the exiled Hoar observed, "was intended merely to let the administration down 'easy.'" In voting for it, many Republicans probably felt like Speaker of the House James G. Blaine, who wrote after having a "frank chat" with Grant: "I will support the resolution of inquiry, but am against the final acquisition."[116]

Second, though much of this debate turned on legalisms and partisan squabbling, the vanguard of the opposition relied on race. Of this group Schurz was the most ruthless and articulate. The gravest question surrounding annexation in the tropics, he said, was the following: "[I]s the incorporation of that part of the globe and the people inhabiting it quite compatible with the integrity, safety, perpetuity, and progressive development of our institutions which we value so highly?" For several reasons, he argued, the answer was unequivocally no. He suggested that the United States would not be satisfied with one annexation in the tropics; others would follow in time, thus the logic of his opposition: "You annex the rest of the West Indies; more and more; not hundreds of thousands, but now millions of people." Another question presented itself: what to do with these millions? "You cannot exterminate them all," proclaimed the senator, so, he told his colleagues, "you must try to incorporate them with our political system." The Constitution, he warned, allowed just one course of action. "You must admit them as states, such as they are," he said, "upon an equal footing with the States you represent; you must admit them as States," Schurz told his fellow senators, "not only to govern themselves, but to take part in the government of the common concerns of the Republic. Have you thought of what this means?" he asked. "Imagine 'manifest destiny' to have swallowed up Mexico also; and you will not be able to stop when you are once on the inclined plane. And then fancy ten or twelve tropical States added to the southern States we already possess; fancy the Senators and Representatives of ten or twelve millions of tropical people, people of the Latin race mixed with Indian and African blood; people who . . . have neither language, nor traditions, nor habits, nor political institutions, nor morals in common with us; fancy them," he continued, "sitting in the Halls of Congress, throwing the weight of their intelligence, their morality, their political notions and habits, their prejudices and passions, into the scale of destinies of this Republic . . . fancy this, and then tell me, does not your imagination recoil from the picture?"[117]

Elated by the speech, Grant's former secretary of the interior, Jacob Cox, wrote to Schurz, congratulating him for placing "squarely before the country" what he believed was the most crucial issue of the debates: "that extension into tropical regions is proven by all experience to be dangerous to republican institutions." Like Schurz, he too opposed "any attempt to dilute our republicanism with an admixture of West Indian, of Mexican, or of South American turbulence."[118] This was more than a simple gesture of support or expression of admiration. Cox's letter reveals that a second influential member of Grant's cabinet resisted annexation on racial grounds.

Grant never made peace with this defeat. Words spoken by Grant and others written by his own hand reveal the churning disappointment and bitterness he felt. In late March 1871 he told a confidant: "[M]y belief that the Country would demand the admission of Santo Domingo if the question were thoroughly understood, led me to ask for a commission to visit that republic. My desire," he continued, "was to vindicate myself and the gentlemen whom I had selected to visit that country."[119] Here the president revealed the emotion that would bind him to the Dominican treaty from that moment to the end of his life. It was not the bullish pursuit of victory that drove Grant or a need to force Congress to reverse its decision but his furious desire for vindication.

To realize that Grant craved vindication is far less important than understanding the strange and even tragic manner in which he pursued it. Early on, he blamed others for his failure. In the message Grant sent to Congress on 4 April 1871 along with the Santo Domingo Commission's report, the president cast himself as the statesman and visionary thwarted by the maneuvers of a gang of craven politicos. Grant explained that when he accepted the "arduous and responsible position" of president, he "did not dream of instituting steps for the acquisition of insular possessions."[120] Annexation was thrust upon him by dire circumstances (Fabens and Cazneau are conspicuously though predictably missing from this message). The Dominican Republic was weak, he said: impoverished, vulnerable, and, Grant insisted, ready "to pass from a condition of independence to one of ownership . . . under a European power." Given this, the president wrote, "I felt that a sense of duty and due regard for our great National interests"—specifically an "earnest desire" to uphold the Monroe Doctrine—"required me to negotiate a treaty for the acquisition of the Dominican Republic." But despite its wisdom and historic sanction, the policy was overthrown, he told Congress, when men opposed to annexation lied to and misled the public, spread "allegations calculated to prejudice the merits of the case," and cast baleful "aspersions upon those whose duty had connected them to it." To his reckoning, this justified both the Morton resolution and the creation of the committee whose report he was then submitting to Congress. The result of its investigations, the president argued, "fully vindicates" before the people the "purity of the motives and actions of those who represented the United States in the negotiation." The president confessed that he held on to a slim hope that the people, "that tribunal whose convictions seldom err," in possession of the facts, would rally to him and offer deliverance. Grant conceded, "It is not the theory of our Constitution that the will of the people . . . is the supreme law," but "I have ever believed that 'all men are wiser than any one man'; and if the people, upon a full representation of the facts, shall decide that the annexation of the Republic is not desirable, every department of the government ought to acquiesce in that decision."[121]

The people did not rise in support, and their silence, probably a sign of profound indifference, surely felt like condemnation to Grant. Six years later, in his last annual address to the nation as president, he could neither forget nor find within himself the integrity to let the matter rest. He eulogized his treaty in this message, he insisted, not to reopen the issue (or old wounds, presumably) but "to vindicate [his] previous actions in regard to it." The president revisited points worn thin years before regarding the commercial and strategic advantages of acquisition before he arrived at a significant and unexpected moment. Here, Grant finally broke the silence he had maintained on race and annexation through eight years and two administrations. He ended it not in vague, tentative, or abstract terms but directly and explicitly, declaring, just as he had in the "Reasons Why" memorandum, how the annexation of the Dominican Republic would have raised the material and political fortunes of millions of African Americans. "The emancipated race of the South," he wrote, "would have found there a congenial home, where their civil rights would not be disputed and where their labor would be so much sought after that the poorest among them could have found the means to go." In instances of "great oppression and cruelty, such as has been practiced upon them in many places within the last eleven years," he predicted, "whole communities would have sought refuge in Santo Domingo." Grant said that he did not believe that "the whole race would have gone." Because "[t]heir labor is desirable—indispensable almost —where they are now," the president did not think that African Americans should abandon the South. But annexation would have given them options tantamount to power that they needed desperately in the face of their enemies and tormentors: it would have made blacks, according to Grant, "'master of the situation,' by enabling them to demand [their] rights at home on pain of finding them elsewhere."[122]

What compelled Grant to end his silence on race? Annexation was dead, a fact that simultaneously bore through him and liberated him. The president, at the twilight of his public life, could say anything on this issue because he could no longer be hurt by his words. By the fall of 1876 his two most formidable enemies were gone from politics: Schurz had retired from the Senate the previous year, and Sumner had been dead for two. The politicians from the battles of 1870 and 1871 still lurking in the halls of Congress had put this ugly matter behind them. There was at least no harm in indulging the president one last time. But in the final account the best explanation for why Grant revealed the race element in his annexation scheme is found in his own writings: they demonstrate with absolute clarity how deeply he craved and ached for vindication. From the end of his presidency to the end of his life, Grant acted out the belief that by exploiting race he could have it.

On this point, Grant was nothing if not practical. His use of race, like that of the imperialists who followed him, functioned in reaction to one question: would it take him further away from or move him closer to his object? So long as annexation was the object the answer was the former (put another way, fixing African Americans and the benefits, rights, and opportunities they might enjoy at the center of policy during the Reconstruction era would have destroyed the treaty with the white public even before Schurz and others attacked it on racial grounds). When the object became vindication, it was the latter.

After retiring from the presidency, Grant spoke of race and annexation on at least two more occasions. In 1878, while on an around-the-world tour, he told a reporter from the *New York Herald* that the annexation of Santo Domingo would have solved "many problems that now disturb" the nation. Reconstruction was over, the last northern troops were being removed from the South, and white Democrats and secret vigilante groups were aggressively and often violently unraveling the work of the previous decade. African Americans and a few dedicated whites struggled to defend the fragments of political and citizenship rights that survived southern "redemption." Surveying all this, Grant maintained that the violence and bloodletting would have been avoided had the Senate simply ratified his treaty. The island, he said, "would have given a new home to the blacks who . . . are still oppressed in the South." Had even a small number, two or three thousand, emigrated, he said, "the Southern people would learn the crime of KuKluxism, because they would see how necessary the black man is to their own prosperity."[123] What this suggests is that more than a dozen years after emancipation, Grant still did not comprehend the true and complex nature of antiblack violence: how terrorism and political and economic disfranchisement were the prime mechanisms of control, destroying both the theory and practice of free labor.

Grants last words on the Dominican Republic appear in his *Personal Memoirs*, the book he completed only days before his death in 1885. Observing the cycle of cruelty, exploitation, poverty, and violence African Americans faced two decades removed from slavery, Grant predicted that they would not suffer such injustices in silence forever. Retribution would come. Given this, he wrote, the "condition of the colored man within our borders may become a source of anxiety, to say the least." This was the preface to another dramatic shift in the former president's mind, to another—and startling—rationalization of his lost imperialist policy. Here his motive was no longer driven by sympathy for the former slaves and the desire to provide them with a safe haven as had been the case in 1869, 1876, and, to a certain extent, 1878. Here Grant declared that he pursued annexation with the ardor and stubbornness that he did to save the nation from a calamitous race war: from "a conflict between the races [that] may come up in the future as it did between freedom and slavery before." It was "looking to a settlement of this question," he said, "that led me to urge the annexation of Santo Domingo during the time I was President of the United States."[124]

Grant, wasting from cancer yet by nearly every account still lucid and decisive, chose to return to the Santo Domingo policy in the closing pages of a book largely devoted to the Civil War. Also, the integrity of his final statement on it, regarding his motives, is betrayed by the extant evidence. These facts are significant and revealing. With respect to what they tell us about the workings of Grant's mind in his final days, they give us sound reason to believe that this is how he wanted his presidency and the annexation plot remembered in history. In the larger scheme of things, these statements represent continuity that would stretch backward and forward in time. Grant, like those before him and after, justified empire not for the benefit and uplift of people of color but rather for the advancement of the nation, specifically a *white* nation in which African Americans were reduced to a source of "anxiety," a word that directly reflects the period's obsession with the so-called Negro problem.

When he wrote those words Grant was fully aware that he was in the last hours of his life, a time which many have counted, not without good reason, to be among his finest and most courageous. But if we take account of all the facts, we must acknowledge that Grant also succumbed to profound weakness. On Santo Domingo and the fate of African Americans his courage and better judgment failed him. He made the deliberate decision to exploit a peculiar species of racism—one of the most ancient yet most deeply rooted fears held by whites, race war—in a final attempt to vindicate himself and have in death what he could not achieve while alive.

After his father's death, Jesse Grant lived a largely unremarkable existence. He traveled, moved in and out of occupations, and briefly, in middle age, was the subject of fanciful rumors that made him a candidate for the vice presidency of the United States on a ticket to be led by Robert Lincoln, the son of Abraham Lincoln. Eventually, late in life, sixty-seven years old, a widower living in California, he tried his hand at biography. *In the Days of My Father General Grant* was published in 1925. It is an important book in that it provides an indispensable firsthand account of Grant's presidency, and nowhere more so than in the pages that touch upon the subject of this chapter. In them, Jesse Grant recalled a day in the White House when he asked his father why he was so determined to have the Dominican Republic. "Because they should belong to us. There is not sound argument against annexation, and one day we shall need it badly," the president said, adding, "I fear we may bay heavily for the failure to act as justice and common sense indicated."[125]

This epitaph to the Santo Domingo scheme was more than just a defense of a father and a president. It revealed that the passage of time had not diminished at all the fierce desire for vindication that Grant felt and apparently bequeathed his youngest child. Engaged in the simplest activities of everyday life, Jesse Grant brooded over what were, to him, the most visible and distasteful consequences of his father's defeat a half century earlier. He wondered if "the time is not approaching when the Northern states will face a race problem more serious than that of Reconstruction days." What troubled the old man as he moved through his world was not the fear of a coming race war but the constant reminders that an old and familiar social order—in which the rules of Victorian etiquette and the color line were inviolable—had passed away. "I think of San Domingo and of father's persistent efforts to bring about annexation," he wrote, "every time I ride upon the Elevated or in the Subway, and see white women stand while negroes occupy the seats."[126]

CHAPTER THREE

The Policy of Last Resort

The January 1893 revolution that overthrew Hawaii's queen, Liliuokalani, precipitated from her attempt to proclaim a new constitution and restore native authority in the islands. Her intentions were to reclaim the monarchy's dominance over the elective legislature, the House of Nobles, and limit suffrage to her native subjects, effectively disfranchising the white population. When she discovered that her ministers and closest advisers would not support this plan, the queen backed down. She told her subjects that the new constitution must wait, asked them to end their public demonstrations, withdraw from the streets, maintain peace and order, and be patient for a more opportune moment.

The powerful white classes responsible for the coup, a congregation of planters and landholders, traders and businessmen, most of them of American descent, resented sharing power with the monarchy. After the revolution they would testify that their actions were correct and just—that they had been provoked to action by the personality of the queen, her emotional instability, and a long pattern of outrages, excesses, and abuses of power and a series of immoral acts. In response, to protect both their interests and potentially their lives, they formed the Committee of Safety, organized in the words of one of its leaders "to take steps to preserve the public peace and secure the maintenance of law and order against the revolutionary acts of the sovereign."[1] On 16 January 1893, on the orders of John L. Stevens, the U.S. minister to Hawaii, marines from the USS *Boston* came ashore and stationed themselves within sight of the Government Building, ostensibly to protect American life and property, deliberately to intimidate the royalists in anticipation of the coup d'état. The presence of this cordon of marines guaranteed that there would be no resistance. The revolutionaries entered and took over the capital the following day, announced that the monarchy had been deposed, and proclaimed the establishment of a provisional government. To close the circle on his intervention, Stevens cited the existence of a de facto government and extended official diplomatic recognition. Representatives of other foreign nations—including Germany, Italy, Russia, China, Spain, Sweden, Norway, Denmark, Mexico, Chile, and Peru—quickly did the same."[2]

Liliuokalani was helpless to respond. Indeed, any attempt to retake the Government Building would certainly have led to a confrontation between her loyalists and armed American soldiers. Rather than do anything that her enemies could construe as an act of war against the United States, the queen wisely chose to yield under protest. She sent an appeal directly to the United States government, calling on it to "undo the action of its representative," Stevens, and restore her as Hawaii's legitimate constitutional monarch. Her initial protests were ignored.[3]

The provisional government acted with all deliberate speed and rushed a delegation to Washington, D.C., to negotiate the terms of Hawaii's annexation to the United States. Its five members made a restless and exhausting journey across half an ocean and then a continent. They arrived in the capital on 3 February and immediately began talks with Secretary of State John W. Foster. Foster wanted the islands, but he had to work both quickly and with great care. He had to craft a treaty that would not antagonize Congress, one that it would ratify before President Benjamin Harrison, defeated for reelection by Democrat Grover Cleveland the previous fall, left office on 4 March.

Difficulties complicated the negotiations from the start; the most significant involved money. The delegation requested that Hawaii be included in the McKinley tariff, in particular its lucrative sugar bounty: a two cents per pound subsidy that the government paid domestic growers as a bulwark against the foreign product. Here the Hawaiians' motives were transparent: to regain—as an added benefit along with annexation—a privilege they once had, but lost. Before the tariff went into effect in 1890, the islands had enjoyed a favored position in the American market; Hawaii's agricultural economy flourished, and the sugar growers' accounts grew fat. Afterward, the effect of the tariff was, as one historian put it, like a violent "body blow on the Hawaiian sugar economy."[4] Growers lost millions of dollars per year; Minister Stevens estimated it to be as much as $12 million.

Two more requests from the Hawaiian negotiators would have required prying dollars from the grip of a stingy Congress. They asked for a grant to fund improvement in Pearl Harbor. A treaty drafted in 1884—but not ratified until 1887—gave the United States exclusive rights to the harbor that was, nine years later, still unnavigable and, therefore, practically useless. They also wanted an appropriation for laying an oceanic cable that would connect Honolulu to the United States. Foster rejected all three proposals. They would be too expensive and too controversial given the time he had left. The inclusion of any of the three proposals in the final treaty would excite a commotion in Congress and carry the debate beyond his deadline.

Foster dismissed another proposal that, for the purposes of this book, was most significant: a provision that would have kept in place Hawaii's contract labor system and promiscuous immigration policy, which together had brought tens of thousands of Chinese, Japanese, and Portuguese "coolie" workers to the islands. Cheap labor was vital to the health and prosperity of the sugar industry. Foster understood this. He appreciated both the urgency and necessity behind the request, but he also understood, far better than the Hawaiians, the political dangers that shadowed it.

Only months before, Congress had renewed the Chinese Exclusion Act. The original exclusion bill, passed in 1882, was only in part the result of anxiety over the Chinese presence. In objective terms involving actual numbers, there was very little to fear since the Chinese made up only .002 percent of the American population. But, as Ronald Takaki observed, Congress was responding to fears and forces that had little or no relationship to the Chinese: to the stressful reality of class tensions and conflict within white society during an era of economic crisis. Recent history had taught all Americans, the working classes especially, a hard lesson: that enormous expansions of the economy were followed by intense and painful contractions, which in turn generated social convulsions such as the violent Railroad Strike of 1877.[5]

The first Chinese Exclusion Act did not exclude all Chinese. It prohibited only the entry of Chinese laborers (Chinese businessmen—called "treaty merchants"—and their families would still be allowed to enter the United States; thus, American commerce would be protected by inclusion, labor by exclusion) and denied naturalized citizenship to the Chinese already in the United States. "Support for the law," Takaki tells us, "was overwhelming."

The House vote was 201 yeas, thirty-two nays, and fifty-one absent. While congressmen from the West and South gave it unanimous support, a large majority from the East (fifty-three out of seventy-seven) and the Midwest (fifty-nine out of seventy-two) also voted for the prohibition. Significantly, support for the anti-Chinese legislation was national, coming not only from the western states but also from the states where there were few or no Chinese. In the debate, congressmen revealed fears that were much deeper than race. The exclusionists warned that the presence of an "industrial army of Asiatic laborers" was exacerbating the class conflict between white labor and white capital. White workers had been "forced to the wall" by Chinese labor. The struggle between labor unions and the industrial "nabobs" and "grandees" was erupting into "disorder, strikes, riot and bloodshed" in the industrial cities of America. Congressmen still remembered the armed clashes between troops and striking railroad workers in 1877, and were aware of the labor unrest that would shortly erupt in Chicago's Haymarket Riot of 1886, and the Homestead and Pullman strikes of the 1890s. "The gate," exclusionists in Congress declared, "must be closed." The Chinese Exclusion Act was in actuality symptomatic of a larger conflict between white labor and white capital: removal of the Chinese was designed not only to defuse an issue agitating white workers but also to alleviate class tensions within white society.[6]

Foster was convinced that any stipulation that appeared either to favor Chinese labor or to undermine this pillar of the racist social order "would have the same effect upon the [treaty's] opposition that a red flag would have upon a bull."[7] President Harrison, in good republican fashion, asked if Foster might include an article allowing for a general plebiscite, to prove to the doubters and anti-imperialists that annexation was consistent with the will of the Hawaiian people. At Foster's insistence—because of the time constraints and almost certainly because such a vote would have gone against their cause—this was left out as well.[8]

The treaty, signed on 14 February 1893, declared that America and Hawaii were bound together by a historic relationship and called for the annexation of the latter "as an integral part of the territory of the United States." There was no mention of or any explicit provision for statehood. There can be little doubt that this omission was also deliberate. Foster labored hard to craft as precise and acceptable a document as time and difference of opinion allowed. In a note to the president, Foster stated that the treaty was written "with as few conditions as possible and with full reservation to congress of its legislative prerogatives." The treaty would give Congress, therefore, full

Queen Liliuokalani
(Hawaiian Historical Society)

discretion in resolving matters that recent history had shown to be most divisive, which included, Foster said, "all questions affecting the form of government of the annexed territory, the citizenship, and elective franchise of its inhabitants."[9]

Articles included in the treaty ceded all public and government land in the islands to the United States. The United States assumed responsibility for the public debt and agreed to pay the deposed queen twenty thousand dollars annually for life. For Liliuokalani, this was poor compensation for her kingdom, but for the Americans and white Hawaiians, it represented an investment: an exchange whereby the queen accepted her situation and agreed to live out her remaining years in peace, without stirring up the resentments of her people. Lastly, a special article prohibited all future immigration from East Asia into Hawaii and from the islands into the United States.[10] This represented a promise that the Chinese Exclusion Act would not be undermined, that the domestic racial order would be unaffected by empire. White labor and the hundreds of men who represented (and feared) it in Congress would have no cause to oppose the treaty on those grounds. Again, we see that policymakers saw racism, racist beliefs, and the laws, customs, and structures that upheld the dominant social order as stumbling blocks— barriers that they had to anticipate, account for, and remove if their imperialist plans would succeed.

The Republican-controlled Senate Committee on Foreign Relations gave its advice and consent quickly, in two days, with only a single dissenting vote, and passed the treaty to the upper house of Congress on 17 February. At first its prospects appeared bright. The *New York Herald* reported that according to its canvass all but three of eighty-six senators supported acquisition.[11] Unconvinced by the wisdom dispensed in the *Herald*, the secretary of state courted influential Senate Democrats John Tyler Morgan of Alabama, the senior Democrat on the Foreign Relations Committee, and Arthur Gorman of Maryland. Foster recalled in his *Diplomatic Memoirs* that neither man anticipated serious opposition from his party.[12] Indeed, in the days following the treaty's appearance, Democrats Johnson Camden of West Virginia, John Chipman of Michigan, and Matthew Butler of South Carolina announced their intentions to vote in its favor. The majority of their party brethren, however, withheld their opinions and waited for direction from their leadership.

Grover Cleveland, the president-elect, immersed in his preinaugural labors, said nothing in public on the Hawaiian treaty, not while it was being negotiated or after it reached the Senate. On 22 February he met with Walter Gresham and John Carlisle, the men he had designated as his secretaries of state and treasury, respectively, to discuss the questions that his administration would face, among them "the case of the Hawaiian Queen."[13] By this time, with Republicans pushing for immediate action, Democrats were anxious to know Cleveland's intentions regarding the treaty and how he wanted them to proceed. Congressman James McCreary, the incoming chair of the House Foreign Relations Committee, advised the president-elect to have the treaty stopped until the new administration took office. Cleveland agreed, and the Senate Democrats kept the treaty from coming to a vote.

Five days after his inauguration, President Cleveland withdrew the treaty from the Senate "for the purpose of re-examination."[14] Some, the Republicans in particular, interpreted this to be an act of crude, naked partisanship.

Cleveland recalled the treaty, they said, in order to deny Harrison and his party a great and historic victory and perhaps to claim it for himself and the Democrats.[15] Foster believed that the motivation behind the president's decision was private rather than public and above all else personal, that Cleveland had been "influenced by Gresham's hostility to Harrison."[16] But the balance of evidence leads toward other conclusions. It suggests, instead, that Cleveland and Gresham simply did not know what to do with Hawaii or the treaty; that they wanted time to investigate and consider the matter on their own terms. In other words, they wanted to arrive at a decision on annexation based on reason, facts, and their own conception of national (and party) interest. Neither man wanted simply to usher through a policy forfeited by another administration, a rival party, in a riot of jingo emotion.

From the standpoint of the public, Cleveland's taking a cautious posture turned out to be a wise short-term strategy. Harrison and Foster had been sharply criticized for the "indecent haste" with which they tried to snatch Hawaii and with which they tried to ram the treaty through the Senate before the question could be discussed publicly, calmly, and rationally. By comparison, Cleveland's reserve made him appear statesmanlike, like a politician concerned more with national rather than partisan interest. A conservative on matters related to the United States Treasury, the president was mindful of the costs that would accompany imperialism. By itself this aspect of his stand would have won the president allies across lines of section, class, and party. Finally, Cleveland must have been intensely aware of the troubles that would descend on him if he annexed, without investigation or question, a territory that was, first, so distant and, second, inhabited by a conglomeration of native Hawaiians, Japanese, and Chinese. Such a leap, if taken impulsively, could have been a political catastrophe for either party, but especially so for Cleveland's Democrats, the party of white supremacy.[17]

Another important factor explained and justified the administration's caution. Neither Cleveland nor Gresham was satisfied with Stevens's account of the revolution. Their suspicions were raised further by Queen Liliuokalani's provocative and articulate protest, addressed directly to the new president.[18] They decided that many questions needed to be answered before a decision could be made on Hawaii. On 11 March, Cleveland appointed James H. Blount, a Democrat and former Confederate, former congressman from Georgia, and retired chair of the House Committee on Foreign Relations, as special commissioner with "paramount" authority over all American affairs in Hawaii. Blount was instructed to go to the islands, assess the situation there, and report back on "all that can fully enlighten the President touching the subject of [his] mission."[19]

Blount would be in Hawaii for about four months, interviewing witnesses, royalists, and participants in the revolution and gathering other evidence. Over that time the Cleveland administration remained conspicuously silent on Hawaii. This reflected, in part, the president's determination to have all the facts at his disposal before deciding on a course of action. More important, his energies were consumed in responding to the economic collapse that began on 3 May 1893, the stock market crash that thrust the United States into the worst depression in its history to date. In its first month businesses failed at a rate of a dozen per day. Shops, factories, mines, and other workplaces shut down in staggering numbers. The farm sector suffered even worse. By the end of 1893 it is estimated that five hundred banks and more than sixteen thousand businesses had gone into bankruptcy. By the middle of 1894, 150 railroad companies would follow.

A grim Samuel Gompers, head of the American Federation of Labor, estimated that there were more than three million unemployed in 1893. Labor and agrarian radicalism, catalyzed by the disaster, excited both hope and fear across the nation: the march of Coxy's Army on Washington, D.C., demanding that the federal government create work relief; the Pullman strike, which set federal troops and United States marshals into battle with desperate railroad workers; and the resurgence of the Populists in national politics. A public largely indifferent to foreign affairs, even in the best of times, had, in the middle years of the 1890s, even more reason to turn its attentions inward. In any event, the fate of the Hawaii treaty would wait until Blount completed his mission. Then Cleveland would decide whether the nation would refuse the islands or annex them and take up the burdens of a great imperial power.

The first great fact of the Pacific Ocean is its enormousness. In area it occupies seventy million square miles, about one-third of the earth's surface. It is the planet's dominant feature. Hawaii's predominant feature is its isolation. The archipelago consists of eight islands and tiny, scattered islets, the visible summits of a chain of underwater volcanoes rising out of the Pacific, twenty-four hundred miles southwest of San Francisco and over five thousand miles east of the Philippines. The first human inhabitants were Polynesian voyagers who probably arrived around A.D. 400. From these beginnings a society evolved that was ruled by chiefs and priests and whose culture was defined by oral traditions, elaborate myths, and primitive technology. The arrival of British explorer Captain James Cook in January 1778 brought Hawaii's seclusion to an end. Intermittent contact with traders and merchants interested in the islands' valuable sandalwood followed until the first missionaries arrived in 1820.

The story of U.S. policy in Hawaii began twenty-two years later, a half century before the revolution, with an initiative meant to remove the last vestiges of the islands' isolation. The first step was taken by Hawaii, not the United States, the result of King Kamehameha III's desire to see his country "formally acknowledged by the civilized nations of the world as a sovereign and independent State" and to formalize its diplomatic relations.[20] To achieve these ends the king sent two representatives, Prince Timoteo Haalilio and William Richards, to Washington, D.C., in December 1842 to present their mission to Secretary of State Daniel Webster. Under Kamehameha's instruction his emissaries were to continue on to England and France to secure recognition from those nations, negotiate formal treaties to replace obsolete conventions, and arrange for the exchange of qualified envoys. The American capital was to be only the first stop in a great and historic mission for the island kingdom.[21]

Richards knew the city well and had influential friends on whom to call for the necessary introductions and counsel. It was Haalilio, however, who captured the greatest attention. During their stay the young prince was in great demand socially and the object of widespread interest and curiosity. Julia Gardiner, who only months later would marry President John Tyler, though somewhat discomfited by his appearance, was positively beguiled by Haalilio. "His complexion," she wrote in her diary, "is about as dark as a negro, but with Indian hair though at a distance being short and thick it seems the *true wool*." His manner, she said, was "modest and graceful," which left the impression that he was "quite a man of the world in comparison with his Interpreter," a reference to Richards.[22] John Quincy Adams was similarly taken by the sight of the prince, seeing him, interestingly, as a man "nearly black as an Ethiopian, but with a European face and wool for hair."[23]

Haalilio and Richards's first meeting with Webster was frustrating for them, as the secretary of state, according to Richards, "appeared to know little about the islands."[24] When the two parties finally reached discussion, the Hawaiians made their case for formal diplomatic recognition. They justified their cause on the grounds of the natives' moral and material progress; their written language and laws, constitutional monarchy, legislature and courts, schools, and knowledge of the Christian Bible proved their capacity for civilization and self-government. They reminded the secretary of state of the islands' geographic position at the "great center of the whale fisher for most of the world . . . on the principal line of communication" between America and Asia. "There is no other place in all that part of the Pacific Ocean where repair of vessels can be made to so good an advantage, or supplies be obtained in such abundance, and on such favorable terms." Webster, a Whig from Massachusetts, a state whose economy thrived on the fishing and whaling industries and whose merchant class was desirous of pursuing trade in East Asia, could not be indifferent to these arguments. Furthermore, they said, Kamehameha's kingdom had protected both the persons and the property of foreign citizens, a matter of particular concern for the United States. On the matter of persons, they cited "some 1,400 American citizens . . . at the various parts of the islands, requiring constantly . . . the protection of his Majesty." The property they owned, which Haalilio and Richards said was "more or less dependent on the protection of [the king's] Government," was worth, Webster learned, "not less than five to seven million dollars annually."[25]

Webster was most affected by Hawaii's importance in America's Pacific trade. Indeed, he said, the preponderance of this trade made the United States "more interested in the fate of the islands, and of their Government, than any other nation can be." On this basis Webster defined "the sense of . . . the United States" regarding its future position toward Hawaii: "that the Government of the Sandwich Islands [Cook had named the islands after the earl of Sandwich] ought to be respected; that no power ought to seek any undue control over the existing Government, or any exclusive privileges or preferences in matters of commerce."[26] The 31 December 1842 message that would come to be called the Tyler Doctrine (a document written largely by Webster) repeated these ideas and raised them to the level of policy. President Tyler declared that an independent Hawaii must be the "true interest" of all the commercial powers and that the kingdom's "growth and prosperity as an independent state" was "in a high degree useful to all those whose trade is extended" into the Pacific and East Asia. Furthermore, he said, the United States would be (in an odd choice of words) "dissatisfied" by any attempt by another power "to take possession of the islands, colonize them, and subvert the native government."[27]

Despite its ambiguity, particularly around the word "dissatisfied," the

Tyler Doctrine created the basic framework for America's Hawaii policy until 1898. It brought the islands onto the nation's policy horizon and extended the implicit pledge to support and protect Hawaii's independence. It was also intended to ward off rival powers, in particular France and England, who had competitive economic and political interests in Hawaii. Both nations had recently shown aggressive and predatory tendencies in the Pacific: England annexed New Zealand in 1841, and France seized the Marquesas in 1842. If the Tyler administration feared that either power might attempt to take Hawaii, its anxiety could be justified (the content of Webster's memorandum to Haalilio and Richards and the Tyler Doctrine indicate that this was a vital consideration). This would be a pivotal theme in United States–Hawaiian relations, a significant factor in American intervention in the revolution of 1893 and the push for annexation in 1897–98.

The Tyler message did not extend recognition to Hawaii as an independent state, which was evidence that American policy was less than fully formed. Webster's ignorance concerning the islands and his circumspect treatment of Haalilio and Richards might account for some of this tentativeness. Richards suspected that the secretary of state's political instincts and ambition were at the root of his caution. "[T]he great Daniel is looking for popularity," he observed, "and he will not do, nor fail to do anything, which can affect that without considerable reflection." John Quincy Adams also speculated on Webster's posture and its potential effects on the power rivalries in the Pacific. Characteristically stern, Adams "did not see the wisdom of leaving to Great Britain the option of assuming the islands under her protection, like the Ionian Islands." Interesting even though it is only a suspicion is Adams's insight into Webster's avoiding the tangled question of extending formal diplomatic recognition to the Hawaiians: "which is that they are black."[28]

Despite Haalilio and Richards's presence in the capital and their capable work in support of King Kamehameha III and his people, Webster and Tyler extended little substantive consideration to the native Hawaiians. Webster offered cursory thanks to them for their "numerous acts of hospitality to the citizens of the United States." Tyler's message noted favorably their "progress towards civilization," their rising competence in matters regarding "regular and orderly civil government," and their government's dedication to introducing "knowledge, . . . religious and moral institutions, means of education, and the arts of civilized life."[29] Neither, however, described in any detail the role that the native population would play in policy they had outlined.

Looking back to the winter of 1842, vagaries and silences in the historic record are quite naturally to be expected. The president and secretary of state lived more than five thousand miles from the islands. There was no direct or regular communication with them; indeed, this episode began with the Hawaiians' wish to give order to the sporadic nature of their relations with the United States. California, whose political and economic evolutions would provide vital reference points for determining the nation's interests with the island kingdom, would not join the Union for another eight years. Regardless of these factors—yet in many ways *because* of them—no one could ignore the fact that the integrity of the Tyler Doctrine depended not on American commercial or military power but on the native Hawaiians: on the very same people who (in words attributed to Tyler) had just "emerg[ed] from a state of barbarism." Indeed everything would depend on the native Hawaiians—on their advancement, stability, prosperity, and survival. United States policy would yaw and tack dramatically over the next five decades, and it would do so consistently in response to the state of the native Hawaiian population; its course was straight and stable when their numbers were large, rolling and wavering when Hawaii fell into its tragic and calamitous decline.

Figures on Hawaii's population prior to Cook's arrival have been elusive and controversial for more than two centuries. In 1779 one of Cook's officers, Lieutenant James King, who relied on intuitive observation alone, estimated that there were approximately 400,000 natives inhabiting the eight islands. His accounting was attacked almost from the moment it first appeared in print. Captain George Dixon, a visitor to the islands in 1787, called King's estimate "greatly exaggerated." To his reckoning the population numbered closer to 200,000. William Bligh, who later captained the infamous HMS *Bounty*, was aboard the *Resolution* during Cook's last voyage. He arrived at a far more precise number: 242,200. This figure is suspect, historian David Stannard tells us, because of its precision but mostly because Bligh failed to explain how he had arrived at it.[30] The missionary Rufus Anderson cited the 400,000 with skepticism in his writings on Hawaii, but he stopped short of dismissing that number entirely. There was sufficient reason to think the number "somewhat excessive," he said, but then he offered the startling observation that "a traveler, forty years after [Cook's] time, found traces everywhere of deserted villages, and of enclosures, once under cultivation, then lying waste." Their ruins were, to Anderson, sound and poignant evidence that in the recent past there had been perhaps tens of thousands more native Hawaiians living, working, and cultivating the land. The lowest figures on the islands' population always came from missionaries, who estimated that there were only 120,000 and perhaps as many as 150,000 native peoples in the islands in 1820, the year that the first of their number arrived.

Abandoned lands, scattered shards of relics, eyewitness accounts, and intuition aggregated to form the conclusion that the Hawaiian people were dying off at a calamitous rate. Census figures compiled and surveyed over more than a half century provided daunting confirmation. What caused such devastation, and what accounts for its severity? The first cause was the introduction of infectious diseases, common in the West but unknown to the islands prior to 1778, against which the native population had no immunity. Exposure to microscopic arrivals killed the people in numbers that would exceed the rate of natural increase. In 1806, an epidemic, believed to be either cholera or bubonic plague, was said to have swept away half the native population on Oahu. Epidemics in 1826, 1839, and the late 1840s killed thousands of children, women, and men. Measles, influenza, smallpox, and syphilis killed through the direct effects of their pathologies and indirectly by disabling labor and disrupting agricultural cycles, which lead to famine, malnutrition, sickness, and more death.[31]

Knowledge of medicine, science, and history, encounters with the cruel cycle of disease, famine, morbidity, and death, might have taught those who witnessed these events in Hawaii what would happen when epidemics ravaged vulnerable populations. When witnesses tried to come to terms with this catastrophe, reason and science carried far less explanatory power than race. In *The Hawaiian Islands: Their Progress and Condition under Missionary Labors*, Rufus Anderson cited a physician's study of diseases found on the islands. The doctors believed that the climate was "eminently favorable to health," thus the disproportionate amount of disease among the natives arose, they concluded, out of the victims' moral deficiencies, from their "low estimate of life, and the consequent reckless habit of living."[32] The Reverend Artemis Bishop, writing in the *Hawaiian Spectator* in 1838, attributed their decline to a high rate of infant mortality, which could have resulted from natural causes or ritual infanticide. Either way, Bishop declared, both tragedies arose from the "unrestrained licentiousness of . . . older and middle-aged women."[33]

To Bishop, though the Hawaiian people were themselves the authors of their own tragedy, the women carried the greater share of the blame. Their

TABLE 1 Decline of the Native Hawaiian Population, 1832–1890

1832	130,313
1850	84,165
1853	71,091
1860	69,800
1872	56,896
1884	40,014
1890	34,436

Sources: Kuykendall and Day, *Hawaii: A History*, 298; House Executive Documents, 53d Cong., 3d sess.; *FRUS*, 1894, App. 1, 256.

alcoholism and "diseases propagated through impure intercourse with white men," he wrote, accounted for much of the decline in the adult population. Such was the nature, he said, of "a barbarous or semi-barbarous people who have no command over their appetites." They were incapable of consuming alcohol "with any degree of moderation," Bishop said, only in excess and eventually "to a fatal result." Their sexual hunger was just as devastating. In a few years "a dreadful mortality, heightened," he asserted, "by their unholy intercourse, swept away one half of the population, leaving the dead unburied for want of those able to perform the rights of sepulture."[34]

Mark Twain, in his eminently popular Sandwich Island lecture, talked of Hawaiians' decline with dark and gruesome levity. Twain told curious and fascinated audiences in the United States and England that their fall from 400,000 began with the arrival of the first white men and their motley and deadly companions: "various complicated diseases, and education, and civilization, and all sorts of calamities." With only 55,000 remaining when he gave the lecture—more than one hundred times between 1866 and 1873—Twain remarked that though disease was "retiring them from the business pretty fast," some "proposed to send a few more missionaries to finish them." Their extinction was inevitable, Twain said, a sad eventuality but not without its benefits. "When they pick up and leave we will take possession [of the islands] as their lawful heirs."[35] In the 1880s and 1890s, policymakers would try to ennoble this process by giving it a name: "Americanization."

Traveler and writer Isabella Bird, in *Six Months in the Sandwich Islands* (1881), called the "dwindling of the [Hawaiian] race" a pitiful and "most pathetic subject." At the time of her visit, only about 49,000 remained. Bird's fascination with their disappearance was romantic rather than morbid. She likened "the laughing, flower-clad hordes . . . who make the town gay with their presence" to "butterflies fluttering out their short lives in the sunshine . . . a wreck and residue / Whose only business is to perish."[36]

Just beneath her poetry Bird set her conclusions on cold, hard statistics and personal observation. Working down from King's high estimate, Bird calculated that the Hawaiians would vanish entirely as a race in 1897. What distinguished her narrative was her belief that the natives were a worthy and noble people. They had shown, she said, a "singular aptitude for politics and civilization." Had fate been more merciful it would have been interesting, Bird wrote, "to watch the development of a strictly Polynesian monarchy staring under passably fair conditions." Instead, "[w]hites . . . convey[ed] to these shores slow but infallible destruction on the one hand, and on the other the knowledge of the life that is to come . . . rival influences of blessing and cursing . . . producing results with which most reading people are familiar."[37] In government, policymaking, and business circles, to the way-ward traveler and the lyceum attendee, to the reader perusing the many books, pamphlets, and articles that took up the subject of Hawaii, the de-cline of the native population was an indisputable fact, confirmed by a confluence of spontaneous observation and objective census figures, all gathered over decades. In truth, their disappearance was a more complex phenomenon. Some native Hawaiians—the precise numbers will probably never be known—had simply emigrated, leaving the islands to pursue work, and it is not unreasonable to think, given the daunting insularity of their homeland, adventure, elsewhere. After 1850, some would go to the Pacific coast and find work as agricultural laborers. Still others lived away from the islands for long periods, months and perhaps years, aboard commercial and whaling ships. Many who stayed on the islands resisted being drawn into the plantation system that was expanding over the islands, with its hard labor, long hours, and small wages. They chose to maintain themselves by keeping to traditional work, raising taro, sweet potatoes, and other products on small parcels of land that had not been integrated into the mainstream economy, sugar production.

Regardless of its causes, the native population's descent was something more than just a strange and tragic curiosity. It created a string of practical problems for the survivors, Hawaii's native rulers, as well as the white mi-nority. This was true for the missionaries, certainly. As the calamity unfolded they showed various degrees of compassion toward the native peoples. Some concentrated on providing the natives with physical relief from their suffering, along with spiritual guidance and assurances of God's love and mercy. Others saw only God's judgment on a race they considered debauched and inferior and consoled themselves with the idea that the Hawaiians' destruction was their own doing. Either way, there would be fewer souls to save and over time a progressively smaller role for the missionary in the islands.

The planters' dilemma was more immediate and, from the standpoint of what was to follow, indispensable to understanding the evolution of U.S. policy leading up to Hawaii's annexation. The planters' need for agricultural workers reached a critical phase at the same time its most proximate and inexpensive source of labor was disappearing. The sugar growers were compelled by economic necessity to find hands to work and harvest their cane fields, quickly. The only choice was to import them. In 1855 King Kamehameha IV seized the moment to address, simultaneously, the problems of the labor shortage and depopulation—the needs of the planter class and the priorities of the Hawaiian monarchy, whose paramount concern had become saving native peoples from extinction.

As to the labor crisis, it was not unprecedented. A previous shortage had been addressed by bringing workers from China, so-called coolie laborers. The monarchy proposed initiating a similar, but not identical, policy. The king asked the Hawaiian legislature to consider importing workers to the islands, but he insisted that they not be Chinese. Those emigrants, he argued, had "not realized the hopes of those who incurred the expense of their introduction." Kamehameha's primary objection was that they could not be assimilated. "They are not so kind and tractable as it was anticipated they would be," but worse still, he said, "they seem to have no affinities, attractions, or tendencies to blend with this, or any other race." He asked that the legislature instead recruit labor from what he called more "compatible" Polynesian groups, from "a class of persons more nearly assimilated with the Hawaiian race." A people such as this would serve everyone's purpose: "besides supplying the present demand for labor," they "would pave the way for a future population of native born Hawaiians."[38]

Efforts to meet the requirements of the monarchy and the planters never ceased, but the latter's always took precedence.[39] So over the king's wishes, urgings, and prejudice, labor was again brought from China. Eventually a wider net was cast, and the first shipload of Japanese workers arrived in 1868:

141 men, 6 women, and a child. Both groups would increase in size by thousands over the next three decades but especially after 1875, when reciprocity opened American markets to Hawaii's products, the most important being sugar.

Policymakers in the United States were slow to realize the effects that depopulation and the coming of tens of thousands of Asian workers would have on the goals set down by the Tyler Doctrine. The Hawaiians' demise had deleterious effects on the economic, political, and social order, and this vulnerability could, the Americans feared, encourage an intervention by a rival power, possibly over the most trivial matter. Over time, as these dangers became more real, the American foreign policy establishment became only more sensitive toward defending its "paramount" interest in Hawaii.

Several episodes seemed to confirm their fears and justify their vigilance and occasional belligerence. In the summer of 1880, James Comly, the U.S. minister in Honolulu, sent urgent cables to Secretary of State William Evarts about a crisis that began when the German consul sold a cache of goods to natives living on one of the islands. When the consul demanded immediate payment and the Hawaiians found that they did not have the resources to satisfy him, Comly reported, "he fined them 200,000 pounds of copra [the dried white flesh of the coconut, which is the source of coconut oil], an amount more than the total production of the island." Once the impossibility of the demand became clear, the consul "took possession of certain lands and harbors in the name of the German government."[40] This matter was settled peacefully and without any detriment to Hawaii's sovereignty, but soon a more ominous threat—from the Americans' perspective—arose.

In the spring of 1881 a group of British merchants demanded that the Hawaiian government grant their products the same favored treatment offered to American goods under its reciprocity treaty of 1875. Their claim was based on an 1852 treaty which guaranteed that English products would receive "most-favored nation" privileges. Although the British government pursued its claims peacefully and through diplomatic channels, politicians in Washington, D.C., sensed a challenge to the United States. In April, Secretary of State James G. Blaine began writing cables to the American minister in London, James Russell Lowell, instructing him to warn the British away from any mischief they might have contemplated and reiterating the content of the Tyler Doctrine. Hawaii's position "in the vicinity of our Pacific coast" and America's commercial relations with the islands, Blaine said, "lead this government to watch with grave interest, and to regard unfavorably, any movement, negotiation, or discussion aiming to transfer them in any eventuality whatever to another power."[41]

The secretary of state reaffirmed the American position again that year when he learned that King Kalakaua was about to depart on a tour of Asia and Europe. Blaine suspected that the monarch might give territory to another power in exchange for trade and investments. He drafted and circulated a note to his envoys, stationed in the countries that the king was scheduled to visit, in which he reminded them that the 1875 treaty forbade any "alienation of territory." Blaine conceded that the contract was not permanent, that Kalakaua could terminate it if and when he desired. The disadvantages of this arrangement left him deeply unsettled. He instructed the diplomats to be watchful of Kalakaua's activities during his journey and, if it became necessary, to warn any nation that tried to negotiate with him of the United States' attitude on matters regarding Hawaii, its sovereignty, and their country's preeminent position among its foreign rivals.[42]

Comly, who had carried out Blaine's instructions from his post in Honolulu, noted what he called "discomfort" among the British residents of the islands.[43] Its cause, he said, was jealousy over America's predominance. He told Blaine that England's trade commissioners kept themselves busy by constantly seeking some "means of undermining this influence and fostering British interests." Comly's concern in this instance turned on how the British were attempting to raise their stature by exploiting Hawaii's chronic labor crisis. He saw British representatives engaged in what he called a "systematic and indomitable struggle to force" the Hawaiian government to accept its "East Indian coolies." To his reckoning, these maneuvers were designed to usurp the Americans and grant the British "innumerable opportunities for meddlesome interference with the internal affairs of [Hawaii's] government." Since there appeared to be support for this initiative within the islands (The Hawaiian press put it bluntly: "The United States has given us a reciprocity treaty—why should we not allow Great Britain to give us labor?"), Comly warned the secretary of state that "coolly [sic] immigration from British India" represented nothing less than "a great and increasing danger" to American interests.[44]

Blaine found this "coolie convention" (his term) intolerable. It would have given England semijudicial supervision over its subjects, brought to the islands as laborers, and "extend[ed] to them advantages not possessed by the subjects of any other power." His fear was that this "extreme privilege" could at some future time bring about the end of Hawaii's independence. Blaine

Uncle Sam defends Hawaii from imperial Britain.
"Uncle Sam: I guess I had better take care of this one."
(*New York Herald*, 5 February 1893)

repeated that the United States would not stand idle and allow the islands to
be pulled into the orbit of one of Europe's great powers. The consequent
dangers were too great. The "just and necessary influence of the United
States" in the Pacific would be reduced, first of all. But more significant,
declared Blaine, "in case of international difficulty it would be a positive
threat to interests too large and important to be lightly risked." The method
by which America was displaced, "by diplomatic finesse or legal technical-
ity," hardly mattered to the secretary of state. Even "a scheme by which a
large mass of British subjects [was brought into Hawaii], forming in time . . .
the majority of its population," would undermine friendly relations.[45] Such
a challenge would come not from the great powers of Europe but from
across the Pacific and in the form of Asian immigration, which accelerated
dramatically after 1875. In the 1880s, but especially the 1890s, when annexation was the dominant issue of United States–Hawaiian relations, the Asian
presence was pivotal.

The arrival of "coolie labor" reached a crucial juncture when, on 14 February 1881, Comly sent an urgent message to Blaine stating that over the
previous three weeks "about 1,700 adult male Chinese immigrants had been

added to the population." Fifteen hundred more were said to be on their way, thus a "majority of the adult male population of the islands is now Chinese." He warned Blaine that there would be no end to the movement as he could see it so long as the "chief demand of the islands shall continue to be *more laborers*."[46]

Blaine's reply was significant in a number of ways: in terms of his description of the nature of the crisis, his delineation of the policy options he would and would *not* pursue, and the influence of race over all of it. His opening is especially revealing. The secretary of state said that although Hawaii was "the key to the maritime domination of the Pacific States," the United States did not want "material possession" of them "any more [than the nation wanted] Cuba." Of the demographic changes that were transforming the islands, Blaine declared that the nation must be concerned over "any tendency toward introducing . . . new social elements, destructive of [Hawaii's] necessarily American character." Though he expressed sympathy toward the plight of the native population ("a cause of great alarm to the Government and the kingdom") and understood their attempt to reverse it ("it is no wonder that a solution should be sought with eagerness in any apparently practicable quarter"), Blaine insisted that the problem could not be solved "by a substitution of Mongolian supremacy for native control," a perilous situation that had been brought about by "the rapid increase of Chinese immigration to the islands." Blaine was adamant that the Hawaiian Islands "cannot be joined to the Asiatic system." He preferred that they remain independent of all foreign influence, but if they did "drift from their independent station," he said, "it must be toward assimilation and identification with the American system, to which they . . . must belong by the operation of political necessity."[47]

In a confidential note to Comly, separate from the official communication just cited and written the same day, Blaine discussed in more precise terms what was, to his mind, "the essential question": "the gradual and seemingly inevitable decadence and extinction of the native race and its replacement by another, to which the powers of Government would necessarily descend." Put more simply: which race, the Asian or the Anglo-Saxon, would control Hawaii once the native population was gone? The census, he noted, contained two undeniable facts: the first, the "alarming diminution of the indigenous element," and the second, that an "adventitious labor element," the Chinese, was taking its place at such a rate that labor in the most productive and lucrative agricultural fields, rice and sugar, was dominated by aliens.

"The worst state of things," Blaine said, "is that it must inevitably keep on in this increasing ratio, the native classes growing smaller, . . . and the immigration to supply the want of labor greater every year."[48]

According to Blaine, Hawaii was "entirely . . . part of the productive and commercial system of the American states." Trade between the two countries, facilitated by reciprocity, made the islands "practically members of the American zollverein, an outlying district of the State of California." Often the historical literature cites this statement as a prologue to accounts of the imperialism of the 1890s and, more specifically, Hawaii's annexation in 1898. Rarely if ever is the statement fixed in its proper context. When isolated, these remarks imply that Blaine was articulating an aggressive policy bent on control or annexation when, in reality, his point was something else altogether: that up to the winter of 1881, these were the results of a just and wise Hawaiian policy, that more control was unnecessary and unwise.

Thirty years before, said Blaine, when the United States faced a choice between annexation or commercial assimilation, it pursued the latter, or in his words the "*less* responsible alternative. The soundness of the choice however," he declared, "evidently depends on the perpetuity of the rule of the native race as an independent government." Then the secretary of state arrived at a critical realization. The downward spiral of the native population, he feared, was "an inevitable fact, in view of the teachings of ethnological history." This, the erosion of monarchical power, and the peaceful invasion, taken together, meant that "the whole framework of our relations to Hawaii has [been] changed, if not destroyed."

Annexation would not be the solution. The secretary of state suggested—consistent with tradition—another less responsible alternative. The answer he preferred required "a replenishment of the vital forces of Hawaii," and the initiative had to come from the United States, not Asia, Britain, or even Hawaii. This meant sending thousands, perhaps tens of thousands of Americans to the islands, an inoculation against the "yellow peril." Blaine argued that a "purely American form of colonization would meet all phases of the problem," that all the capital, "the intelligence, and activity" necessary to reverse Hawaii's descent into an Asian sphere of influence already existed within America. Better still, he said, the labor—as this was always a question of labor as well as race and politics—that would displace the Chinese would arrive already prepared for the rigors of work in a tropical clime: they would be men and women "trained in the rice swamps and cane fields of the Southern States."[49]

The last statement is tantalizing, for it suggests that African Americans be taken from the South and colonized to serve the nation's purposes in Hawaii. For generations they had been put to work in the rice swamps and cane fields in the steamy South, in a climate they were allegedly perfectly suited for by nature. And they had been employed in recent years to solve other labor crises, albeit as strikebreakers, but the principle was remarkably similar: use blacks as a solution to a desperate labor problem that threatened the status quo. Race very likely worked on Blaine's mind when he dismissed annexation as a policy option. Precedent would have supported the secretary of state if he wanted to suggest it as a response. Elsewhere he had even expressed optimism regarding the potential benefits of annexation and seemed confident that labor and industry would both profit from it, but Blaine never called for annexation outright; indeed, as we have just seen, he refused to consider it, even in a confidential letter. Why he did this is unclear but not indecipherable, and in any speculation the Chinese presence would seem to be the crucial factor.

We know that the Chinese, their immigration, and the impact of their growing numbers on Hawaii's social order had been a matter of great concern for Blaine and Comly and a vital topic in their correspondence throughout 1881. As a matter of domestic politics, Blaine's feelings toward the Chinese and his opposition to their immigration into the United States was well established, a matter of public record, and part of his political vita. Like millions of his fellow citizens, Blaine believed that the Chinese were unsuited to be citizens, that they were incapable of meeting the grand responsibilities of republican government. He said many times that their presence degraded American labor, that it was hostile to the material interests of the white working classes. On these grounds Blaine made himself a fixture in the Chinese exclusion debate. Speaking before the Senate in February 1878 he declared: "I will not admit a man by immigration to this country whom I am not willing to place on the basis of a citizen." He went on: "we ought not to permit in this country of universal suffrage the immigration of a great people, great in numbers, whom we ourselves declare to be utterly unfit for citizenship."[50]

Blaine pursued power and in particular the presidency at a time when one's position on the so-called Chinaman question could make or break his standing in national politics. Although the exclusion issue was pivotal in all parts of the country, he realized the sensitivity this issue had in the Pacific and western states. Thus Blaine told the *San Francisco Chronicle* in December 1878 of his great sympathy for the plight of white labor. A people, he said, "who eat beef and bread and drink beer cannot labor alongside of those who live on rice, and if the experiment [in Asian immigration] is attempted on a large scale, the American laborer will have to drop his knife and fork and take up the chop sticks."[51]

China represented one type of threat, Japan another, and in the late 1880s and early 1890s, the latter would eclipse the former in the minds of policy-makers as the main threat to Hawaiian independence and American pre-dominance. Japan's presence and interests in the islands grew in stages after its first group of citizens arrived there in 1868. Mostly for ideological rea-sons—the government's belief that allowing its people to migrate to foreign lands as lowly contract laborers would damage the nation's prestige—Japa-nese immigration did not reach significant numbers until 1884. This oc-curred because between 1881 and 1885 thousands of Japanese were dislocated and reduced to poverty by the workings of the Meiji restoration and a simultaneous economic depression. Agriculture and small business suffered with the result being widespread unemployment and the threat of social chaos. In December 1884 the *Japan Weekly Mail* issued a bleak report that the depression in trade showed "no signs of abatement," and if any other coun-try was able to provide work for Japan's impoverished farmers, "it would be a judicious step to get them there as fast as possible."[52] That same year the Japanese government informed Hawaii's representative in Tokyo that it would no longer oppose large-scale contract immigration. The gates were open, and the results of this, considerable. Between 1885 and 1894, over thirty thousand Japanese immigrants entered Hawaii. By 1896, Japanese nationals accounted for 60 percent of the islands' labor force.[53] The weight of these numbers would effectively alter the course of American policy, directing and then ultimately pushing it toward annexation.

In November 1892, Minister Stevens cabled Secretary of State Foster and presented his opinion, based on an "intelligent and impartial examination of the facts," that United States policy "will soon demand some change, if not the adoption of decisive measures, with the aim to secure American interests and future supremacy."[54] Chinese and Japanese immigration had brought Hawaii to a juncture where, Stevens warned, there could be a "part-ing of the ways," with the islands going either "to Asia or . . . [to] America." Unless restrained quickly, the Asian population would make Hawaii into "a Singapore, or a Hongkong," suitable for foreign domination but "unfit to be an American Territory or an American State under our constitutional system." Stevens saw annexation as the only course and predicted: "If the American flag floats here at no distant day . . . the Asiatic tendencies can be arrested and controlled without retarding the material development . . . surely advancing [Hawaii's] prosperity . . . opening the public lands to small farmers from Europe and the United States, thus increasing the responsible [meaning white—a critical factor and the subject of the next chapter] voting population, and constituting a solid basis for American methods of government."[55]

Stevens expressed his fear of the alternative as he told Foster that "[t]wo-fifths of the people now here are Chinese and Japanese." If "the present state of things is allowed to go on," he continued, "the Asiatics will soon be largely preponderate," helped along by the demand curve of the sugar industry and its gluttony for "the cheapest possible labor—that of the Japanese, the Chinese, and India coolies." To avert this result, disaster in Stevens's mind, he called for an aggressive initiative to "Americanize the islands." His proposal was simple and direct: the United States should intervene immediately, "assume control of the 'Crown lands,' [and] dispose of them in small lots for . . . [American] settlers and freeholders." The islands would be transformed by the creation of a "permanent preponderance of a population and civilization which will make the islands like southern California . . . bringing everything here into harmony with American life and prosperity." Hesitation or delay, he warned, would only "add to present unfavorable tendencies and make future possession more difficult."[56] Thus the Asian presence, expanding unchecked, threatening to overtake the islands and pull them out of the American sphere of influence, compelled Stevens to call for annexation just two months before Queen Liliuokalani was overthrown. The fears that all this ignited in Stevens no doubt provided crucial motivation for his actions in January 1893: his intervention, without which the revolution would probably have failed.

Grover Cleveland was not a subtle man. If his first, strong inclination was against taking the islands, there is little reason to doubt that he would have communicated this decision to Gresham, Carlisle, and the Senate Democrats early on and in no uncertain terms. But Cleveland did not do this because he was indecisive over Hawaii. On 19 March 1893 the president told Carl Schurz: "I do not hold annexation in all circumstances and at any time unwise, but I am sure we ought to stop and look and think. That's exactly what we are doing now."[57] Cleveland, then, accepted the policy framework that he inherited from Tyler, Seward, Fish, and Blaine, without amendment or criticism. More specifically, he accepted annexation as a viable option, consistent within the nation's long-standing policy in Hawaii.

Annexation had been considered before 1893. In several instances the catalyst was a threat, real or imagined, from a European power to America's predominant position in the islands. In each instance where race insinuated itself into policy formation, it acted as a hindrance to annexation. Acquisition was contemplated briefly in 1851, the direct result of French aggression, with the apparent goal of undermining Hawaii's independence. Threatened with a takeover, agents of King Kamehameha III delivered a deed of cession to the U.S. minister to Honolulu, Luther Severence. The Hawaiians intended this to be a defensive measure, but Americans on the islands, specifically those with business interests, sensed an opportunity. The minister told Secretary of State Webster that the sugar planters, nearly all of them American, "have a strong interest in annexation to the United States," that "the subject of annexation is here often hinted at, and sometimes freely discussed in private." As Whigs in the years shortly after the Mexican War—a conflict in which the Democrats used "manifest destiny" to justify the seizure of distant territories—Severance realized that "[w]e must not take the islands in virtue of the 'manifest destiny' principle, but," he asked, "can we not accept their voluntary offer [to attach the islands to the United States]?" Webster's answer was no.[58]

Congress considered Hawaii's annexation for the first time in August 1852 when J. W. McCorkle, a Democrat from California, made an explicit request for their acquisition, calling it a matter "of the highest importance" to both his state "and the Pacific." Possession would help secure the West Coast in the event of some future war, "especially a war with Great Britain." The islands would also serve as an essential outpost for trade. Hawaii's economic relations with California, then the newest state in the Union, "[are] of a vast importance, and their possession [is] almost necessary to the United States in a successful prosecution of commercial enterprise with Asia and the Pacific Islands."[59]

In October 1863, Secretary of State Seward received word from the U.S. minister in Honolulu, James McBride, that the activities of Britain's representatives in the islands presented a threat to American interests there. McBride was convinced that the British would exploit the vulnerabilities in Hawaii that had been brought about by the declining health of the king and the condition of the native population, which was "decreasing so rapidly as to produce the general, if not universal, belief that within a short period, say from twenty to forty years, there will not be enough of them remaining to perpetuate this Government." The Civil War prevented Seward from opening any new initiative. He pursued annexation very briefly after the war, in 1867–68, but as noted earlier, his plans faltered under the accumulated weight of Reconstruction and congressional and partisan opposition.

We need not cover each episode in which annexation was considered in great detail. But given the object of this book, two instances in which racism complicated efforts to formalize relations with Hawaii further and draw the islands closer to the United States deserve brief consideration. The first involves an annexation attempt and the second a reciprocity treaty. In 1854, Secretary of State William Marcy, anticipating that Britain would attempt to impose demands on the Hawaiian government, outlined how the United States would respond in the event of "any change in the political affairs of the Sandwich Islands." He told the U.S. minister stationed in Honolulu, David L. Gregg, that if "in the course of events" the loss of its independence by Hawaii should become "unavoidable, this Government would much prefer to acquire the sovereignty of these islands for the United States, rather than see it transferred to another power. If any foreign connection is to be formed," Marcy concluded, "the geographical position of these islands indicates that it should be with us."[60]

Gregg's cables to Washington, D.C., warned that such a moment was imminent. They indicated that Hawaii's government was weakening rapidly, that its ruling authorities were convinced of the islands' "inability to sustain themselves . . . as an independent State." If the United States did not act immediately and decisively to take them, said Gregg, the Hawaiians would appeal to a rival power. They were prepared to come to the United States either for protection or "to seek incorporation into our political system." Their preference, according to Gregg, was annexation, and the secretary of state was prepared to accommodate them.

By the fall of 1854, Gregg had negotiated the agreement and sent it on to the capital. It was a standard document of its kind except for three remarkable provisions. The first, article 2, promised the islands admission "into the American Union as a State, enjoying the same degree of sovereignty as other States, and admitted . . . to all the rights, privileges, and immunities . . . on a perfect equality with the other States of the Union."[61] The next element, article 3, stated that all Hawaiians, "the King of the Hawaiian Islands, his chiefs and subjects of every class" included, "shall possess . . . all the rights and privileges of citizens of the United States, on terms of perfect equality, in all respects, with other American citizens." Finally, article 8, in some ways the most extraordinary of the three, required the United States to appropriate seventy-five thousand dollars annually for ten years "for the benefit of a college or university . . . [and] for the support of common schools." The stated purpose for this, said the article, was to give the native Hawaiians "the means of education, present and future, so as to enable them the more perfectly to enjoy and discharge the rights and duties consequent upon a change from monarchical to republican institutions."[62]

In Washington the treaty received a cold reception from the secretary of state and President Franklin Pierce. Both objected most pointedly to the special provisions insisted upon by the Hawaiians. "If ratified in its present shape at Honolulu and sent hither," Marcy informed Gregg, "[the president] would probably not submit it to the Senate."[63] This was a revealing statement, coming from an administration generally believed to be dedicated to expansion and territorial acquisition, under the banner of "manifest destiny." Cuba was its primary object, but the president and his followers did not limit their ambitions to the Caribbean. At a Democratic Party celebration in Albany, New York, following Pierce's election in 1852, a toast was offered: "Cuba and the Sandwich Isles—may they soon be added to the galaxy of States."[64] Once installed in office, Pierce gave encouragement to expansionism. He stacked his cabinet with men well known for their expansionism. William Marcy had supported James K. Polk's attempt to purchase Cuba in 1848. While a congressman, Secretary of War Jefferson Davis had called for the purchase of the same. Attorney General Caleb Cushing was similarly inclined.[65] Then, in his inaugural address, Pierce announced that the policy of his administration would "not be controlled by any timid forebodings of evil from expansion. Indeed," he continued, "it is not to be disguised that our attitude as a nation and our position on the globe render the acquisition of certain possessions not within our jurisdiction eminently important for our protection, if not in the future essential for the preservation of the rights of commerce and the peace of the world."[66]

Despite the mighty words, Pierce refused the Hawaiian treaty. He found article 2 especially unacceptable. Marcy tells us why: "There is in his mind strong objections to the immediate incorporation of the islands in the present condition into the Union as an Independent State." Both the secretary of state and the president had expected the kingdom to offer itself to the United States as a territory, not as a state demanding for itself and its people immediate and full equality. Both had hoped that the Hawaiians would have left such questions to the United States, so that the administration could push ahead with the acquisition unencumbered and "unembarrassed by stipulations on that point." The secretary of state believed that such an understanding would serve both nations, whereas "a treaty which would embarrass the United States in their action on this question would . . . be objectionable."[67] For his part, Pierce measured the effects that the treaty—as it was written— would have on domestic politics. He knew that if Hawaii was admitted as a state, with its multiracial populace, on the basis of equality, he would offend and potentially divide his party. Annexation collapsed as a result.[68]

Reciprocity had been attempted twice prior to 1875. Both treaties failed. In 1855, Secretary of State Marcy submitted a treaty he had negotiated with the Hawaiians, but the Senate ignored it into oblivion.[69] Seward's efforts in 1867 met formidable opposition from several directions. The politics of Reconstruction, the determination of American sugar producers to keep foreign competition out of the domestic market, and a small band of annexationists who believed that reciprocity would delay acquisition all came together to defeat the second initiative.[70]

Beyond these and other local considerations and its overt purpose—facilitating economic expansion—reciprocity must be appreciated, as it was in the years after the Civil War, as a defensive strategy. Hamilton Fish acknowledged the defensive aspects of this policy option when he opened reciprocity negotiations with Hawaii and when he declared that the islands could not go to a rival commercial or military power. "Such a transfer," he said, "would threaten a military surveillance in the Pacific, similar to that which Bermuda [a British possession] has afforded in the Atlantic." The United States endured the incursion off its eastern shores "from necessity," but, he continued, "we desire no additional similar outposts in the hands of those who may at some future time use them to our disadvantage."[71] Given that the great powers coveted Hawaii primarily because of its position on the trade routes through the Pacific Ocean—hence the decades of diplomatic competition over the islands—America's official policy toward those islands must be considered in light of their military significance. Annexation was the most aggressive means of securing the nation's position in Hawaii and addressing concerns about the safety of the Pacific coast, but few men in politics seemed ready or able to bind the United States to such a commitment, despite "manifest destiny," regardless of their worries over defense.

Hawaii was too distant, too tropical, too unknown, too strange, its population too heterogeneous. All this made annexation too radical a policy option for most. Reciprocity, by comparison, was a conservative and therefore safer alternative: a politically workable method of achieving the same ends.

In the debate over Fish's treaty, Congressman James A. Garfield counted himself among those who favored reciprocity with Hawaii, but not because it would lead to annexation, as other supporters had come to believe. "I disclaim any purpose or suggestion of annexing the Hawaiian Islands as any part of my reason for supporting the treaty," he said. "On the contrary, one of the reasons why I favor the treaty is that it will be a satisfactory *substitute* for all probable schemes of annexation." Like many others, Garfield was not opposed to territorial acquisition in principle, just when it crept beyond certain boundaries. Here, we again see policymakers exercising the ancient conviction that climate dictated the boundaries beyond which certain races should not adventure.

Garfield approved of expansion to the north, within the temperate zone; it was expansion into tropical places that alarmed him. Referring to the south, to "the whole group of West India Islands and the whole of the Mexican territory contiguous to the United States," Garfield told the House, "I trust that we have seen the last of our annexations." The point of his objection was clear: such lands were in the hot zone. Those islands and Mexico, he said, "are inhabited by people of the Latin races strangely degenerated by their mixture with native races . . . a population occupying a territory that I earnestly hope may never be made an integral part of the United States." If Cuba, long coveted by expansionists, were offered to the nation "with the consent of all the powers of the world, and $100,000,000 in gold were offered as a bonus for its acceptance," declared Garfield, "I would unhesitatingly vote to decline the offer."[72] The racial and cultural differences that made the West Indian, the Cuban, and the Mexican peoples undesirable, Garfield carried over to native Hawaiians.

Defensive and strategic concerns moved Garfield to support the letter of the treaty, but to his reckoning its spirit, the basis of the special relationship it embodied, arose out of racial sympathy that bound the United States to the islands' white population. It was fortunate, he told the assembled congressmen, that Hawaii was "dominated in all its leading influences by Americans, our own brethren. Their hearts warm toward us as their first choice in forming alliances." "Our own brethren": the statement excluded native

Hawaiians, Chinese, and other peoples of color. "They [the islands] are ours in blood and sympathy," Garfield said, "and in this treaty they offer us the first place, an exceptionally favorable place, in their relations to the world."[73]

Before closing his speech, Garfield said once more that he favored the treaty because "it would obviate any necessity for annexing the islands." Reciprocity "and the respect which the name of the United States carries with it among the nations of the earth," he argued, "will prevent any attempt on the part of any other nation to obtain control there." He warned, however, that if Congress failed to ratify the treaty, European "schemes of annexation will vex us from year to year, until we shall be compelled to annex these islands as a matter of self-protection." Garfield, then, supported one policy in order to make a second, more radical policy option unnecessary, and he argued forcefully that other congressmen do the same. Garfield's racial beliefs are representative in terms of when and how they intersected with expansionism in the postwar era. His conviction that the inhabitants of the tropical zones comprised a dangerous and unassimilable mass made Hawaii's annexation a distasteful and fearful option.

Over the several weeks that the annexation question was before the public in 1893, race emerged as the most contentious issue. The Senate held its deliberations in executive session; they were brief and of little consequence compared with the public debate. *The Nation* dropped race into the discourse early. An editorial published on 9 February warned its readership of the consequences of annexation: Hawaii would become a territory, then eventually a state with powers that included "deciding our Presidential elections in case of a close division of the Electoral College." Such pessimism was based on the publication's low opinion of the islands' population "of natives recently emerged from savagery, speaking foreign tongues, Japanese, Chinese, and Portuguese."[74]

Where *The Nation* led, others followed. The *Chicago Herald* stated that the islands would form a "pigmy State of the Union" and called their absorption "ridiculous." The paper dismissed compromises such as the suggestion that Hawaii might be "formed into a county and attached to California." Again, it was the population that engendered caution and hostility. The *Herald* proclaimed that the islands' "benighted voting mass" would make this kind of arrangement "difficult and dangerous." The *McKeesport (Pa.) Morning Herald* said only that Hawaii was not qualified for statehood: it was scarcely fit to make a respectable territory because "[i]ts people have no capacity for self-government."[75] The *Chicago Evening Journal* joined strategic concerns with racial fears. By "annexing this sugar plantation with its mixed population," it said, "we risk all in case of war. On this continent we are supreme; in the midst of the Pacific Ocean we would be at the mercy of the Chinese population of Hawaii."[76] The *New York Herald* saw the Asian presence as the main impediment: "How can the United States admit the 20,000 Chinese residents of Hawaii to citizenship? How can we extend the invitation to these people to come into our fold while our present laws remain on the statute books?"[77] The *New York Evening Post* reported that racial and other considerations had turned many senators away from annexation even before the treaty was submitted to them. The pressures coming from the domestic sugar industry, "taken together with the Pacific Coast's experience with the Chinese and a sense among some Southern Senators that we have enough race problems on our hands already without adding the Kanaka to the negro, Indian, and Mongolian question, make the prospect of annexation rather doubtful for the present."[78]

Another writer, a *New York Herald* correspondent living in Paris and identifying himself only as "A Disciple of Daniel Webster," chided the American press for its "jingo fever" and for its basing the islands' annexation on a misguided fear that "some foreign power" might take them. Acquisition was unnecessary and perilous, he insisted: unnecessary because earlier agreements had given the United States "all the practical benefits of a protectorate," making it safe from outside interference; perilous because of the consequences that would result from governing the sundry races inhabiting the islands. America would have to administer the islands "as a sort of 'crown colony,' with a very restricted suffrage based on race or color exclusion." The correspondent objected to annexation, first, because this condition would violate the Fourteenth and Fifteenth Amendments to the Constitution. A second consequence of annexation disturbed the "Disciple" even more: the possibility that statehood would follow, conferring citizenship and political power on a variety of peoples he considered wretchedly inferior. "It would be a curious thing indeed," he wrote, "to some day have a close election for President of the United States settled by the votes of semi-barbaric Sandwich Islanders, whose grandfathers were cannibals, aided by Chinese and Japanese and Papuan laborers."[79]

Twenty-three years after battling President Grant, Carl Schurz, now the editor of *Harper's Weekly*, emerged again to stand against imperialism in the tropical zone. He took full advantage of his position and published two articles in the spring and fall of 1893 in which elaborated reasons, old and new, to oppose Hawaii's annexation. "The Annexation Policy" concentrated on military and economic questions and was aggressively supportive of Cleveland's withdrawing the treaty. He took on the expansionists who excoriated the president for withdrawing the treaty from the Senate, arguing that he was a statesman of uncommon courage who, instead of derision, deserved "the thanks of the country." Schurz was confident that time would prove "that all [the] commercial advantages which, according to the advocates of the scheme, annexation would secure to us can be had without cost to ourselves, and . . . without burdening this republic with the grave responsibilities which the annexation of the islands would involve."[80]

It was a powerful article, but Schurz was not wholly satisfied with it. He told Cleveland in a private letter that its approach was too narrow, that it failed to convey the full force of his arguments. "Of the political aspects," Schurz explained to the president, "much more might have been said that would apply to all acquisitions of territory outside of the continent, especially in tropical countries."[81] The second article, "Manifest Destiny," appeared in October 1983, and in it Schurz was determined to address the consequences of empire that he had overlooked in the first piece.[82]

The article's title was ironic by intention. Schurz used it to attack the annexationists, accusing them of chanting "manifest destiny" like a mantra in order to beguile the public and "produce the impression that all opposition to [annexing foreign territory] is a struggle against fate." Grave and substantive differences of opinion existed, he said, and they demanded to be heard in a sober national debate. To Schurz's mind the debate was over what effects a "vigorous foreign policy" characterized by an "indiscriminate acquisition of distant territory" would have on the nation's character, politics, and prevailing social order.

Schurz rested his argument on the Constitution, which he saw as providing for only one outcome with respect to seizing distant lands: the territory annexed must eventually be admitted to the Union, welcomed as a state that must stand on an equal basis with every other state. The land, he insisted, was not the issue that should concern Americans. The people who would occupy those lands—or, in this case, who *already* occupied those lands—were the true cause for alarm. For they would have the power to "take part in the government of the whole country through Senators and Representatives," Schurz warned, "as well as through the votes cast in the election of our

Presidents and in adopting or rejecting constitutional amendments." They would have to be admitted, he said, as "equal members to [the] national household, to its family circle."[83] The turns of phrase here, which conjure up images of intimate domesticity, prefaced Schurz's determination to distinguish natives from strangers and his intention to cast all the inhabitants of the world's tropical places firmly, permanently in the latter category.

As in 1870, Schurz said that he did not oppose imperialism on principle. He would welcome the absorption of desirable territories, he said, and oppose indefatigably the addition of undesirable places. Again, climate and race marked the distinction between the two. Canada, Schurz repeated, would be a fine acquisition because "there would, as to the character to the country and of the people, be no reasonable doubt of the fitness, or even the desirability of the association." Schurz outlined his criteria: "Their country [Canada] has those attributes of soil and climate which are most apt to stimulate and keep steadily at work all the energies of human nature. The people are substantially of the same stock as ours, and akin to us in their traditions, their notions of law and morals, their interests and habits of life. . . . They would mingle and become one with our [white] people without difficulty. The new States brought by them into the Union would soon be hardly distinguishable from the old in any point of importance. Their accession would make our national household larger, but it would not seriously change its character."[84] In contrast, according to Schurz, the logic of "manifest destiny" carried to the tropical zone would bring only catastrophe in the form of "States inhabited by people so utterly different from ours in origin, in customs and habits, in traditions, language, morals, impulses, ways of thinking—in almost everything that constitutes social and political life": unlike the case of Canada, their absorption was unthinkable. Climatic influences . . . have made them what they are," he said, "and render an essential change of their character," one necessary for their assimilation, "impossible."[85]

Shortly after the article appeared, Schurz wrote to Secretary of State Gresham to say that he purposefully made "the population of a group of islands on the highway of the Pacific Ocean" the centerpiece of his argument, because he hoped to "provoke a continuation of the public discussion of these important questions, which might serve to draw more serious public attention to them." In a flattering reply to its author, Gresham called "Manifest Destiny" the "best article of the kind that I have seen," predicting "it will do a great deal of good. After all," he wrote, "public opinion is made and controlled by the thoughtful men of the country, and what you said cannot fail to impress people of that class."[86]

Taken together, the racial arguments that were set against imperialism at the start of the 1890s were not only familiar but, as Schurz's article reveals, had also not evolved much since 1870. Racism and its place in the politics of annexation would change dramatically after 1893 as imperialists began to develop a strategy that finally enabled them to exploit race to their advantage: not with the arrival of social Darwinism, the language of "mission," "uplift," or "the white man's burden," as the conventional narrative argues. These concepts would have fixed nonwhites at the center of imperial policy, a problematic place for them to be in the era of Chinese exclusion, racial lynching, Jim Crow, immigration restriction, resurgent nativism, and the Mississippi Plan. Instead, the spokesmen for Hawaii's acquisition began to talk of the courage of the revolutionaries, the fortitude of the provisional government, and how white civilization in the islands was mortally threatened by indigenous heathenism and a stealth invasion from East Asia. This strategy was intended to subvert and dull the serrated attacks of Schurz and the other vigilant anti-imperialists, diminish the role of the unassimilable mass living on the islands, and place the white minority at the center of policy. The expansionists began to formulate arguments which declared that annexation was an absolute necessity, not for the sake of uplifting Hawaii's native population but for the sake of the whites.

In 1891 Sereno Bishop wrote a portrait of the Hawaiian queen for the American journal *Review of Reviews*.[87] It reported that Liliuokalani meant "Lily of the Sky," that she was commonly and affectionately known as "Queen Lydia," that she had long held "a prominent place in Honolulu society" and associated with "the more cultivated ladies of the capital, among whom . . . she received her early education." She was a religious woman, a characteristic that Bishop found encouraging. Her command of the English language and knowledge of literature and music were considered admirable, her manner "particularly winning, her bearing noble and becoming." The queen had "deeply in her heart the moral welfare of her people."[88] The article was respectful and flattering; remarkable in contrast with a second account of the queen written less than two years later.

Just weeks after Liliuokalani was overthrown, the *New York Evening Post* published a letter from Bishop which set down one of the first public calls for Hawaii's annexation based heavily on racial sympathy. Bishop characterized the revolution as racial, as a struggle of whites against a "reactionary heathen element" in which the queen was the main culprit. He explained away the *Review of Reviews* article by saying that at the time it was necessary to "put the most favorable construction which truth would allow" on Liliuokalani's character, while leaving "some unseemly 'skeletons' . . . covered up."[89]

The revolution was instigated, he insisted, by a series of actions by the queen, each one intended to affront the white population. For example, Bishop cited her desire to end the segregation of lepers, "a step which would drive the whites out of the country for fear of infection." Worse were the moral offenses. Bishop claimed that the royal palace was overrun with kahuna sorcerers, that it was "the breeding place of poisonous influences . . . destroying the people with sorcery, lust, and drunkenness." He accused the queen of participating in ritual sacrifices to Pele, the volcano god, in which pigs and birds where "thrown by her alive upon the burning lava."

But the themes Bishop returned to, and concluded with, were race antagonism and the threat to white civilization. Liliuokalani and the "baser element of the natives inflamed by the heathen influence," he said, were determined to "destroy the white share of influence in the government, and put the forty millions of white capital and all *our* beautiful civilization which has created this Paradise under the boot of their ignorance and brutality."

Other accusations made against the queen carried more weight: first, because they were consistent with the image of the sensuous heathen that Hiram Bingham, Rufus Anderson, Mark Twain, Sereno Bishop, Isabella Bird, and others had portrayed since the 1820s; second, because these accusations were verifiable. Liliuokalani was charged with supporting two iniquitous laws, one licensing the sale of opium on the islands and the other chartering a lottery company.[90] The bill regulating the importation and sale of the exotic drug alarmed Hawaii's "best people," whereas the queen chose to think of the bill in terms of the revenue it would generate. In her memoir she argued that attempts to prohibit and criminalize opium had utterly failed. The decision, however regrettable, had been forced on her by the significant Asian presence in the islands. "With a Chinese population of over twenty thousand persons," she declared, "it is absolutely impossible to prevent smuggling, unlawful trade, bribery, corruption, and every abuse." Liliuokalani concluded that the bill was not immoral. Indeed, she remarked, defending her controversial act, it was realistic and "wise to adopt measures for restricting and controlling a trade which it was impossible to suppress."[91] The lottery bill was also cast in terms of its progressive elements and power to generate revenue. The queen signed the legislation believing that it would fund public works projects, improve Hawaii's infrastructure, and provide gainful employment for her people. A fact that the annexationists managed to obscure was that before the revolution both measures had the support of the islands' prominent white citizens. After the coup, this class denied their complicity and then used these "crimes" to justify overthrowing the queen. That these hypocrisies were largely overlooked or ignored testifies to the effectiveness of Bishop and other propagandists as well as to the ignorance of most Americans regarding Hawaii. It appears that most observers in the United States, like the *New York Herald*, swallowed their stories whole. "The Queen simply went from bad to worse," it said, "and the white population rebelled at further degradation. Hence her disposition."[92] Hawaii's annexation was justified increasingly, then, as a means to rescue white civilization from both the immoralities that accompanied the Asian infiltration and the barbarism of the native peoples.

Alfred Thayer Mahan's calls for annexation were also motivated by a desire to maintain white civilization in Hawaii. Indeed, in his mind and in this instance, strategy and race were conjoined. Mahan's greatest fear was that if the United States failed to take the islands, they would fall under the control of a foreign power. The chief danger came from East Asia, from a race and not simply a commercial or military rival. In a letter printed in the *New York Times*, Mahan said that one key element of the Hawaiian revolution that had been "kept out of sight" was the islands' relation to China, "evident form the great number of Chinese, relative to the whole population, now settled in the islands." The great question before the United States, he said, was whether Hawaii should "in the future be an outpost of European civilization, or of the comparative barbarism of China." His mind churned over the prospect that any day the "vast mass of China" would rise up "to one of those impulses which have in the past ages buried civilization under a wave of barbaric invasion." Hawaii could easily become the vital stepping-stone in China's eventual crusade against Western civilization, he said. "In such a moment it would be impossible to exaggerate the momentous issues dependent upon a firm hold of the Sandwich Islands by a great, civilized, maritime power." The United States, Mahan declared, had to be such a power. "By its nearness to the scene, and by the determined animosity to the Chinese movement which close contact seems to inspire," he said, "our own country, with its Pacific coast, is naturally indicated as the proper guardian for this important position."[93]

On 3 February 1893, Senator John Tyler Morgan of Alabama spoke in favor of Hawaii's annexation, but his support was conditional and articulated well within the bounds of the traditional policy framework. This imperialist of the South told the press that he did not particularly want the islands, that he preferred that they remain "under an independent form of government," but he would support taking them "if the alternative is the acquisition of Hawaii by some foreign power." He justified his imperialism further by proclaiming his sympathy for the white revolutionaries. The commission that was at that moment negotiating the annexation treaty with Secretary of State Foster, he said, represented "the best class of Hawaii" and "voic[ed] the desires of the intelligent and enterprising portion of the Hawaiian population." Morgan stated that that portion was white, not native, and "made up of foreigners who have gone to that country and those who were born there of American and European parentage." He also attempted to obscure the importance of the native's role and power in the islands. The senator told the *Times* that this class "do not appreciate law and order as it is understood in this country or by the better class of the population of Hawaii."[94]

Rather than reading this final statement simply as evidence of white supremacy being applied to an imperialist policy, Morgan's comments must be placed in the context of the moment in which they were made. His support for annexation was, first of all, catalyzed by his fear that America's predominant position in Hawaii might be undermined by the actions of a rival nation. In short, his first priority was that the islands remain American, and Morgan could feel this way because he believed that they were American already. Americans and other white peoples had civilized the islands. Their representatives, not those of the natives, had come to the United States and proposed annexation. Even while he was diminishing the native Hawaiians by speaking of their unfitness, Morgan showed that his first concern was for the whites, justifying annexation as a noble and necessary effort to rescue white civilization.

Samuel Chapman Armstrong confessed in the *Southern Workman* that his "thoughts had been much occupied . . . with the recent Hawaiian Revolution." His concerns and their significance are easily explained. Armstrong was born in Maui in 1839, the son of Presbyterian missionaries. His father served for a time as Hawaii's minister of education. The son applied the lessons learned from his father in his administration of Hampton Normal and Agricultural Institute, founded as a school for former slaves. Armstrong was also guided by the similarities he believed he found between African

Americans and the Polynesians among whom he had grown up. In "Lessons from the Hawaiian Islands," written in 1884, he observed: "Of both it is true that not mere ignorance, but deficiency of character is the chief difficulty, and that to build up character is the true objective point of education." Morality and industry went together, "[e]specially in the weak tropical races."[95]

Armstrong's sympathies were decidedly with his white brethren who were "seek[ing] annexation and . . . vigorously courting the United States for that purpose." He feared that tradition and history were against them and that they would fail because "the American policy of refusing new territory seem[ed] likely to prevail." He judged the provisional government to be "sound and clean," and President Dole, an old schoolmate, "one of the soundest and best of men." In the *New York Evening Post*, Armstrong continued to advocate the whites' cause. He told its readers that the islands' exceptional progress was due solely to "the control of its affairs by white people," mostly Americans, and that "the conquest by American missionaries of the Hawaiian Islands . . . gives the United States both a claim and an obligation in the matter—a claim to be considered first in the final disposition of that country, an obligation to save decency and civilization in that utterly broken-down monarchy."[96]

The whites had no choice but to rule the islands, he argued, as no other element of the population was capable of upholding a stable and effective government. "Universal suffrage has been tried . . . Asiatics being wisely left out," he wrote, but that experiment had failed. Armstrong affirmed his point with a graphic and unsettling analogy: "Give a child a razor and he will hurt himself. Give the African or Polynesian unlimited political power and, unless restrained, political death will follow." Armstrong maintained that republican government could survive in Hawaii "no doubt a good many years." All that was required, even though they were overwhelmed in terms of numbers by the other races in Hawaii, were "determined, well armed[,] capable Europeans and Americans to govern and hold the weak, impulsive natives in check."[97] These sentiments, taken together, anticipated arguments that would be pressed more fully and forcefully when annexation was attempted again in 1897.

By the summer of 1893, the Cleveland administration had committed itself to abandoning annexation and the treaty. Gresham received Blount's report on 17 July 1893. Over the preceding months, Blount had communicated with the secretary of state, sending informal accounts of his investigations. By the time the final report was ready, Gresham was convinced that Stevens had acted illegally, that he had collaborated with the revolutionaries to force the queen to surrender, and that the majority of Hawaiians were opposed to annexation. Blount told Gresham that if the matter were put to a popular vote, the results would be "at least two to one" against.

To Gresham's mind, then, a great wrong had been done to Liliuokalani, thus the United States had a moral obligation to restore her to power. Attempts to convince the secretary otherwise proved futile. Lorrin Thurston, chairman of the Hawaiian delegation that negotiated the treaty with Foster, pleaded with Gresham throughout the summer of 1893 but failed to overturn his decision to support the queen against the provisional government. Bluford Wilson wrote to the secretary of state to ask if he was truly prepared to position the United States "alone among civilized nations" by turning its back on its own citizens (and at the same time imperiling the nation's security). "Are we to repulse our founders of new states and drive them into the arms of foreign and hostile empires already wide open to receive them? Are we to have a second Bermuda built up in the Pacific Ocean as an eternal menace to our . . . Pacific Coast? May God and Gresham forbid."[98] No amount of provocation would move the secretary of state, who was stubbornly fixed on the morality of the question. "Should not this great wrong be undone?" he asked Carl Schurz. Not waiting for an answer, Gresham declared: " 'Yes,' I say decidedly."[99] Justice demanded that the United States restore Liliuokalani and the islands' constitutional government to power.

The story of Cleveland's restoration policy and its failure can be summarized briefly. Gresham presented his recommendations to the president and the cabinet on 6 October. All agreed that Stevens's participation in the queen's overthrow was decisive, illegal, and wrong. Disagreement emerged over what the administration should do to correct the matter. Gresham may have considered armed intervention, but the other secretaries, especially Attorney General Richard Olney, thought the use of force too extreme.[100] Olney questioned the constitutionality of using troops without the consent of Congress. Another consideration weighing on the attorney general's mind had to do with the effects that intervention would have on Hawaii: restoring the queen's government in "a country . . . devastated and a people . . . diminished in number and alienated in feeling by a contest of arms" would almost defeat the administration's purpose.[101]

These objections led the administration to attempt a diplomatic solution.

The cabinet met again on 18 October, reaffirmed the restoration policy, and decided on its course of action. Gresham drafted instructions for the new minister to Hawaii, Albert S. Willis, informing him that the president would not send the treaty back to the Senate, thus annexation was done as a policy option. Willis was told to inform the queen of this and to convey Cleveland's regrets that she was removed from her throne by American troops and forced "to rely on the justice of this government to undo the flagrant wrong." Willis was then instructed to get one concession from Liliuokalani, indispensable to the administration: that she must "pursue a magnanimous course by granting full amnesty to all who participated in the movement against her, including persons . . . connected with the provisional government, depriving them of no right or privilege which they enjoyed before the so-called revolution."[102]

Willis arrived in Hawaii on 4 November and met with Liliuokalani nine days later. As instructed he communicated the president's greetings, regrets, and request that, if restored, she grant "full amnesty as to life and property" to all those who had acted to overthrow her. According to Willis, Liliuokalani replied that she could not concede to Cleveland's request as she was bound by certain laws. "[A]s the law directs," she said calmly, "such persons should be beheaded and their property confiscated." The minister would later take it upon himself to research the penal codes, presumably in search of some loophole or ambiguity. He found none. "There are under this law no degrees of treason," Willis told Gresham. "Plotting alone carries with it the death sentence." During his meeting with the queen, Willis asked if she felt that this was the proper course of action to take toward these people. She replied simply, "It is."[103]

The provisional government proved to be no less obstinate. Predictably, it refused to surrender power and allow Cleveland to restore the queen. Sanford Dole, the minister of foreign affairs, told Willis that his government did not recognize the president's authority to interfere in Hawaii's domestic affairs. Furthermore, Dole insisted that the revolution would have succeeded even without the interposition of American forces, "for the . . . causes for it had nothing to do with their presence." Cleveland may have stopped annexation, but, Dole promised Willis, the matter was not closed for the people he represented. "We shall . . . continue the project of political union with the United States as a conspicuous feature of our foreign policy," Dole said, "confidently hoping that sooner or later it will be crowned a success, to the lasting benefit of both countries."[104]

The president's annual message gave Hawaii little consideration, but his 18

December 1893 address, a substantial document of six thousand words, confronted the issue directly. In it he reviewed the facts of the revolution and Stevens's role in it, relying heavily on the findings contained in the Blount report. Cleveland then described the grounds on which his administration objected to this annexation. Not only would the acquisition of Hawaii run contrary to the nation's tradition of contiguous landed expansion restrained to the North American continent, he said, but it would also appear to endorse the unjust actions of an agent of the United States, a man who acted wrongly in support of a government that did not represent the will of the Hawaiian people.[105] The president's attempt to restore the monarchy failed, he said, not because of the resistance of the white Hawaiians but chiefly because "the conditions [amnesty] have not proved acceptable to the Queen." Confessing that he had little confidence in "the prospects of successful Executive mediation" of the problem, Cleveland washed his hands of it and referred "this subject to the extended powers and wide discretion of the Congress." Before closing, the president promised that he would cooperate gladly with any plan Congress might devise to solve the Hawaiian question "which is consistent with American honor, integrity, and morality."[106]

A month earlier, Secretary of State Gresham had received a letter from Oliver Morton, one of many who congratulated him for his stand against imperialism. To Morton, Hawaii's revolutionaries had forced a very dangerous choice upon the nation: "Either the United States must disavow the work done in its name, by overthrowing a usurping monarchy, or . . . accept their work by annexing the dominions." To avoid the even greater perils that were conjoined to the islands' annexation, he said, "[s]ome substantive action was necessary." He then explained to Gresham what he thought these fearful prospects were: "When the United States attempts to govern a foreign dependency whose subjects are aliens in race and tongue, and who are not qualified for exercising the suffrage, nor indeed for fulfilling any of the functions of citizenship in a free republic, then is our government taking the initial step in founding an empire. Such a precedent would not be mere dangerous," Morton concluded, "but fatal."[107]

Gresham was bound to agree. He relied on the same justifications cited by this correspondent, including race. Early in his political career, the secretary of state had been a committed nativist, a member of the Know-Nothings before the Civil War, and afterward a supporter of Andrew Johnson's "restoration" policy. In 1866, as a Union Party candidate for office in Indiana (he considered himself a Republican at the time), Gresham showed that he understood the power of racism in politics and worked consciously and hard to capitalize on it. He matched the Democrats' appeals to negrophobia by denying that his party supported voting rights for blacks. Indeed, he declared his conviction that the white race was superior and pledged to his followers that the Union Party had "no disposition to make the negro the equal to the white man."[108]

Years later these sentiments still registered with the secretary. In public he defended the administration's position against empire on the grounds of justice and morality. In private he said that it was right to stop the treaty for the additional reason that Hawaii's population was unsuited to join the United States. Their inability to maintain a republican form of government made statehood impossible, therefore annexation was impossible. While he was the subject of savage attacks by political enemies, these sentiments must have provided refuge for Gresham. In the end he found comfort in his conviction that he had followed a just and moral path and the knowledge that his adversaries had been defeated. "[A]nnexation is dead," he wrote, "whatever else may occur."[109]

CHAPTER FOUR

Hawaii Annexed

The provisional government was an expedient necessity, organized to give the revolutionaries the authority and power they needed to pursue their main objective following the overthrow of Queen Liliuokalani. Its paramount goal was annexing Hawaii to the United States. It failed in 1893, but the initiative was hardly dead, despite Gresham's curt eulogy. The oligarchs believed that time would be the deciding factor and that it was clearly on their side. A year after the revolt they were firmly in command of the islands, in defiance of President Cleveland. And through their struggles the revolutionaries had made important and powerful friends in the United States, especially among Republicans. Their strategy was a simple one: wait, because Grover Cleveland could not remain president forever. In the meantime, the white faction would put its political house in order.

"[P]roclaim a republic and bide your time for a change in the administration which is shure [sic] to come with the next Presidential election," Samuel Blisk told his cousin, Sanford Dole. "[T]he sympathy of the great majority of the people of the United States are [sic] with you." He closed impatiently: "I trust you will soon modify and qualify the franchise and proclaim a new republic."[1] Some believed that powers greater than the people were at work. Dole told a Mrs. Mills in January 1894: "I believe in our cause; it is the Lord's work, and I feel His hand is leading us. . . . We now have the difficult and important work on our hands of so m[o]difying our government as to give it a more representative and permanent character."[2]

Admonitions from other interested onlookers (including concerned relatives) reminded Dole of what he already knew both intuitively and from recent experience: that race was wrapped like a Gordian knot around the annexation question. Charles Fletcher Dole told his cousin that despite the natural concern he had for family, "[m]uch of the talk in favor of annexation I have to confess does not much move me." By this he meant that he was not convinced by the threadbare argument that the islands had to be taken if for no other reason than to build a new naval base in the Pacific. "I am not belligerent enough for that," he wrote, "neither do I see it as likely that this attempt to maintain a naval station at distant points tends towards that era of peace and good will which I hold that our nation ought to stand for." Whereas "military necessity" mattered little to this Dole, race loomed large. "I should like to be united in some form with Canada. I should like for similar reasons to have all of you good Honolulu men under the flag. But," he continued, "I am sobered when I think of you someday knocking for statehood and bringing in another ill-assorted population of unfit citizens! We have such a crowd of them already."[3]

More practical advice also found its way into Sanford Dole's hands. In early November 1893, he received from W. D. Armstrong—the son of a missionary, the brother of a planter, and determined supporter of the new regime—a letter intended to offer moral support and political guidance. Armstrong directed his compatriot to enclosures he had included with his note. Among them he pointed to "extracts from the present Constitution of Mississippi, which is said to have the effect of disfranchising a majority of the negroes of that state."[4] Armstrong's meaning was clear: to advance white interests, both short term and long, Dole should build racial exclusions into Hawaii's new political order. The Mississippi Plan would provide the model. There was no need to reinvent this particular wheel, though both men knew, given their real ambitions, it would have to carry Hawaii significantly further. For Mississippi, establishing white domination through African American exclusion was an end unto itself. For the provisional government, establishing white domination by disfranchising the native peoples, the Chinese, the Japanese, and the Portuguese—in effect creating the appearance of a "lily white" citizenry—was vital to establishing an independent republic, and also a shrewd and necessary precondition for annexation to the United States.

Dole and his officers immersed themselves in the task of placing the new regime on more permanent and, with several very conspicuous exclusions, republican foundations. In March he announced the assembly of a convention to draft a new constitution. From the very start precautions were taken to protect and institutionalize the interests of the islands' dominant class, the

Sanford Dole
(Hawaiian Historical Society)

white minority. A majority of the delegates, nineteen, were members of the provisional government. The remaining eighteen were selected through a general vote in which the franchise was open to every male resident of the islands "of Hawaiian, American, or European birth or descent." Asian males, Chinese and Japanese, were purposefully excluded. Furthermore, deliberate steps were taken to squash dissent. Each voter was required to swear an oath before God pledging that he would "support and bear true allegiance to the Provisional Government" and oppose any movement to reestablish the monarchy. Angered by the suffrage restrictions, between two and three thousand royalists met on 9 April to protest the convention. They argued that the franchise provisions were "calculated and intended to prevent full and fair representation of the people," that these rules created, in effect, the "practical disfranchisement of the [native] Hawaiian people" and anyone else with monarchist sympathies.[5]

The protesters were correct. The convention was, indeed, manipulated from the start to safeguard and expand white rule. Their suspicions were confirmed in a letter that first appeared in the *Hawaiian Gazette* (the note was reprinted in the *Nation* in July 1894 for American consumption). Its author, W. N. Armstrong, described as "one of the truest and most forward patriots now in Hawaii," admitted that the constitution was undemocratic, but insisted that this was unavoidable "based on the necessities of the case." "If we were alone here," he said, referring to the white American and European population, "very little government would be quite sufficient, because the true Anglo-Saxon does not require much government; each man rules himself." Since they were not alone, necessity demanded that "the whites . . . create a form of government through which they can rule the natives, Chinese, Japanese, and Portuguese, in order to prevent being 'snowed under.'" This, Armstrong declared, required "an uncommonly strong central government" that placed "very large powers in the hands of a few."[6]

Evidence that the constitution was designed with these priorities at the fore appears in Dole's correspondence with John W. Burgess, then the dean of the faculty of political science at Columbia University. While contemplating the formation of a Hawaiian republic, Dole sought instruction in Burgess's *Political Science and Constitutional Law*, a book, he told its author, that "has been a great help to me." In a letter dated 31 March 1894, Dole shared his burden with the professor: that "many natives and the Portuguese" had been enfranchised under the previous system and that these groups, "comparatively ignorant of the principles of government," because of their numerical strength and collective incapacities, would be a "menace to good government."[7]

Burgess's reply, filtered through his own racial attitudes, showed profound sympathy for Dole's concerns and intentions. "If I understand your situation," Burgess wrote, "it is as follows: You have a population of nearly 100,000 persons, of whom about 5,000 are Teutons, i.e., Americans, English, Germans, and Scandinavians, about 9,000 are Portuguese[,] about 30,000 are Chinese and Japanese, about 8,000 are native born of foreign parents, and the rest are natives. . . . With this situation, I understand your problem to be the construction of a constitution which will place the government in the hands of the Teutons, and preserve it there, at least for the present."[8] This could be achieved, Burgess said, "with the existing material that you have provided the Teutons are substantial[ly] united in purpose and will act harmoniously." He went on to suggest two prohibitions that would further secure white rule: imposing even more rigid voting qualifications and "appoint[ing] only Teutons to military office."[9] Dole thanked Burgess with the truest appreciation. "Your letters," he told the scholar, "showed a clear knowledge of our peculiar political circumstances."[10]

The constitution, proclaimed on the auspicious date of 4 July 1894, fulfilled Dole's efforts to convert the principle of control by the "responsible" element into an actual frame of government. In *American Expansion in Hawaii*, the historian Sylvester Stevens discerned the connection between the provisional government's racial agenda and annexation. "The obvious purpose behind the establishment of the conservative Republic," he wrote, "was the organization of such a government as would hold the turbulent racial and other forces in Hawaii in check until better relations could be established in the United States."[11] The constitution also contained an article that "expressly authorized and empowered" the president and his cabinet "to make a treaty of political and commercial union" with the United States.[12] Dole was a committed and aggressive annexationist in 1893, and as president of the Republic of Hawaii, the first and only man to hold that office, he gave himself the constitutional authority to attach the islands to America. His task would be a formidable one.

Familiar obstacles stood between the imperialists and Hawaii's annexation: warring political parties, a worsening economic depression, social upheaval, anxiety, ignorance, a conservative tradition in foreign affairs, and racism. A point made earlier in this book bears repeating here: in the 1890s—an era marked by Wounded Knee, the infamous Mississippi Plan and Chinese Exclusion Acts, the deliberate prohibition of African Americans from the World Columbian Exposition, the founding of the Immigration Restriction League, Jim Crow, and lynching and other forms of terrorism—it was clearly unwise, even self-destructive, to place despised racial and ethnic groups at the center of policy, particularly when a policy was already divisive and controversial.

Both the political landscape and racial climate of the 1890s were hostile to imperialism, especially when policymakers went after territories such as Hawaii: distant, unfamiliar, alien, and exotic places populated by a conglomeration of "inferior" races. Worse still for the expansionists, annexation was inevitably tangled up in questions of statehood and citizenship, and the effect was always damaging. *New York Tribune* editor Whitelaw Reid complained bitterly over how difficult it was "to get anybody in Congress to admit the possibility of dealing with [the Hawaiian Islands] in any other way than by making them a state of the union." He believed that the same presumptions tied policymakers' hands in the Caribbean: "Everybody seemed to consider it natural, as well as certain," Reid grumbled, "that Cuba would come in some day as a state." His frustration arose from deeply held convictions regarding race and nationalism, beliefs that led him to conclude that making states out of distant territories and granting citizenship rights and equal protections to alien races was foolish, "humanitarianism run mad, a degeneration and degradation of the homogeneous, continental Republic of our pride."[13] Reid the imperialist understood that popular racial attitudes and racist laws and structures conspired to hinder expansionism. His imperialist brethren knew this as well, as their actions and words attest.

In this chapter I show how the imperialists confronted and, to an extent, effectively overcame the barriers raised by racism and the racial social order of their time. I contend that when the imperialists renewed their efforts to take Hawaii in 1897, they abandoned the rhetoric of racial uplift, Christian mission, the "white man's burden," benevolent assimilation, and any other language that placed nonwhites at the center of their initiatives. Race was central to their strategy and rhetoric, but not in the way that is commonly assumed. Imperialists justified Hawaii's annexation not for the redemption of the native peoples but for the sake of the island's whites.

On 9 January 1895 President Cleveland informed Congress that the Hawaiian government wished to lease to Great Britain a small and uninhabitable possession that lay four hundred miles from the archipelago called Necker Island. The English had come up with an ambitious plan to lay a submarine cable from Canada to Australia and wanted the island for a station. Cleveland asked Congress to modify the reciprocity treaty of 1884, specifically a section that forbade Hawaii to "lease or otherwise dispose of any . . . port, harbor, or other territory in [its] dominion" to another power. The president could find no reason to obstruct the British plan; in fact he suggested practical and positive reasons to support it. "[I]solated Hawaii would gain through telegraphic communication with the rest of the world," he said, and America's communications with those islands would be "greatly improved without apparent detriment" to its national interests. He asked Congress to act promptly and "permit the proposed lease."[14]

The response from Congress was prompt, but otherwise it was not what

Cleveland had anticipated. On 21 January, Senator Henry Cabot Lodge introduced a resolution calling for the construction of a rival American-owned cable from San Francisco to Honolulu. It declared that the United States should not surrender its treaty rights "in order to enable another government to secure a foothold . . . upon any part of the Hawaiian Islands." The resolution then went on to demand a radical preemptive action, calling on the Senate "to secure possession of the Sandwich Islands by their annexation to the United States."[15] The Lodge resolution ignited a fierce partisan ruckus in the Senate, and only after several days of debate did the legislators turn their attention back to the original question regarding the cable. Those who embraced the idea of an American cable extracted it from the original resolution and attached it to a far less controversial appropriations bill. The amendment called for five hundred thousand dollars to begin construction. The benefits to trade and commerce were considered obvious and accounted for the strongest argument in its favor. Opposition sprung up, nevertheless.

The cable amendment—one of a total of fifteen fastened to a simple appropriations bill—was the only one to excite controversy. Its presentation in the Senate set off weeks of debate. So much frustration accrued after a time that a question arose: should the Senate continue to debate over a rather humdrum appropriations bill that happened to contain a troublesome amendment, or should it just remove the amendment entirely? Senator Richard Pettigrew of South Dakota broke ranks with his fellow Republicans over this issue. Siding with the Democrats, he attacked the cable appropriation on several points, first on economic and political grounds. Pettigrew questioned forecasts of the cable's profitability, thinking them far too optimistic. Construction alone, he said, would cost the United States government between three and four million dollars, "while the business of the cable would not bring revenue enough to pay for the rent of the offices at each end of it." Reviving one of the more damaging controversies of 1893, Pettigrew went so far as to suggest that the cable amendment was most likely the work of the special interest groups in Hawaii conniving with sympathetic politicians in Washington, D.C. "[T]his is but a scheme," declared the senator, "to connect Claus Spreckles's sugar plantation in these islands with his sugar refineries in San Francisco."[16]

Pettigrew was just as dismissive of pro-amendment senators who based their urgings on anti-British prejudice. This group argued that a cable would be built through Hawaii, if not by the United States, then by the British, and therein lay the danger: this would lead ultimately to British control of the islands, colonization, the destruction of America's generations-old policy, and the end of free security along the nation's Pacific coast. Pettigrew was unconvinced. He conceded that England would take its cable through Hawaii, but this, he insisted, would be good for the United States. "[W]e shall be able to communicate with those islands," he observed, "and every commercial interest will be as well served." And at no cost to the United States Treasury, a point he failed to mention but one that could not have gone totally unnoticed. On the matter of national defense Pettigrew was adamant: the United States had absolutely nothing to fear. If Britain seized Hawaii, he said, the islands would be a point of weakness, not strength, "for they would be hard to defend." Finally, he blasted politicians who based their arguments on prejudice and ideology rather than fact and reason, men who "whenever they wish to put through a measure which they advocate, talk to the American people about the fear of England," a sentiment he dismissed as "absurd and ridiculous." In attacking this stratagem, Pettigrew was acknowledging its power. The rhetoric of national honor and Anglophobia—"this bugaboo of sophomores, who are everlastingly 'hoisting' the American flag, and dying before they will allow it to be pulled down!"—had a profound influence over the American people.[17]

The senator's speech then took a rather remarkable turn. To defeat the cable appropriation—a measure designed to facilitate commerce across the Pacific, to open markets for home products at a time when the nation was slogging through a terrible depression—Pettigrew resorted to racism. According to Pettigrew, the Lodge resolution contained another agenda, very poorly hidden: that the cable appropriation was, in fact, the first stage of an imperialist policy set toward annexing Hawaii. So to stop both schemes the senator proposed "to show the character of the people who inhabit the Sandwich Islands," to prove that they were, in his words, "utterly worthless, utterly incompetent, and not capable of self-government."

Pettigrew's arguments were based largely on the writings and speeches of Hawaii's missionaries.[18] At length he read from a report by the Reverend C. M. Hyde, the last resident missionary from the Board of Foreign Missions, regarding a native Hawaiian Sunday school superintendent who got drunk on sweet-potato beer. The man could not be punished, cried the senator, because "drunkenness was so common that it could not be treated as an offense."[19] Further along, he cited a paper by the Reverend Sereno Bishop "on the cause of the decline of the race of Hawaiians." Pettigrew focused on the most lurid passages, those that would be most shocking and appalling to the gentlemen of the Senate. Chastity, he said, "had absolutely no recognition" among the native people, and any woman "who withheld herself was counted sour and ungracious." Foreign men had gone to the islands and "enormously aggravated and inflamed the normal unchastity of the people." In the presence of "the white hordes," according to Pettigrew's sources, "life had become hideously brutalized. To multitudes of young women, gathered into the seaports for profits, from half the households of the country, life became a continuous orgie of beastly excess. . . . The stormy and reckless passion of the white men, exulting in his onwonted license, imparted itself to the warm but sluggish Hawaiian nature. Life became a wasteful riot of impurity, propagated from the seaports to the end of the land. . . . The inevitable consequence was depopulation. The population of brothels and slums has no internal power of multiplying."[20]

To Pettigrew, the native Hawaiians were not the only detestable human element in the islands. Its contract laborers were "the scum of the world" and "little less than slaves."[21] The thousands of Portuguese, the senator remarked, "are not Portuguese at all" but recruits from the Madeira and Azore islands, "a mixture of races—Portuguese and black and other races of Africa . . . the lowest of all the population upon the [Hawaiian] islands except, perhaps . . . the natives themselves." On the tens of thousands of Asians, Pettigrew read aloud from the Blount report: "The character of the people of these islands is and must be overwhelmingly Asiatic." Although the majority had arrived as contract laborers, Blount determined that the Chinese, Japanese, and Portuguese did not "disappear at the end of their contract terms." More than 75 percent of the Japanese who arrived in the islands as temporary laborers remained after their contracts ended. The Chinese, who occupied a range of skilled and unskilled trades, working, for example, as farmers, mechanics, teachers, fishermen, and ranchers and engaged "the largest part of the retail trade," also appeared to be permanent, Blount concluded.[22]

"Is it the desire of the jingoists in this Chamber," Pettigrew asked, "that they shall have the pleasure of seeing this worthless population represented on this floor?" Could they imagine watching "the Senator from Hawaii pleading for an additional appropriation for the relief of 1,200 lepers"? (Pettigrew ignored the fact that this hypothetical senator would most likely be white; it was not as dramatic an image, certainly, nor would it have helped his argument.) Furthermore, the nation had "problems enough" and could not "afford to add more dark-skinned races to [its] population." Pettigrew continued: "With the negroes of the South, the Chinese of the Pacific Coast, the Indians of the West, and the dagoes of the East, I believe that every problem we are able to solve will be presented to us in the near future; and that . . . our duty rather than to add this unfit population to ours [must be] to maintain our present area and pass those laws which will give every man an equal opportunity and promote the more even distribution of wealth throughout our borders."[23]

It would be an error to cast Pettigrew as just another politician whose anti-imperialism was grounded in racist thought when he was much more: a Republican who broke with his party at a time of fierce partisan hostility, a time when Congress was nearly equally divided between Republicans and Democrats and party loyalty and discipline were cardinal virtues. More important and more telling was the cause of his defection: racism connected to empire. Republican imperialists were reminded once again that they had to act with extreme caution when dealing with questions of race and empire. If they did not, they risked losing crucial support within their own party or, worse still, splitting it apart.

Henry Cabot Lodge rose to defend his amendment just moments after Pettigrew closed his assault. The Massachusetts senator wanted to rescue his policy but he would not be lured into an argument he could not win, so he sidestepped the issue of Hawaii's inhabitants. After Pettigrew's attack (backed up, such as it was, by the authoritative eyewitness testimonies of Christian missionaries, some with ancestral roots in Lodge's home state), quarreling over the essential character of the islands' largest racial groups would not have helped his cause. Lodge thought no better of the native Hawaiians, the Chinese, the Japanese, and the Portuguese than did Pettigrew. Introducing them into his rebuttal could have no beneficial effect; indeed, it is not difficult to imagine how this fight would have damaged Lodge's case further. Such a tactic would have taken the senator far away from the military and strategic issues he preferred to emphasize, no doubt in part for political reasons. Furthermore, Lodge knew race was a treacherous obstacle in the way of expansion. Thus, he told his fellow senators that he would not "enter into the discussion of the people of Hawaii." His reason, he insisted, was because they were not part of "the vital questions involved." All that mattered was the British threat and Hawaii's strategic position "at the heart of the Pacific, the controlling point of commerce in that great ocean." After that, Lodge said, it did not matter if the islands were desert rocks or "populated by a low race of savages."[24]

Historians have typically cast Lodge, alongside Theodore Roosevelt and Alfred Thayer Mahan, as the archetypal social Darwinist-imperialist of the 1890s. He has been called a "rabid imperialist", is said to have proclaimed the "large policy" program "in its most ambitious form," and "preached with the greatest fervor the twin gospels of expansion and sea power."[25] Characterizations like these place Lodge in direct (narrative) opposition to racist anti-imperialists such as Carl Schurz and E. L. Godkin, men with whom he shared certain pronounced racial attitudes.[26] This leads us to an important realization: the conventional narrative has consistently ignored or overlooked one critical fact in its accounts—that Lodge's racism had a limiting effect on his expansionist ideas.

The grand declaration of Lodge's imperialism described in other histories is drawn from his article "Our Blundering Foreign Policy," which appeared in the *Forum* in March 1895. Said to have foreshadowed the aggressive new departure in American foreign affairs and the annexations of 1898, the article is considered by some to be indispensable to understanding the imperialism of the 1890s as Mahan's *Influence of Sea Power upon History* and the Reverend Josiah Strong's *Our Country*.[27] A more accurate interpretation of Lodge's piece would emphasize its undiluted partisanship, for it reveals—as the title indicates—far more about the tense atmosphere of domestic politics and combative party rivalry that it does about the state of American foreign relations three years before the imperialists' triumph.

Lodge set forth a simple thesis: Cleveland's and the Democrats' diplomacy was nothing more than "a policy of retreat and surrender." The president's failure two years earlier to carry through Hawaii's annexation, his hostility toward the Dole government, and his attempt to restore what the senator called "the corrupt rule of the deposed queen" were, in sum, a repudiation of "the unbroken policy of the United States for fifty years."[28] The list of denunciations went further: Cleveland had dishonorably surrendered America's position in Samoa, crippling the nation's Pacific trade. The administration's misguided policies "entered into the legislation of the Democratic party in Congress," where "[t]hey lose no opportunity injuring us."[29] And the damage was being done at perhaps the worst time possible: while "[t]he great nations are rapidly absorbing for their future expansion and their present defense all the waste places of the earth." According to the senator, this was a "movement which makes for civilization and the advancement of the race. As one of the great nations of the world the United States must not fall out of the line of march."[30]

Having created a narrative of impending doom, Lodge made great claims for his party: "All the great constructive legislation of this country, with hardly an exception," he said, "has been the work of the Republican party and its predecessors." He maintained that this would be no different with respect to foreign affairs. Lodge did indeed see expansion as natural, competitive, and beneficial to "the race." He especially celebrated "the march of the American people" as part of this grand legacy and proclaimed in his best spread-eagle rhetoric: "We have a record of conquest, colonization, and territorial expansion unequaled by any people in the nineteenth century."[31] However emphatic his imperialist declarations may appear at first glance, Lodge believed, and clearly expressed his belief, that there were demonstrable limits to this movement: lines drawn by history, tradition, and ultimately race.

He noted two types of limitations, the first being political. Unlike England, Lodge stated, it was not the policy of the United States to enter "upon the general acquisition of distant possessions in all parts of the world." The American government, he said, was "not adapted to such a policy, and we have no need of it, for we have ample field at home."[32] Apparently Lodge was unaffected by both the 1890 census, important for announcing the closing of the American frontier, and Frederick Jackson Turner's famous lecture on the subject and its historic implications, presented in 1893. The second limitation to American expansionism Lodge noted in his famous article involved race and racism, twin forces that determined, in his mind, where expansionism should stop as well as where it might properly and beneficially advance. Lodge was unmistakably clear on this point: "We desire no extension to the south." His reasoning was equally clear: "[F]or neither the population nor the lands of Central or South America would be desirable additions to the United States." By contrast, contiguous expansion within the temperate zone, into regions where assimilable whites were in the majority, was a very different matter, just as it was to "anti-imperialists" such as Sumner, Schurz, Garfield, and Godkin. From "the Rio Grande to the Artic Ocean," Lodge wrote, "there should be one flag and one country," because "[n]either race nor climate forbids this extension and every consideration of national growth and national welfare demands it."[33]

One more point regarding Lodge's convictions on expansion and race:

while he did call for an aggressive policy "in the interests of our commerce," the senator remained simultaneously sensitive and evasive regarding race. The isthmian canal was the centerpiece of Lodge's designs, and to secure the waterway he said that the United States should "control" Hawaii (rather than annex it) and "maintain [its] influence in Samoa." Britain's presence in the Caribbean was a constant source of concern, so Lodge wanted "among those islands at least one strong naval station." After the canal was built, then, Cuba would become, according to Lodge, "a necessity." Perhaps antic-ipating racist objections to what even this vague language implied—annexa-tion—Lodge insisted, quite disingenuously but significantly, that Cuba was only "*sparsely settled.*"[34] Lodge was not the only influential thinker of the time to comprehend and express publicly his conviction that race was a dangerous obstacle to empire; he was, however, among the men who were openly committed to expansion, the most forward and honest in confront-ing the matter.

Others understood the problem in much the same manner as Lodge. In 1893, in "Grave Obstacles to Hawaiian Annexation," Judge Thomas Cooley presented racial objections to colonial expansion in stark and candid terms. Cooley found many elements of Harrison's annexation scheme unaccept-able, even distasteful: the irregularity of the administration's methods, the complete disregard for the native Hawaiians, the questionable authority of the provisional government that had negotiated the treaty of annexation, and inconsistencies he noticed in the strategic and military arguments the imperialists used to justify the acquisition. More important, Cooley feared that if the treaty were simultaneously ratified it break with tradition and in its place would create two very dangerous precedents. First, it would estab-lish a framework for entangling relationships with any nation on the globe; second, he declared, its passage would "justify our annexing other countries regardless of the differences of race and the discordant elements that might be brought into the Union by the act."[35]

Cooley's objections involved the coming together of contemporary racial ideology and a strict interpretation of the Constitution. The judge assumed an Anglo-Saxon notion of American citizenship: the United States was a white man's nation, and the federal Constitution was his document, exclu-sively. This he applied to expansion. The Constitution was formed, he said, solely "for the government of a Union of harmonious and contiguous states [on] the North American continent." Annexing Hawaii would undercut this grand principle because it involved "bringing incongruous elements into a

Union never framed to receive them." The acquisition of other territories inhabited largely by nonwhites would be equally and perhaps even more unacceptable: it would mean attaching to the United States "countries inhabited by races radically different in physical and . . . mental characteristics to those by and for whom the Union was established."[36]

Cooley argued that the treaty-making power established in the Constitution was a natural extension of Anglo-Saxon nationality and citizenship and that no treaty or policy that contradicted these principles could stand. The judge wrote that neither the Constitution nor "any of the actions or discussions which led up to its formation" indicated that its framers contemplated anything other than a "Union composed of contiguous states made up of people mainly of one race." This, he insisted, "was the general plan of the Union." Distant acquisitions would eviscerate the framers' intentions by making the nation "the ruler" of territories that could never join the Union as "harmonious members of a family of contiguous states constituting together one common country." A policy that brought a significant body of nonwhites into the polity, said Cooley, "would seem to be as much . . . forbidden as would be anything that directly antagonized" the Constitution.[37]

In "The Policy of Annexation for America," written in 1897, James Bryce offered two reasons to oppose territorial imperialism. First, acquiring far-off territories would mean sacrificing its invulnerability, the one great advantage the United States enjoyed over the author's native country, Great Britain. America had no distant possessions to defend from hostile nations, and rather than a weakness, the people should recognize this as a manifest strength. Also, America, he said, did not need more territory: "The continental territories of the United States are so far from being filled up," he wrote, "that the question of finding fresh dwellings for her inhabitants belongs to a distant future." Thus a second learned and leading thinker appears to have been unaffected by alleged anxieties drummed up by the closing of the frontier.[38]

The second, contiguous reason for avoiding empire, Bryce argued, involved race. He disagreed with the contention made by certain annexationists that Cuba and Hawaii were "desirable properties, fit for American citizens to migrate to and settle in." They could not be Americanized because neither island was climatically fit to receive white colonization. "Their climates," he asserted, "are much too hot for the Anglo-American race to work in; and both of them are peopled already by races from much hotter countries, fitter to stand the heat." Though Hawaii had a "more agreeable climate

. . . tempered by the trade winds," Bryce determined that white occupation was still unworkable. "[A]ny additional agricultural population must be a population," he insisted, "of Asiatic or Polynesian race, since men of Teutonic stock cannot do field labor under so hot a sun."[39]

Simply put, Bryce, the author of the magisterial *The American Commonwealth* (1888), concluded that expansion could not work when it took the United States into places where neither white men nor their institutions could flourish. That these territories were already occupied by various inferior races made such a project only more perilous, as their presence suggested, to his mind, a more substantial question: if Cuba or Hawaii were annexed, how could they be governed? Admitting them as states was the obvious solution but from the American standpoint, because of race, it was also the most detestable. Cuba was populated by "many Creole Spaniards . . . [and] many more negroes and mulattoes," and no one, Bryce asserted, wanted to "increase the black element in the American Union." There were, he said, "already more than seven millions of negroes in the South," which the white population held in check by holding "the colored vote under control by one kind of device or another." This "large, capable, and energetic white population of Anglo-American stock," said Bryce, wisely kept the mechanisms of government out of the hands of African Americans to prevent a recurrence of the alleged excesses of "black rule" and carpetbag government seen during the Reconstruction era. "In Cuba," he insisted, "there would be no such American element." The "Creole Spaniards and negroes," as Bryce called them, would rule in their own way, and to his reckoning, "it would not be a way consonant with the spirit of American institutions."[40]

Bryce included in his article a reproduction of Hawaii's 1896 census. Only one-sixteenth of the population, he concluded, "belong to the three European stocks which are capable of working self-governing democratic institutions."[41] Bryce, interestingly, did not include the Portuguese among them. Four-fifths were "Polynesians and Asiatics," unacceptable and "obviously unfit for free representative government." With statehood out of the question, would territorial status address the problem? Bryce responded no; sooner or later such a policy would have to be squared with the Constitution, the provisions of which, he said, "secure equal rights for citizens irrespective of race and color." Its requirements, furthermore, were "no less applicable to Territories than to States." Territorial status was meant to be temporary, transitional—"intended to lead up in due time, when the region become more densely populated by competent citizens, to the higher status of state-

TABLE 2 Racial and Ethnic Profile of Hawaii from the 1896 Census

Native Hawaiian	31,000
Japanese	24,400
Portuguese	15,100
Chinese	21,600
Mixed race	8,400
American	3,000
British	2,200
German	1,400
Norwegian and French	479
All other nationalities	1,055

Source: "Annexation of Hawaii," Senate Report 681, 55th Cong., 2d sess., 43.

hood." Bryce saw no reason to believe that even the passage of eighty years would be enough to make Cuba or Hawaii worthy of statehood. Race and the American system of governance, he reckoned, had come to an insoluble impasse. American institutions, he said, were "pervaded all through by the principle of equality and the habits of self-government." This defining characteristic meant that they were, in Bryce's words, "quite unsuited" to govern distant colonies. American institutions "do not adapt themselves to countries where the population consists of elements utterly unequal and dissimilar, as is the case of Hawaii," where "the overwhelming majority of the inhabitants, whether negroes or Asiatics, ought not to be trusted to govern even themselves, much less their white neighbors."[42]

Mindful of the constraints imposed by racism, the Republican Party committed itself to an expansionist foreign policy. Its national platforms after 1892 called for the extension of trade through reciprocity, the restoration of the merchant marine, the creation of a navy capable of protecting "[n]ational interest and the honor of our flag," the construction of a canal through Central America, and vigilant enforcement of the Monroe Doctrine.[43] These platforms suggest the broadest rendering of what has come to be known as the "large policy," the aggressive phase of expansion and imperialism described in many accounts of this period. Close examination, once again, reveals that the execution of this framework was marked by hesitance, conservatism, caution, and many expressions of concern over the costs of these adventures. Some asked what a very aggressive policy would do to the great traditions of American foreign relations and whether expansion outside the hemisphere would lead to the kind of entangling alliance Washington and Jefferson warned against. Others asked more practical, direct, gut-level questions: how much would a new navy cost, and who would pay for it? The middle years of the 1890s were still marred by economic depression. Business and labor both expressed concern over the potential for new and higher taxes. Many wondered out loud what other sacrifices an expansive policy might demand.

This created, at bottom, an atmosphere of cautious optimism in matters of diplomacy and expansion. Despite the chesty partisan attacks delivered by Senator Lodge and others who castigated the Democrats for failing to annex Hawaii and for their "policy of retreat," the best and strongest language the Republicans could muster for their national platform in 1896 declared that the island should be "controlled" by the United States. Clearly there was politics in the language. "Controlled" was vague and could be interpreted to mean several things: adherence to a traditional, conservative policy; merely sustaining the status quo for some indefinite period; or more decisive action—the declaration of a protectorate or perhaps, at some far-off and undetermined time, annexation. The imprecision of this plank and the absence of the stronger "annexation" indicates that the Republicans were not of one mind on the Hawaii issue (this also suggests that Senator Pettigrew was far from alone on this matter). Events that took place over the next two years help to substantiate this observation. But the presidential campaign between Republican William McKinley and Democrat William Jennings Bryan had little to do with Hawaii or any other foreign issue. The election turned on economics: the money question, the debate over free silver, free trade versus protectionism, and Cleveland's inability to lift the nation out of a devastating depression. In 1896, in the midst of a critical election, the Republican Party would not jeopardize victory by dividing itself or its constituencies over foreign affairs.

On 26 October 1896, a week before the presidential election, John W. Foster sailed out of San Francisco en route to Hawaii. According to his *Diplomatic Memoirs*, he departed feeling "considerable anxiety as to the result." The news of McKinley's victory did not get to Foster for twelve days, and only after having taken an extraordinary journey. "[T]he news was brought to us," Foster recalled, "by a steamer from Yokohama, having been sent under the Atlantic, through Europe, and across Asia." The incident reminded the former secretary of state of Hawaii's continued isolation and "the desirability of telegraphic communication with the outside world."[44] It reaffirmed, as well, his belief that the United States should renew its efforts to annex the islands. Foster and other annexationists were emboldened by McKinley's election even though, on the surface, the new president did not seem to be the sort of man most likely to lead them in this pursuit.

As a candidate, McKinley had said little about foreign policy and seems to have been unconcerned with the expansionist articles of the Republican platform. He brought with him to his office no extensive knowledge of or experience in foreign affairs, and he seems to have known little about the actual workings of diplomacy.[45] But prepared or not, it was not long before questions concerning foreign affairs sought out the new president. Shortly after the election McKinley told a delegation from the islands that he had "ideas about Hawaii" but thought it best, at that moment, to keep the details of his policy to himself.[46] Soon after his inauguration the president was in New York City to attend the dedication of Grant's Tomb. While there he invited Carl Schurz to the Windsor Hotel, where they sat, smoked cigars together, and talked casually about the problems facing the country. McKinley told Schurz that he would not stand for any annexationist scheming and promised him, with regard to Hawaii, that "you may be sure there will be no jingo nonsense under my administration."[47]

Despite the vagaries, reticence, and denials put forth by the president, men who wanted the islands annexed swooped down on the new administration in an attempt to persuade it to act. On 11 March, a week after the inauguration, Senator William Frye and John W. Foster met with McKinley specifically to discuss the Hawaii issue. Both were heartened by the president's apparent interest and concern. The Republic of Hawaii wasted no time sending representatives to present its case to the new administration. On 25 March 1897, Francis Hatch, Hawaii's minister to the United States, and William Smith, a member of the republic's newly formed annexation commission, met with the president. They, too, left the meeting with the impression that they had found an ally in McKinley. In his report to Hawaii's minister of foreign affairs, Smith compared the difference between the McKinley and Cleveland administrations as "like that of the difference between daylight and darkness."[48]

McKinley expressed sympathy for Hawaii, but his first concerns were domestic and involved policies that might bring the nation out of its four-year-long depression. He kept the annexationists at bay for months by insisting that the first order of business was restoring the American economy. Any treaty with Hawaii, he said, would have to wait until after a new tariff was secured. Then suddenly, in June 1897, McKinley ordered Assistant Secretary of State William Rufus Day to begin negotiations toward the acquisition of Hawaii.[49]

Day, with the help of John W. Foster, quickly produced a treaty. It was negotiated, signed on 16 June 1897, and sent to the Senate the same day, accompanied by two documents. The first, a perfunctory message from the president, called annexation "the fitting and necessary sequel" to a succession of policies directed toward Hawaii, and "the inevitable consequence" of a relationship "steadfastly maintained with that mid-Pacific domain for three-quarters of a century." Annexation, he said, was not a departure from tradition but "a consummation."[50] The second document, which carried the signature of the enfeebled secretary of state, John Sherman, presented an account thick with the administration's reasons for acquiring the islands. It said that the government that negotiated the treaty was now (unlike in 1893) firmly established and constitutionally empowered to pursue annexation. More important, Sherman declared, annexation had become necessary as no other option—neither commercial union nor granting Hawaii protectorate status—would satisfy its or America's present or future needs. Only the annexation of the islands "and their complete absorption into the United States" could provide a solution that promised "permanency and mutual benefit."[51]

The notion of "mutual benefit" required making concessions to certain prejudices and racist structures that were vitally important to the United States. Sherman's report told the Senate that the new treaty was like the 1893 agreement in all its basic features. But the document carefully stated that the new version kept intact articles protecting the Chinese Exclusion Acts, also a central feature of the first treaty. The report called on the Senate to note "that express stipulation is made [in the new treaty] prohibiting the coming of Chinese laborers from the Hawaiian Islands to any other part of our national territory." This provision was "proper and necessary" in view of the exclusion acts, "and it behooved the negotiators to see to it that this treaty, which in turn is to become . . . a supreme law of the land, shall not alter or amend existing law in this most important regard."[52] The treaty was sent to the Committee on Foreign Relations just two days after it arrived in the

Senate. The committee made its report on 14 July, recommending its ratifi-cation. The initiative appeared to be moving smoothly and quickly toward ratification when everything came to an abrupt halt. The treaty lay in wait for ten days when Congress adjourned having taken no further action on it.

The end of the story, so far, is less intriguing than its beginning. After holding off the Hawaiians for months, McKinley's sudden decision to open negotiations with them startled friends as well as potential opponents of the treaty. The one senator who should have been advised that negotiations were beginning—Cushman Davis, a leading annexationist and chair of the For-eign Relations Committee—was kept in the dark until they were nearly over. McKinley, furthermore, had neglected to prepare (or warn) the Senate for the treaty's arrival, and once it appeared, it was clear to all that it had come far too late in the session for it to be ratified in 1897.

Could all of this been the result of a sudden and unexplainable impulse followed by calendrical blundering on the part of the president? Very likely it was not. According to historian William Morgan, McKinley's timing and the entire episode make very little sense unless the treaty is viewed not as an instrument of annexation but as a powerful hands-off warning to Japan, which the administration believed was about to subvert the Hawaiian gov-ernment.[53]

Since it had taken power, the Dole government had shown itself to be conspicuously weak on the matter of controlling immigration into the is-lands. Japanese citizens were entering Hawaii at a rate of roughly one thou-sand per month, and by the spring of 1897 they had become the second largest population group in the islands behind only the native Hawaiians. Men made up the overwhelming majority of the Japanese arrivals, and about this time, supported by official pressure from Tokyo, they began to demand voting rights. The ruling white minority grew fearful and began making urgent requests to the State Department through Minister Francis Hatch, pleading for negotiation of an annexation treaty. Hatch's cables to Washington, D.C., document the Hawaiian government's panic over the Japanese threat and its desire that the United States take action "at the earliest moment" to prevent a great calamity. Hatch concurred, writing: "[I]n view of the momentous character of the questions likely to arise at any moment in Hawaii," there should be no delay. This could only refer to the dangers coming from Japan.[54]

Here is when Hawaii's white minority began to push and tug and pressure the administration aggressively, appealing to every sentiment and prejudice it could to force the United States to act on annexation. Honolulu warned that America's dominant position on the islands—the substance of a half century of policy—was rapidly breaking apart. If Japan seized Hawaii, then a potential (and powerful) enemy would jeopardize the peace and security of America's Pacific coastline. These were some of the more compelling arguments that McKinley and the American public heard in the spring and summer of 1897, but they were not the only ones, nor were they, perhaps, the most compelling.

Alongside pleas for annexation based on national pride and interest, Hawaiian annexationists began characterizing their struggle as a epochal conflict between two races. As they called for acquisition with greater and greater urgency, race became the focus of their writings and speeches. The United States must annex Hawaii, they said, for the sake of the islands' whites, to rescue Anglo-Saxon civilization from the creeping Asian hordes.

In May 1897 the Hawaiian branch of the Sons of the American Revolution (SAR) adopted and published an address for the compatriots in America. It wanted to provide an "authoritative statement" that presented the "unanimity of spirit among the thinking portion of the Hawaiian population."[55] The address called for annexation mainly by emphasizing the republic's essential "whiteness," by pointing to the dominance of American institutions on the islands, and by appealing to racial sympathies that bound Hawaii and the United States together with imagined ties of blood and brotherhood.

Hawaii, said the SAR, was an "advanced post of American civilization in the Pacific" and "a signal example of the pervading and transforming power of those principles which it is the object of our Society 'to maintain and extend.' " This group of annexationists established its case, then, by demonstrating the achievements that over the course of fifty years had transformed the islands from a heathen paradise into a small-scale model of the United States. "[U]nder the fostering care of the mother country," declared the SAR, Americans had brought Christianity and civilization to Hawaii; their philanthropy rescued "the native race from the rapid extinction which threatened them," and assisted them in creating a modern constitutional government. American influences had guaranteed property rights and the rule of law and had instituted "compulsory education in the English language for all." Americans commanded two-thirds of the capital invested in the islands, according to the address, and most of the islands' trade went to the United States. The 1893 revolution that had removed the "Hawaiian monarchy . . .

after it had become a demoralizing sham" and replaced it with a republican form of government was likened by the SAR to the American Revolution.[56] The Dole administration was, in contrast to what came before it, "distinguished by great ability . . . [and] integrity." All this made annexation not just possible, said the annexationists, but highly desirable because the islands were "a vigorous *American* colony"—wealthy, intelligent, and capable of self-government. The dominant character of the island-republic was, the document stated again and again, not native Hawaiian but American.[57]

Hawaii was in peril, and if the United States did not acquire it, warned the SAR, a rival power soon would. The theme was a familiar one. As the previous chapter showed, American policymakers had perceived the threat for some time; they recognized that a daunting challenge was coming from Asia in the form of tens of thousands of laborers from China and Japan and that they had to act decisively to counter the "peaceful invasion" and maintain the nation's predominant position in the islands. American policymakers (and their counterparts in Hawaii) also cast the imminent contest over Hawaii in racial terms: as a struggle to secure what James Blaine called its "necessarily American character" against "Mongolian supremacy." It is hardly surprising, then, that the SAR followed this lead. It recognized the confluence of race sentiment and strategic imperative and attempted to exploit the feelings they stirred up to beguile and provoke the United States to take action. Fundamental to its arguments, however, was the fiction that Hawaii was white.

The Asian presence threatened both the racial fiction and the republic's continued integrity. The SAR told its audience that Hawaii had finally arrived at a crucial "turning point" from which it could see an "irrepressible contest between the Asiatic and American civilizations." The Dole government had fought to hold back the Asians with the tools it had, including initiatives designed to increase the islands' white population. One course of action involved abolishing the contract labor system and replacing the Chinese and Japanese with "white workers from the United States." A second effort followed "to attract industrious farmers from the United States to develop our coffee lands." Despite these attempts at Americanization, the SAR feared the worst: "[I]f our overtures for a closer union with the mother country are spurned, if our products are discriminated against in American markets, and we are treated as aliens. . . . [t]he uncertainty that will hang over the fate of this country will deter the most desirable class of settlers from coming here."[58]

The most dire consequence was already being felt. "The native press of Japan and many of her people residing here plainly avow their intention to possess Hawaii," according to the address. Tokyo's method was stealth: "quietly pouring in her people" in an attempt to conquer the islands without overt force. The SAR predicted that if the forces at work were not reversed, every Japanese male would have the vote, and the islands would be run "by loyal subjects of the Makido." And just as the Asian would supplant the white in the workforce, things Japanese would replace everything American. "Hawaiian markets would be filled with Japanese products, its industries carried on by Japanese planters and manufacturers, and its ports with ships carrying the victorious flag of the Rising Sun." Eventually, Tokyo would annex Hawaii, and no one, declared the SAR, would have the right to interfere. America's " 'dog-in-the-manger' policy," it said, "will not succeed in the long run."59

In the address the SAR argued that the common objections to annexation found in the United States—noncontiguity, undesirable population, unfitness for statehood—should have no practical effects on the movement to take the islands. To ease the apprehensions of skeptics, SAR explained that annexation would not "per se confer American citizenship" on the undesirable elements in the population. Federal immigration and naturalization laws, once applied, would eliminate the contract labor system, forcing out the Asians and smoothing the road to Hawaii's acquisition. Afterward, "[u]nder the security of the starry flag, American skill and enterprise will work . . . wonders here," and the "process of Americanization will be rapid." The United States had to, then, secure "this outpost of its western frontier, not only for the security and development of commerce, but for the sake of maintaining and extending American principles at this central meeting place of races."60

Lorrin Thurston recognized the same racial imperative in his *Handbook on the Annexation of Hawaii*. According to Thurston, the relationship between the two nations had grown close, even familial over the previous half century: their connection was "like that of an indulgent and protecting elder brother towards a little sister." Hawaiian civilization was not only "the direct product of American effort" but also "a child of America . . . the one 'American Colony' beyond the borders of the Union."61

For all intents and purposes, Thurston said, Hawaii *was* America. Americans controlled nearly all the wealth and trade. "All legal documents are modeled on those in use in the United States," he said. "Most of the lawyers and judges are either from the United States or educated therein. The public school system is based upon that in the United States.... More than half of the teachers are Americans. English is the official language of the schools and courts, and the common language of business. The railroad cars, engines, waterworks, waterpipes, dynamos, telephones . . . are all American made. United States currency is the currency of the country.... All American holidays, Washington's Birthday, Decoration Day, Fourth of July and Thanksgiving Day are as fully and enthusiastically celebrated in Hawaii as in any part of the United States."[62]

Beyond political compatibility, the linchpin of Thurston's argument was that Hawaii was a white republic; its future had to be protected for the sake of white civilization, and annexation was the only means left to achieve this end. To Thurston, the contest over Hawaii was a competition between nations, but moveover, it was a contest between races in which Japan presented the greatest threat. He said that Japanese were arriving at a rate of two thousand per month, a movement that "was not immigration, but invasion."[63] Dole's constitution explicitly barred them from becoming citizens, but Thurston doubted that the barrier would hold. "An energetic, ambitious, warlike, and progressive people like the Japanese," he warned, "can not indefinitely be prevented from participating in the government of a country in which they become dominant in numbers, and the ownership of property." The drift "Japan-wards," said Thurston, would have to be stopped by some decisive act, otherwise it would mean "the ultimate supremacy of the Japanese . . . [and] the absolute substitution of the Asiatic in the place of the white man."[64]

Thurston's claim that Hawaii was an Anglo-Saxon nation was weakened most by the heterogeneity of the islands' population—whites constituted only a small minority of the more than one hundred thousand inhabitants. The way Thurston attempted to address, to defuse, this problem is the most interesting aspect of his article. His tactic will, by now, appear familiar: reduce or erase the incongruous elements of the population—the people of color whose presence would demoralize a sector of the imperialist movement and catalyze the fiercest opposition among their enemies—and raise, by any means available, the number of whites, even if this meant inventing them.

Thurston's work in this regard is distinguished by his efforts to make the native Hawaiians appear acceptable, fit, and assimilable to his readers. The thirty-three thousand native people were "conservative, peaceful, and generous," he said. They had rejected the "retrogressive tendencies" of the monarchy and had learned to support both the republic and annexation. Thurston felt compelled to explain that the native population "are not Africans, but Polynesians. They are brown, not black." The color line did not exist in Hawaii as it did in American, he said. Native peoples and whites worked as equals and "freely intermarry," which accounted for the "7000 of mixed blood." And this group, he insisted, would "easily and rapidly assimilate with and adopt American ways and methods."[65] Nothing was said regarding the republic having disfranchised the native Hawaiians or their continued opposition to Dole's government.

Thurston was far more charitable than Dole when it came to the Portuguese, a difference in treatment best explained by the differences in time and circumstances. Ironically, both treated the Portuguese in the manner they did to achieve the same end: both wanted to make Hawaii appear as white, racially speaking, as possible. In 1893, Dole lumped them in with the natives, wanting to disfranchise the whole lot. Four years later Thurston, in an attempt to inflate the number of people who could be considered white, added the fifteen thousand Portuguese to the European groups. He did not stop with mathematics but attempted to remake the Portuguese socially and culturally as well. Seven thousand of them, Thurston wrote, had been born in Hawaii and educated in its public schools "so that they speak English as readily as does the average American child." He described their collective character in terms meant to communicate white racial identity. The Portuguese, to Thurston's reckoning, were "a hard-working, industrious, home-creating and home-loving people, who would be of advantage to any developing country." They constituted, he said, "the best laboring element in Hawaii."[66]

The Chinese and Japanese were beyond this sort of redemption. No amount of reasoning or clever turn of phrase could make them appear even remotely American, European, white, or assimilable. Linking Asians to any policy would lead to ruin, whereas removing them, diminishing their numbers, constituted an effort to do away with a formidable obstacle to annexation. Thurston understood this. The Asians in Hawaii were "an undesirable population . . . because they do not understand American principles of government," but their presence should not hinder the United States, Thurston felt. After annexation was confirmed, he said, they would not remain in the islands. Most were sojourners, "laborers who are in the country for what they can make out of it." Once they made a few hundred dollars, Thurston promised, they returned home. He predicted that within ten years "there will not be Asiatics enough left in Hawaii to have any appreciable effect."[67]

The republic Thurston wanted to present, then, was one fit to be part of the United States, racially white by every important measure, a place essentially free of "alien" races. Declaring that the Japanese and Chinese would retreat following annexation meant that the islands would become more white, more American. Their departure would benefit the United States in one additional way, said Thurston: it would provide an open field for American workers. The annexationists were beginning to figure ways to draw labor into the cause of extracontinental expansion. Logically, the working classes could become valuable allies if their prejudices and material interests were accounted for and judiciously handled.

The concern that Thurston showed for labor's sensibilities was deliberate, calculated, and, for the purposes of this book, significant. It revealed an understanding of the connection between American political culture, that racism which focused on Hawaii's nonwhite majority, in particular the Chinese, and imperial policy. Also, when in his *Handbook* Thurston spoke to workers and labor organizations, he revealed a special interest in the western states where the Chinese had become a powerful metaphor for workers' fears. Thurston assured them that Hawaii's annexation would not threaten them. The Chinese, he said, would not emigrate to America because they made "as much or more money in Hawaii than they can in the United States." The exclusion acts would remain secure, he insisted. Indeed, the Asians would see no benefits from this policy. "They are not citizens," he said, "they are aliens in America and aliens in Hawaii; annexation will given them no rights which they do not now possess, either in Hawaii or in the United States."[68] These assurances that annexation would not interfere with Americans' lives, workplaces, wages, laws, or the racial status quo were necessary and showed how racism shaped both policy formation and the actions and words of the imperialists.

Once it appeared, opposition to the treaty erupted with fierce intensity. The editorial pages of newspapers across the country contained dark predictions regarding the impact that Hawaii's joining the United States would have on the latter's domestic sugar industry, various questions of naval and military strategy, and the status of the working classes. Many feared that the islands might shock and unsettle the racial status quo; this caused the greatest commotion in the press. The *Baltimore Sun* asked its readers to ponder what could be done with such a "mixture of races" as existed together in Hawaii. If the islands were annexed, "are the Portuguese to retain the ballot and out-vote the Americans? If we make them into a State," it inquired, "shall we consent to receive at Washington two senators evolved from this mass of Asiatic ignorance?" The *New York World* speculated that annexation was so unthinkable that it could result only from some kind of corrupt bargain; nothing else would compel President McKinley and Secretary of State Sherman to "forc[e] upon us irrevocably this degraded population, this group of islands utterly unfit for membership in our republic." The most likely culprit, according to the *World*, was Hawaii's sugar interests, which seemed to possess some "secret . . . power over the administration" and persuaded McKinley "to foreswear his convictions and deliberately . . . inject into the veins of the nation this leprous and vicious blood of the distant south seas." To the *Philadelphia Record*, the nation's racial social order was in immediate danger from the imperialists. It was a "mockery to build up a rampart of anti-immigration and quarantine laws on the one hand," it said, "and on the other to take in at one gulp the whole mass of diseased and depraved serfs who constitute the greater part of the population of the Hawaiian islands."[69] The *Seattle Post-Intelligencer* declared that the "character of the population" was an aspect that "must inevitably cause this country . . . annoyance." The *Tacoma Ledger* came closest to anticipating the imperialists' political strategy: it suggested that the creation of "some form of territorial government" could give the "Americans on the islands" every protection and benefit they hoped to achieve through annexation while making certain that "the question of citizenship of the other inhabitants shall [never] be raised or considered."[70]

As labor moved toward a position on Hawaii, those unions which favored anti-imperialism understood and justified their stand in highly racialized terms. The response of American Federation of Labor (AFL) was representative. In the fall of 1897 its journal, the *American Federationist*, said that the presence of several thousand American citizens in Hawaii, who controlled more "business on the islands than all other nations can claim," was among a very few "important considerations and incentives for favorable consideration of the [annexation] question." The racial and demographic facts of the case, as well as the editors' question, "what effect would annexation have upon the large masses of our people?," erased any ambivalence they felt. The native Hawaiians were dismissed as "semi-civilized, with no conception of the privileges, much less the rights, hopes, and aspirations of a republican form of government." As laborers they were called "docile and menial, their wants almost primitive," which made them the opposite of the American worker. The Japanese were reckoned as being still worse: "coolie laborers" who toiled without complaint, according to the *Federationist*, and "under conditions wholly at variance with any conception of American manhood." The Portuguese and Chinese "coolies and others equally low in the economic, social, and civilized scale" were just as undesirable. "Who can honestly assert," said the paper, "that they will become under any form of government, congenial, or assimilate to an enlightened homogeneity[?]"[71]

Other labor organizations followed the AFL's lead. In the West, unions feared that annexation would unsettle the United States with both Hawaii' s labor problems "and its twin solutions—contract labor and oriental immigration." The *Coast Seamen's Journal* reported that its rank and file—workers from San Francisco, Sacramento, and Los Angeles—formed a united front "against the [annexation] plot." It insisted that out of its entire membership, not "a single voice has been raised in favor of it," and even "the farmers and businessmen generally . . . have protested against annexation." In June 1897 the San Francisco Central Labor Union announced a series of resolutions, warning its members that acquisition would attach Hawaii to the United States with its contract labor system intact. Some evidence suggests that labor's reaction to annexation may have been affected by such factors as craft and region. The *Iron Molder's Journal* of September 1897 quoted a union spokesman in Cincinnati who "could scarcely share the fear that annexation would seriously threaten our working-men with the same disabilities under which the [Hawaiians] labor." But when annexation was discussed on the floor of the AFL convention two months later, the most vocal opposition came from delegates representing the western states.[72]

These arguments give us a fair indication of how working-class attitudes toward annexation took shape. The white working class was the creator of its own racial ideology and a coarchitect and cobuilder of the late-nineteenth-century American racial social order. An array of groups railed at the corruptions that they insisted attended unrestricted immigration. Nativists, political reformers, and militant Protestants fed popular anxieties based on the alleged destructive habits of various European nationalities and religious groups. Some were natural-born revolutionaries and anarchists. Others were prone to drunkenness, disease, poverty, and violence and knew nothing of the American work ethic. The majority, if allowed to vote, they argued, would only add to the corruption of the cities. Catholics were slaves to the pope. Labor's contribution was the claim that the new arrivals undercut wages, broke strikes, passively accepted terrible workplace conditions, and altogether corroded the status of the native-born white worker.

Labor saw Hawaii's annexation through this optic, tinted dark by decades of nativism, anti-Chinese racism, turning what began as a local movement into national policy. Policymakers were pragmatic men, politicians, partisans, and most of all vote counters who knew that they had to reckon with the exclusion acts. The intelligent policymaker would not undertake any project that might violate them and, as a result, alienate a constituency as powerful and potentially volatile as labor—the strikes of 1877, Haymarket, Pullman, and dozens of other conflicts, less infamous, were still fresh memories. In short, the demands of the racial social order of the 1890s would not allow the imperialists to speak and act in the ways presented in the dominant narrative. If the imperialists tried at the outset to justify annexation on the grounds that it was the nation's duty to uplift, civilize, and carry out a plan of benevolent assimilation on tens of thousands of Japanese and Chinese workers, organized labor would have revolted against the Republicans, fled to the Democrats, and the effect on the party would have been disastrous. The president's actions in December 1897 indicate that at least one leading politician considered this possibility.

In his annual message, McKinley reaffirmed his support for the treaty and prodded Congress to act on it. The Hawaiian senate had ratified the treaty unanimously the previous September, he said, "and only awaits the favorable action of the American Senate to effect the complete absorption." The president was, by this time, clearly aware of the obstacles that stood in the policy's way, particularly those that involved the islands' Asian, native Hawaiian, and Portuguese majority. He told the legislature that it was up to them to determine the "political relation [of Hawaii] to the United States," the "quality and degree of the elective franchise of the inhabitants," and the "regulation of the labor system."[73]

These were perilous questions that McKinley was content to leave at Congress's doorstep. The president cast the maneuver in a more flattering light, basing it, he said, on his faith in "the wisdom of Congress" and his confidence in its ability to ratify the treaty and, at the same time, address the race question: to—as McKinley put it—"avoid the abrupt assimilation of elements perhaps hardly yet fitted to share in the highest franchises of citizenship." Whatever Congress's plan might turn out to be, McKinley insisted that it provide Hawaii with "the most just provisions of self-rule in local matters with the largest political liberties as an integral part of our Nation," because, he said, "[n]o less is due to a people who, after nearly five years of demonstrated capacity to fulfill the obligations of self-governing statehood, come of their free will to merge their destinies with our body-politic."[74]

Two points emerge from these statements; both further reveal what had become the preferred strategy of the imperialists with regard to race. First, throughout this part of the address we see that McKinley's main concern and greatest sympathy was with the white minority. As a politician, an imperialist, a Republican, and president of the United States, he knew that their integrity, character, achievements, and racial identity provided the best case for annexation. Second, on nearly every key point, McKinley attempted to remove the nonwhite majority from the debate. He knew that their presence would only be a source of trouble and injury to his cause. In asking Congress to bar the largest parts of the islands' population from "the highest franchises of citizenship" while allowing the Dole government to maintain control over local matters, the president sought to sustain white dominance and the racial status quo in Hawaii. In calling on Congress to adjudicate the troublesome issues that touched on race, McKinley in effect asked it to ratify the treaty and annex the islands while keeping the nonwhite majority at bay: while denying them, in other words, the rights of equal citizenship, the vote, and access to the domestic labor market. His reference to "nearly five years . . . of self-governing statehood" negated decades of native governance and erased the history and the presence of the native Hawaiians. Given the facts of the revolution, the Americans' role in it, and what followed, McKinley would not have counted the native people among those who came to the United States seeking annexation "of their free will." It was clear to everyone that only the whites had done this; indeed, at the time, they would have been considered the only group on the islands capable of pursuing such a goal. Only whites had "demonstrated the capacity" for self-government. Here was the critical distinction between the capable and the incapable, the incongruous and the assimilable. The president had all but declared that white rule was the necessary prerequisite for annexation.

Congress reconvened in January 1898 and debated over the treaty in executive session. The imperialists believed that they were only a handful of votes short of the sixty that were needed for ratification.[75] This was too optimistic. Deliberations dragged on, and in February no signs indicated that any more senators had been persuaded by the treaty's alleged virtues to move into the imperialist column. It was then that the events which took the

United States into the war against Spain stole attention from Hawaii: the DeLome letter ridiculing President McKinley and the explosion of the USS *Maine* in Havana Harbor, Cuba, which killed more than 250 American sailors. As resistance in the Senate and the imminent war left the annexationists with little hope that they could win a two-thirds vote, they altered their strategy. Rather than press ahead with the treaty, changes were made so that the islands could be acquired by a joint resolution, a method that required only a simple majority in both houses of Congress to pass.

On 16 March 1898 the Senate Committee on Foreign Relations issued its report, supporting the joint resolution and recommending annexation.[76] All of the old and well-explored justifications appeared in the committee's report with one significant difference. The Japanese threat had been moved to the top of the list of the committee's "reasons in favor of the annexation of Hawaii": ahead of justifications based on military and strategic advantage and the role they would play in advancing American trade in East Asia. The report was blunt in this respect: acquisition, it said, would "prevent the establishment of an alien and possibly hostile stronghold in a position commanding the Pacific coast and the commerce of the North Pacific." Further along it became more emphatic. The United States, it said, must act "NOW to preserve the results of its past policy, and to prevent the dominancy in Hawaii of a foreign people."[77] Here was the confluence of national defense and fear of the "yellow peril."

Easily the most remarkable aspect of this document arose out of the committee's attempt to confront the inescapable race issue, the questions that surrounded what it called "the character of population we will acquire from those islands." The committee followed the trajectory established by McKinley and others and justified annexation on the grounds of racial sympathy. The report proclaimed: "in all respects the white race in Hawaii are the equals of any community of like members and pursuits to be found in any country. The success they have achieved in social, religious, educational, and governmental institutions is established in results that are not dwarfed by a comparison with our most advanced communities."[78]

Whiteness was the critical motif of the Foreign Relations Committee's argument. It stated that the islands' whites—the conjunction of Americans, Britains, Norwegians, Germans, French, "and other nationalities"—made up 22 percent of the total population: a minority, but a significant one in terms of numbers but in other ways as well. "These white people are so united in the support of good government," according to the report, "that there is no political distinction of nationalities among them, and harsh differences of opinion on public questions are seldom found."[79] Whiteness was, then, their great common bond and at the same time the solvent that obliterated all less profound distinctions—nationality, religion, culture, ethnicity, language, and history.

Like Thurston, with whom it shared motivations and goals, this Senate committee counted the Portuguese in with the 22 percent, asserting that they "*are also recognized as white citizens*" (a judgment that would certainly have amazed and distressed Sanford Dole). The evidence of this was to be found in what the committee presented as the Portuguese' decidedly Anglo-Saxon qualities. The Portuguese, the report noted, "are thrifty and law-abiding people" who had "intelligent conceptions of the value of liberty regulated by law." Also, their aesthetic sensibilities fit them into the category of white. Readers were told that "[t]heir homes are uniformly comfortable, and usually vine-clad and tasteful in their surroundings." Furthermore, according to the report, "[t]heir advancement in education and in the acquisition of substantial property is very marked since their arrival in Hawaii, and their desire to become citizens of the 'Great Republic' is very earnest."[80] Whiteness had become so vital to the imperialists' cause in 1898 that they would invent it, whereas at another time in another place with a another agenda, the Portuguese would have been cast—as they already had been in Hawaii—as the most debased of peoples and anything but "white."

This emphasis on the virtues of the white minority was only magnified by the comparisons the report made between them and the Asians and native Hawaiians. The Japanese were merely "coolies . . . collected from the lower classes," a "community of ignorant people" and a "dangerous element." Unlike the Portuguese, the Japanese were "not trustworthy as laborers, nor honest in their dealings as merchants." The committee was patronizing toward the Chinese, who were called "the most industrious and thrifty race that has come to Hawaii." The soft touch evidenced here—particularly when compared with what had been said about the Chinese previously in Congress and in the popular and labor press—probably arose from the committee's perception of them as relatively powerless and unthreatening, both with respect to the aggressive Japanese and because, the report declared, they "evince[d] little desire to use the ballot, from which they are excluded." The native Hawaiians occupied the very bottom of the committee's regard.[81]

To the reckoning of the committee, the only race capable of governing the islands and worthy of admission was the white, but they required immediate aid, meaning annexation. "It is beyond question that, as a factor in government, the united white race is indispensable to the safety of the people of Hawaii," said the report. But, it continued, the whites "could not control the islands without the frequent presence, if not the constant attendance, of the warships of the United States and of the European powers," to hold the Japanese at bay. The absence of American control, the committee predicted, would undoubtedly lead to one of two catastrophes: the first would be the beginning of "civil strife and bloodshed . . . and would result in the rule of some white man as dictator"; the second, the more fearful, involved "a Japanese man-of-war . . . stationed at Honolulu" and "the capture of the islands by Japan."[82]

The committee dismissed the arguments put forth by opponents of annexation as "minor objections" that had no "appreciable value" in comparison with the great advantages that would be gained by taking the islands. The benefits the committee referred to were not simply material, according to the report; annexation was "an imperative duty that we owe to Hawaii." The duty was an urgent one, made so by the "sudden influx of Asiatics, and their increasing numbers is an ever present peril to Hawaii." Here, as before, America's obligations were portrayed in the language of family. Protecting the islands and annexation, the report said, "is a duty that has its origin in the noblest sentiments that inspire the love of the father for his children, or a country from its enterprising and honorable citizens, or a church for its missions and the heralds it has sent out with messages of deliverance to those pagans in darkness, or our Great Republic to a younger sister that has established law, liberty, and justice in that beautiful land that a corrupt monarchy was defiling with fraud . . . and dragging down to barbarism. We have solemnly assumed these duties and cannot abandon them without discredit." The consequences of inaction or refusal were too great to disregard. "If we do not interpose to annex Hawaii or to protect her from the influx of Asiatic," the report concluded, the islands' whites "will soon be exterminated."[83]

The Foreign Relations Committee pushed for annexation by conjuring up an image of a Hawaii without Asians and free of native influence: a place both preserved and reserved in the future exclusively for the prosperity of whites. It imagined this picture quite vividly. The report spoke to the islands' fertility "and its abundant fisheries" being great enough to "insure a comfortable living to more than tenfold the present population." Indeed, the "effort of the Republic to fill up the public domain with white people from the United States" had induced "a strong tide of such immigrants. The climate, soil, and the agricultural products," the report insisted, "invite such immigrants." The last point would soon become a matter of contention between the rival parties supporting and opposing annexation.

On 1 May 1898 the United States Asiatic Squadron led by Commodore George Dewey attacked an outgunned and antiquated Spanish fleet in Manila Harbor, the Philippines. Dewey's victory was swift and complete, and it cost only one American life. For the Hawaiian annexationists the conflict came at a fortuitous moment, for the groundswell of nationalism, patriotism, and support for the war effort gave them a long-awaited and precious opportunity to secure their prize.

Three days after the battle, Congressman Francis Newlands of Nevada presented a resolution, almost identical to the one that floundered so badly in the Senate, providing for the annexation of Hawaii. Two weeks later it emerged from the Committee on Foreign Affairs with the endorsement of the majority of its members. Politicians on both sides of the question realized that popular enthusiasm for the war and the people's intense desire to help American forces, regardless of the cost, gave the annexationists the upper hand. The resolution would pass easily in the House of Representatives if only it could come to a vote. When the anti-imperialist Republican Thomas B. Reed, the Speaker of the House and chairman of the Committee on Rules, tried to stop the resolution, fellow congressmen, party leaders, and the McKinley administration pressured him for three weeks until he finally bowed.[84] On 2 June newspapers published polls which revealed that majorities in both the House of Representatives and the Senate favored the resolution. Annexation would be a fact, they said, before Congress adjourned for the summer.[85]

The debates in the House of Representatives and the Senate were remarkably similar in language, content, and tenor. Both were run through with cliché, naked appeals to patriotism, speculations on the economic benefits of annexation and the need to uphold the Tyler and Monroe Doctrines, and the constitutionality of acquiring the islands. Neither debate broke much new ground. The *Congressional Record* reveals senators restating many of the arguments and observations that had been made by congressmen only days earlier. Indeed, in the majority of their often lengthy speeches, politicos in both houses repeated points made in 1870 and 1893, both for and against annexation.

The one unprecedented element in these deliberations was the war. The annexationists did everything they could to exploit the resurgence of patriotic feelings and the new "war spirit." References to the righteousness of the nation's cause, its humanitarianism, and the bravery of America's fighting men consistently drew applause in both chambers. Invoking Commodore Dewey had a similar rousing effect, and his name quickly became a metaphor for national defense, a strong navy, duty, and patriotism. Congressman Robert Hitt favored Hawaii's annexation because the war had shown the people the vulnerability of the Pacific coast and because the nation had to support its soldiers in the Philippines. "There is no one in our country so recreant in his duty as an American," he said, "that he would refuse to support the president in succoring Dewey after his magnificent victory, lying in Manila Bay, holding in control the Spanish power there, but unable to land for want of reinforcements and surrounded by millions of Spanish subjects. Yet," he declared, "it is impossible to send support to Dewey to-day without taking on coal and supplies at Honolulu in the Hawaiian Islands."[86]

In the Senate, John T. Morgan chastised his colleagues whose "fine, silken, glossy arguments about the Constitution" prevented the nation from effectively prosecuting the war. Morgan's first concern, he said, was with the welfare of the soldiers, and Hawaii was essential in order to provide them with both a supply line and a safe haven. "We shall presently be having wounded men and men sick with all manner of tropical diseases coming back from the Philippines . . . and Senators here on this floor [are] filibustering to prevent those men from having a friendly welcome and a landing under their own flag and their own country in Hawaii."[87] Voting against annexation was by implication unpatriotic, a betrayal of Dewey and thousands of American soldiers battling Spanish tyranny half a world away. The opponents of annexation protested what the imperialists were doing by conflating war and empire, by misleading the people, but it was an inadequate response.

Their best weapon, they knew, was to play on the nation's racism and focus their attacks on the facts of the islands' racial composition. Congressman Hugh Dinsmore of Arkansas pointed to the "[f]orty-two percent of the population of the island[s]" that was "Mongolian, Chinese, and Japanese." He accused the annexationists of doing violence to the Chinese Exclusion Acts with their resolution. "Are you to take into full citizenship the Chinese whom your laws exclude from coming to this country?" he demanded to know. "Are you going to confer upon them the immunities and privileges and sovereignty of American citizenship, when you say that they are not good enough even to come among us upon our own territory temporarily?" Congressman Champ Clarke of Missouri scolded the imperialists for, as he put it, laboring "under the delusion that in the twinkling of an eye any sort of human being, no matter how ignorant, vicious, or degraded, can be made worthy of American citizenship."[88]

The prospect that annexation would grant equal citizenship to "degraded" races and weaken the nation's racist structures and social status quo was the theme that ignited the anti-imperialists. Senator Justin Morrill despised the prospect of his nation stained by the "undesirable character of the greater part of [the islands'] ill-gathered races of population." They were too many, said Morrill, and the whites—"Less than 3 per cent of the present number of inhabitants of Hawaii are American in origin"—too few, "not enough to dominate or to boss the 97 per cent of other nationalities." The mass, he warned, would expect to become "full-fledged citizens . . . entitled to share in governing the United States in both Houses of Congress. To this," he declared, "I am irrevocably opposed."[89] Morrill, too, thought it absolutely necessary that the United States control Hawaii, but the racial obstacle was serious enough to make him call for a solution other than annexation, one that involved fewer burdens and would not imperil the United States. "We can be a friend," he said, "without taking them into our family."[90] Senator William Roach of North Dakota chose to taunt his rivals. To justify their stand the resolution's supporters must have convinced themselves, he said, "that the civilization of the United States would be improved by the infusion of . . . the Kanakas; that none of the lepers of that unhappy land would ever scatter leprosy in this country; that rescued from their poverty, they would make us all rich; the brightest star in the blue field of our flag would be that represented by the country of dusky ex-cannibals."[91]

Stephen White of California discoursed in the Senate chamber for four days against annexation; race was the point of departure for his most provocative objections. The nation's great strength, he said, was the result of the "homogeneity of the American people," a population uncorrupted by "the ignorant, venal, and savage, living far removed and alien to us in language and ideas." What, he inquired, could be gained by absorbing the Hawaiian majority? The native peoples, who were on the path toward extinction, would make poor citizens. "Obliteration would come before [the Hawaiian] is qualified to be of us." Not only should the Hawaiians never be "elevated to the position of American citizenship," he said, but "no country tenanted by incompetents should ever be acquired for permanent occupancy" by the United States. "Not every clime, not under every sun, not in the home of every race can the American citizen be found."[92]

White expanded on his racial objections by linking "the character of population we will bring in by annexation" to the interests and prejudices of America's working classes. The Japanese population in the islands, numbering about twenty-four thousand were not excluded under the imperialists' resolution, he said, and their numbers would certainly grow. "We exclude Chinese laborers, but we do not drive away those already there. Therefore the Asiatics in the islands will remain and Chinese and Japanese 'cheap labor' will be incorporated." White was speaking to several constituencies at once: unions and workers in all parts of the nation that had supported Chinese exclusion in the past, but especially his fellow westerners. He wanted to persuade them of the dangers of annexation, to revive their anti-Chinese prejudice and impress it on Congress. "We assume to be fond of our laborers," said White, "and yet we design importing or forcing into this country, by extending our boundary, an element of competition with which our kindred can not possibly hope to compete." He spoke most directly to his fellow politicians, Democrats and Republicans, who wanted these workers' votes. White reminded them that "not very long ago the people of this country agitated the question of the restriction of immigration. It is but a few weeks since it was the subject of discussion in this Chamber. It is but a few years ago when it was almost provocative of a revolution upon the western coast of this country. We then objected to importing Mongolians by the shipload," he said, "and now, as remarked to me by a distinguished Senator, we propose to bring them in by the continent load."[93]

The annexationists did not engage their opponents directly on these arguments, contradict their foundational assumption—that Hawaii's nonwhites were unwanted in the United States both as workers and as citizens—or speak, in the main, of the "white man's burden." The imperialists kept to their best arguments, beginning with the war. The nation was fighting on two oceans, and the resolution's friends believed, rightly, that their most powerful argument was that Hawaii must be taken as a war measure. Operations in the Philippines, they said, required that men and materials be transferred through those islands, an assertion that only magnified their strategic value. After the war, with the fear of the Asian "menace" all but proven, Hawaii would be the nation's first outpost in the defense of the Pacific coast. The imperialists knew from history, distant and recent, that racism acted on policies such as this one like a poison. So they ignored the taunts and refused to be bound to any rationale that would place a mass of humanity universally deemed undesirable at the center of their policy.

They did not, however, surrender the race issue to their adversaries. Whiteness and white racial brotherhood became a leitmotif of pro-resolution debate. Congressman Frederick Gillett of Massachusetts confessed to feeling "a special sympathy with these islands." Much of it had been engendered by memories of the first generation of missionaries who had gone there, men and women from his state. "After many days the bread they cast upon the waters is returning to us again." Their descendants, declared the congressman, had rescued the islands for civilization, overthrowing the "debauched monarchy" and building "a republic modeled on our own." This made annexation correct and just, according to Gillett, because Hawaii's white minority, who were asking "to return to our allegiance" and "share in the honor and protection of our flag," had beyond any doubt "show[n] their love for their native country."[94]

Congressman Robert Hitt raised his arguments from the same ground. He demanded to know from his colleagues: "Are you not as American proud of that little colony, the only true American colony, the only spot on earth beyond our boundaries in the wide world where our country is preferred above all others?" The chamber answered with thunderous applause.[95] Annexation was justified to his reckoning based on the cultural, political, institutional, and racial similarities that bound the two countries together. Hawaii should be annexed for the sake of the "Caucasian element," Hitt said, the "strong intellectual and industrial force on the island . . . men sprung from our blood who have borne themselves with . . . enlightenment, courage, and energy . . . whose only fault is that they love our flag more than their own."[96]

Hitt and others demanded quick action from Congress through pleas that "the rapid growth of the Japanese element" threatened the islands' fundamentally white civilization. Hitt maintained that Tokyo was demanding equality for its citizens living on the islands, pressuring Hawaii's government to allow it to "pour" in thousands more Japanese, and "the right to demand for all Japanese any privileges or rights . . . which could include the right to vote or hold office." Tokyo's success would mean the end of white rule and civilization. Hawaii, he said, "would be converted into a Japanese commonwealth immediately."[97]

DeAlva Alexander of New York ignored the nonwhite majority in his speech; it was, he said, the "Anglo-Saxon residents and their supporters" who were offering the islands to the United States, "an extent of territory larger than Connecticut and Rhode Island combined." White racial sympathy made annexation desirable, for the great extent of land he mentioned was "owned as well as governed by a people who are bone of our bone and flesh of our flesh."[98] The alleged Japanese threat weighed on Alexander heavily. The question, he said, was not only "[s]hall we annex Hawaii" but "are we willing to allow some other nation to annex it?" Throughout 1896 and 1897, he observed, "the Japanese entered Hawaii at a rate of 2,000 per month, until now they number 25,000, or nearly one-quarter of the total population." If this went on unchecked, meaning if annexation failed, "soon the supremacy of Japan will be completed."[99] To Alexander's mind, then, racial duty in the name of preserving white civilization left the United States no other option than to annex Hawaii.

The transformation of Senator George Frisbie Hoar of Massachusetts from anti-imperialist, to imperialist, and back again to fierce anti-imperialist in the case of the Philippines further reveals the power of racial sympathy in the case of Hawaii. In his *Autobiography of Seventy Years*, Hoar recalled a meeting with President McKinley and a conversation that changed his mind about annexation. When Hoar told the president that he did not favor annexation, McKinley was taken aback. "I don't know what I shall do," McKinley said. "We cannot let those islands go to Japan," he told the senator. "Japan has her eye on them. Her people are crowding in there. I am satisfied that they do not go there voluntarily, as ordinary immigrants, but that Japan is pressing them in there in order to get possession before anybody can interfere. If something is not done, there will be before long another revolution and Japan will get control." That rival and predatory nation, he said finally, "is doubtless waiting her opportunity."

The exchange impressed Hoar enough to make him rethink his position. Thoughts of Hawaii's white founders and the predicament of their descendants had a peculiar effect on the senator's mind. They were, to Hoar, people much like himself, men and women from his state, more like neighbors than strangers living in a besieged paradise on the other side of the world. "American missionaries had redeemed the [native] people from barbarism and Paganism," he wrote. "Many of them, and their descendants, had remained on the Islands." Their efforts alone, Hoar believed, created the government that he recognized as honorable and capable of creating a legitimate political contract with the United States. "By the Constitution of Hawaii, the Government had been authorized to make a treaty of annexation with this country," he said, while ignoring the tens of thousands who were disfranchised by that same document. Racial and cultural sympathy mattered more to this senator, who shuddered at the prospect of the islands falling into the orbit of Japan, "not by conquest, but by immigration." The United States had to annex the islands, Hoar reasoned, out of duty, both racial and national, and "deliver them from this oriental menace."[100]

By pushing whiteness to the center of their case, congressional annexationists took up an ingenious strategy, imitating Thurston by overinflating the white population's numbers and inventing whiteness around the Portuguese. Francis Newlands of Nevada was most blunt: "The whites in Hawaii consist of Americans, English, and Portuguese, all of whom can be easily assimilated." When, for example, Congressman Hitt held up the "twenty to twenty-five thousand . . . people of European or American origin" as the best justification for seizing Hawaii, he proclaimed that the former group was composed of "a good many Germans, British, and a large number of Portuguese."[101]

Those who wanted to make the Portuguese white insisted that it was their decades on the islands that had worked the transformation. The Portuguese had learned American ways, embraced its culture, and adapted to its institutions. More than half of the population counted in the 1896 census had been born on the islands and educated there in the schools, which, Hitt told his fellow congressmen, "are similar to the schools here." The children had leaned to speak "English as an ordinary American child." They had also picked up other "white" qualities, such as the aversion or immunity to certain diseases. According to Hitt, leprosy, supposedly brought to the islands by the Chinese, was "a malady that rarely affects people of the Caucasian race of the better class, who use an abundance of soap and water." He announced that "little or no leprosy" existed among the Portuguese, which made them like other "clean, [and] highly civilized people anywhere."[102] Congressman Alexander counted twenty-one thousand "Anglo-Saxons, Germans, Scandinavians, and Portuguese" among those groups "with whom we are familiar, to whom we do not object, and among whom we live and associate, without a thought that they are not homogeneous and desirable."[103] Charles Pierce of Missouri declared that by joining the Portuguese to the islands' British, German, and American communities, "the percentage of intelligence at the present time among these elements is as large as that which exists in any of the new sections of our country."[104]

The annexationists pressed their cause further by arguing that the passage of time would certainly witness the increase of the white population and expansion of white control over the islands. They repeated earlier assertions that the objectionable elements of the present population would only decrease, that some would disappear utterly, making only more room for white settlement. The "Kanakas" were "gradually becoming extinct," said Congressman Newlands, and the Chinese and Japanese had come there only as contract laborers. The overwhelming majority of these emigrants were men, few had brought their families, and most of them, Newlands assured the country, remained "devoted to their own country" and intended to return someday. "The existing Mongolian population, therefore, will necessarily be withdrawn," he said, "and under wise exclusion laws there will be none to take its place." Hitt said that the "Asiatics would rapidly disappear in numbers under the operation of our laws," eliminating contract labor and enforcing the restriction acts.[105] Congressman Alexander suggested that the Chinese would probably leave Hawaii voluntarily, for they were there only "to accumulate . . . a few hundred dollars" while looking forward to the day when "the steamer shall return them to their own people and homes." Within ten years, he continued, there would be a mere handful of Asians left on the islands, and the few who remained would be found "washing the dirty linen of a superior and more prosperous people."[106]

The enemies of annexation rejected these predictions, first, out of their own prejudices; and second, because they, like many others, thinking Hawaii tropical, embraced the conviction that whites withered in hot places. Champ Clarke said that if any valuable lands had escaped the sugar barons' greed, "they are not fit for our children and other white people of our breed, for the all-sufficient reason that they can not endure outdoor work in that sultry climate." John Bell of Missouri asserted that there was not one example in all of history where a white civilization thrived in a tropical zone. "The American civilization, the European civilization, is an incarnation of the temperate zone. It cannot exist anywhere else." Bell concurred that the white race was incapable of laboring successfully in Hawaii. "[I]t will take two or three generations before you get one [white man] that will stand that climate. And when you get that type you will get a type but little better than the native himself." Bell continued: "I want to say that the entire cultivation of Hawaii to-day is [done] by Asiatic labor. You may speculate about the American people Americanizing Cuba, Americanizing Puerto Rico, Americanizing the Philippine Islands, but it is a mere dream. It can never be. And I hope to God the day will never come when we shall have a single foot of tropical climate within the bounds of the exemplary Government." In the Senate, Richard Pettigrew said that because of its tropical temperatures Hawaii was no place for Americans as history had already proven. He observed that although the islands had been open to the United States since 1875, very few Americans had been drawn to them. "The population of Americans in the islands [had] not increased materially under this wonderful influence," he said, referring to reciprocity, because "the climate had no attraction for them."[107]

The House of Representatives passed the joint resolution on 15 June 1898 by an overwhelming margin, 209 to 91. The Senate gave its approval in a vote of 42 to 21 on 6 July. Significantly, despite the obvious importance of the resolution, less than a full Senate voted (twenty-six were absent), yet ironically, that day exactly two-thirds of those present voted in favor. "If all of the Senators had been in their places," according to the *American Monthly Review of Reviews*, "the majority would apparently have fallen a little short of the two-thirds of that body."[108] The imperialists' change of strategy had worked: the joint resolution succeeded where the treaty would surely have failed.[109]

News that Congress had approved annexation arrived in Hawaii by ship, aboard the USS *Coptic*, a full week after the Senate vote. Harold Sewell, the U.S. minister to Hawaii, noted that the Americans and their allies embraced the news "with unbounded enthusiasm," with the ringing of bells, the blowing of factory whistles, with shouts and fireworks. Days and nights of celebration followed. The *Pacific Commercial Advertiser* ran a one-word headline, "ANNEXATION," and beneath it printed: "Honolulu, H.I., USA." Newspaperman Henry Whitney saluted the occasion by scribbling patriotic verse:

> And the Star-Spangled Banner
> In triumph shall wave
> O'er the isles of Hawaii
> And the homes of the brave.[110]

Away from the celebrations the majority of native Hawaiians, royalists, and their sympathizers mourned the news. Liliuokalani, who had been in the United States for more than a year, returned to the islands on 2 August, just ten days before the annexation became formal. Anna Prentice Dole accompanied her husband to the wharf to witness her arrival. Both were curious to see "what reception she would have." Anna Dole recalled what was to her a strange and unsettling silence. "Nobody cheered and a tentlike enclosure had been placed on the wharf so no one would see her come on shore," she said. A crowd had gathered to welcome Liliuokalani, and soon the tent was removed. Seeing her people, and them her, the queen raised her hand and said "aloha." Then "a great shout of Aloha came from the crowd. But that was all." The scene impressed Anna Dole. "I felt sorry for the poor woman," she confessed, "and so did Sanford. But it was all over."[111]

For many in the United States this was a moment for celebration unfettered by conscience. The *New York Sun* cheered annexation on its pages, though not without some partisan gloating. "The flag which the Cleveland Policy of Infamy hauled down in April of 1893 goes up again in July of 1898." The result, said the *Sun*, was the emergence of a new nation. "The America of the twentieth century has taken its first and most significant step towards the grave responsibility and high rewards of manifest destiny."[112] This was representative: the press acclaimed annexation. Religious and business journals that had drawn back in the light of revelations contained in the Blount report in 1893 either took the view that five years had erased moral stains or interpreted Dewey's triumph as a sign from Providence.[113]

Others, clearly a minority of Americans, were not so certain that this was the work of Providence. "Hawaii is ours," Grover Cleveland told Richard Olney, his former secretary of state, two days after the Senate vote. "As I look back upon this miserable business, I am ashamed of the whole affair."[114] The *Boston Transcript* realized that "[t]he Rubicon has at last been crossed. This country," it said, "now enters upon a policy that is entirely new. It has thrown down its former standards, cast aside its old traditions, has extended its first tentacle two thousand miles away, and is growing others for exploration in southern and eastern seas."[115]

The *Transcript* spoke for those who were resigned to rather than enthusiastic over annexation and empire. The events that had led up to the acquisition—the years of nasty inter- and intraparty battles, rumors of corruption, backroom politics, and eccentric diplomatic maneuvers—would, the newspapers predicted, "soil the pages of American history." But it also held out hope that the nation's honor might still be restored "by stopping where we are and dealing with our new and strangely acquired trust in a spirit of highest patriotism, altruism, and honesty." Many believed that Hawaii was not the end but the precursor to more, and even more distant, annexations, "a powerful fulcrum for our insatiate world lifters." Beyond the joint resolution, the *Springfield Republican* saw lying a "larger plan of imperialism, of which the taking of Hawaii forms only a part, and a comparatively small part." The first step was important, said the *Republican*, because "it lends an easiness to the next," but the newspaper was hopeful and certain "that the second line of defense [against imperialism] . . . will prove stronger than the first line." Several leaders in the Senate who had supported Hawaii's annexation had announced, directly after that vote, and anticipating a movement to seize the Philippines, that they would not go further. "The senior Massachusetts senator [Hoar] voted for the Hawaiian resolution, but declares his opposition to further distant annexations. The senior Alabama senator [Morgan] has been a leader in the Hawaiian scheme, but says he is opposed to going so far as the Philippines. Other examples can be cited to the same effect," said the newspaper. "It is accordingly with great hope of success that the anti-imperialists fall back into their second line of intrenchments [*sic*]." At first the *Republican*'s optimism appeared sound and well reasoned. It noted correctly what it called "peculiar influences bolstering up the Hawaiian conspiracy which will be absent from the support of other schemes of annexation."[116] The accrual of history, policy, religion, commerce, and institutions that, over the course of a half century, justified and rationalized annexation did not exist between the United States and the Philippines. There were no sugar interests whose representatives would lobby attentive (and occasionally corruptible) senators, nor was there an annexation commission from Manila rushing to Washington, D.C. There was certainly no union based on racial sympathy, shared Anglo-Saxon blood, or "outposts of American civilization" in jeopardy to be romanticized.

Anti-imperialists had two more reasons to be hopeful. Even with all these "peculiar influences" in its favor, the Hawaiian annexation treaty failed to win the support of two-thirds of the Senate. After the joint resolution's passage, two more senators stated publicly that they would oppose further acquisitions. John Tyler Morgan's promise was especially significant as he was a leading man in foreign affairs, an expert whose opinions would influence other politicians, and one of the most outspoken—if overlooked—expansionists of his time.[117] Most understood that despite the rampant speculation, nothing was certain in the summer of 1898. The war was still being fought. The president's first priority was to bring the conflict to a quick and victorious conclusion. Only then would he decide what should be done with the Philippines.

CHAPTER FIVE

The Philippines

It is significant that not even the leaders of the so-called large policy, the vanguard of aggressive expansionism, argued at first for keeping the Philippines. Before joining his Rough Riders, Theodore Roosevelt told Assistant Secretary of State John Bassett Moore that he thought the archipelago was too distant, too far beyond the American sphere of influence, and he warned against their acquisition. Alfred Thayer Mahan, the oracle of naval power and colonial expansion for men such as Roosevelt and Senator Henry Cabot Lodge, was also hesitant. In a letter to Lodge, Mahan described himself as "rather an expansionist" but then confessed: "I . . . have not fully adjusted myself to the idea of taking them [the Philippines], from our own standpoint of advantage."[1] Months later, he was still not convinced of the wisdom of holding the islands. Near the close of what he called an "extraordinary year," Mahan told a friend that the Philippines still "had not risen above my mental horizon." Though he looked "with anxious speculation toward the Chinese hive," he said that he had never "dreamed that in my day I should see the U.S. planted at the doors of China, advancing her outposts and pledging her future, virtually to meeting the East much more than half way." Throughout the note, Mahan's demeanor is hesitant and cautionary, not celebratory.[2]

For his part, Lodge said that the Philippines offered "vaster possibilities than anything that has happened to this country since the annexation of Louisiana," but he was careful not to discuss this particular view in public.[3] The senator wanted the East Asian markets opened for the benefit of the nation, his party, and his Massachusetts constituents—industrialists, merchants, missionaries, and the state's working classes—and favored taking the entire island chain, temporarily. Lodge's concern was not with the Filipinos or their right to or desire for political independence. He wanted the islands so that the United States could sell them to a friendly power like Great Britain or trade them for other islands that were well within the nation's established sphere of interests: the Bahamas, Jamaica, or the Danish West Indies. Taken together, this testimony from the intellectual leaders of United States imperialism shows that American foreign policy in 1898 was focused overwhelmingly on the Atlantic Ocean and the Caribbean, that East Asia was peripheral even within the ambitious reckoning of the "large policy." Nevertheless, Americans struggled to reorient themselves to the great changes that were at hand.

In the final peace agreement, Spain would relinquish Cuba and Puerto Rico to the United States. This fortified American hegemony in the Caribbean and reaffirmed the Monroe Doctrine, but it did not significantly alter the nation's role in the larger world. Events in the Pacific would. Hawaii's annexation was the culmination of more than a half century of policy, steady economic and cultural infiltration from the United States, the intervention of American marines in a local coup, and the clever political exploitation of the war crisis. Taking Hawaii surely raised the nation's prestige and widened its horizons, but it did not signify a radical departure from established policy. There were no truly unprecedented risks, burdens, or responsibilities involved, nor did it create new entanglements. In this light, McKinley was partly correct when he characterized the acquisition as a consummation rather than a great departure: "partly" because Hawaii's annexation instantly raised the volume and intensity of speculation over the future of the Philippines, whose acquisition would be, if it occurred, a startling departure from all past traditions.

Consideration began soon after news of Dewey's victory arrived, but in those first days and weeks, few saw much reason to keep the islands. The *Springfield (Mass.) Republican* warned that "what to do with the Philippines" was "not so simple a question as may at first appear." They could not go back to Spain because its rule over the islands had been "even more cruel and oppressive than in Cuba." Disposing of them in some other manner, selling them to the highest bidder, for example, created a different but still perilous set of difficulties that included "disturb[ing] the 'balance of power'" in East Asia. Regardless of the hazards involved in solving the problem in "a satisfactory manner," the *Republican* was adamant on one point: "to keep them for ourselves is utterly out of the question." Acquisition, it said, would sink the United States "head, neck, and breeches, into old world affairs, compel us to abandon our policy of comparative isolation and confinement in the western hemisphere," and force the nation "to become a great naval and military power in the Pacific and far east." Moreover, the *Republican* declared, by taking the Philippines the country would have to govern "a population the farthest degree removed from American standards and ideal." To secure the point, the newspaper provoked its readers with a description of the population: "On some 400 islands of the group are from 7,000,000 to 10,000,000 people," composed of "negritos, an almost savage race, the remnant of the aboriginal population . . . Malays, Chinese, and Chinese mestizoes, the latter being descended from Chinese fathers and native mothers." One "would only have to consider for a moment the character of the inhabitants of the Philippines to see that permanent possession is not to be thought of." The *Chicago Inter-Ocean* concurred: "There is no part of the globe less suited to form a part of the United States than these Philippine Islands."

Different methods of disposition were suggested in the press. The *New York Mail and Express* smelled a profit and advised selling the islands "to insure our war indemnity." Each of the great powers fighting for advantage in the Pacific and "participating in the Chinese game," said the paper, "will view with jealous eye its acquisition by another. Hence the bidding will be lively." The *Boston Herald* found the idea of auctioning off the islands and its people thoroughly offensive. "Have those who have been battling for their own freedom no rights? it would be asked. On what ground can we sell them and their country, as if they were serfs, to a foreign government?" Still, concluded the *Herald*, keeping the islands was equally unacceptable because it would "rend the Monroe Doctrine from top to bottom." The Detroit *News* acknowledged that in the past the United States had shown "a decided timidity about acquiring territory outside its continental borders," suggesting that this was a wise tradition and a model for addressing the immediate problem before the country. Regardless of the wealth of natural resources contained in those islands, the editors of the *News* argued that the distance was prohibitive and wanted them to be exchanged for manageable territories, closer to home. "We might as well offer to surrender the Philippines for a small indemnity if Spain would agree to cede Porto Rico to the United States." The *Philadelphia Ledger* was supremely confident that the nation "had no intention of appropriating the Philippines." According to the *Des Moines Register*, America had no desire to be either a colonial power or "a landlord in the far east." "Its greatness lies at home, and in the development of its own resources," it said. "We do not desire to weaken our influence by scattering our power."[4]

Even when the desire for territory was most clearly expressed, as with Lodge and the *Detroit News*, ambitions and imaginations were beholden to a traditional, conservative policy framework. The Monroe Doctrine gave that policy authority and a degree of elasticity, but only within a discrete geographic area. It provided a rationale for imperialism throughout the nation's own hemisphere, but outside those boundaries, the doctrine's power dissipated. Roosevelt's and Mahan's reservations, Lodge's as well, are evidence of this. So was the *Des Moines Register*'s insistence that the nation's greatness lay "at home," a designation that referred to North America (including Canada) and the Caribbean. Imperialism within this sphere was acceptable; activities outside it, however, gave leaders in politics, business, and society, the public, and even the "large policy" men pause.

When the war began, President McKinley is supposed to have said that he could not have guessed the position of the Philippines within two thousand miles. Whether the statement was literally true (the balance of evidence suggests that McKinley was exaggerating) is less important than what it reflected: an ambivalence toward and a lack of basic knowledge about the Pacific that was detectable throughout the nation. Finley Peter Dunne's fictional common man, Mr. Dooley, reminded his friend Hennessy that at the start of the war he did not know whether the Philippines where islands or canned goods, and with it over, their location was still a mystery. "Suppose ye was standin' at th' corner iv State Sthreet and Archey R-road," Dooley asked Hennessy. "[W]ud ye know what car to take to get to the Ph'lippeens? If yer son Packy was to ask ye where th' Ph'lippeens is, cud ye give him anny good idea whether they was in Rooshia or jus' west iv th' tracks?" This perception was something more than the result of exaggeration or fiction. George Catlett Marshall recalled of 1898: "Few of us had ever heard of the Philippines until that year. We had heard of Manila rope, but we did not know where Manila was." In a parade in Uniontown, Pennsylvania, welcoming home soldiers returning from the war, Marshall saw "a grand American small town demonstration of pride in its young men and of the wholesome enthusiasm for their achievements." When the celebrations were over, Marshall contemplated the war in more sober terms. "Most of us

President William McKinley
(Library of Congress, Prints and Photographs Division
[LC-US262-34105])

realized that it was much more," he said, "[that] it reflected the introduction of America into the affairs of the world beyond the seas."[5]

The annexation of the Philippines is the culminating event in the historical literature on race and American imperialism in the late nineteenth century. Its basic thesis bears repeating here: in the aftermath of the Spanish-American War, imperialist exploitation of the dominant racial ideologies of the period—social Darwinism, Anglo-Saxonism, and the "white man's burden"—helped to bring about the ratification of the Treaty of Paris and the seizure of a vast bi-oceanic empire. The extant evidence indicates that nearly the opposite is true: that the imperialists triumphed in 1898, by only a single vote, because knowing how race and empire had intersected in both the distant past and their own time, they worked deliberately, and successfully enough, to *remove* race from the debates. Their work was helped along considerably by the Teller Amendment. Passed at the start of the war without a single dissenting vote, it disclaimed any intention on the part of the United States to annex Cuba and, by extension, its inhabitants. The Cuban people were thus removed as a factor in the debates that came later. The erasure of the Cubans was repeated, after a fashion, at the conclusion of this episode. The Senate's deliberations ended in February 1899 not with annexation of the Philippines but with the passage of a resolution that explicitly denied American citizenship to ten million Filipinos. The story of events in between, in which imperialists ignored, diminished, and evaded race, begins with President McKinley, who made the decision to take all the Philippines.

In October 1897, Thomas Reed, the Republican Speaker of the House of Representatives, sent a pair of newsclippings to Henry Cabot Lodge. The first was about the worsening crisis in Cuba and the violence and anarchy that would soon draw the United States into war. But Reed was more intent on directing Lodge's attention to the second clipping, a story about a recent performance of African American entertainers. "The darky description," Reed insisted lest Lodge set it aside for more urgent business, "is worth read[ing] all through."[6]

The performance it described was a wicked and inventive satire on the two most prominent politicians of the day, a cultural form of political expression created and acted out by a people disfranchised throughout the nation. The "Billy Bryan step," according to the article (which was written in a condescending black "dialect"), was a dance "war you goes two steps forward an' three steps back, and keep a sickly smile on yer face all de time." With the "McKinley step . . . you go along just easy like, don't raise yer feet high off de floor, and just kinder give a double shuffle and let de music of de band kinder push you along."[7] This reflected the common view of McKinley held by many of his contemporaries: a cautious and unassuming man drawn along by forces orchestrated by others. Both Reed and Lodge knew this image and apparently found some humor in it.

McKinley's historic reputation has benefited greatly from more recent assessments of his presidency. He is no longer looked upon as possessing either a chocolate éclair for a backbone (after Theodore Roosevelt's famous remark) or a mind, which, like a bed, had to be made up for him. Nor is he seen as "clay in the hands of a little group of men who knew all too well what use to make of the war," as Julius Pratt once asserted.[8] McKinley emerges from newer historical literature as a pragmatic leader, the possessor of an intelligent and resourceful mind, a sometimes cunning politician, and a skilled manager of men who was more likely to manipulate others than to be manipulated himself. Roosevelt observed that the president loved just "one thing in the world and that is his wife. He treats everyone [else] with equal favor; their worth to him is solely dependent on the advantage he could derive from them."[9] Roosevelt, whose mettle no one doubted, knew the president was a man to be reckoned with.

When the war came, many who had doubted McKinley's fortitude reconsidered their judgments. Henry Adams told John Hay less than a week after Dewey's victory at Manila that although he thought himself to be "rather a reckless political theorist, he [the president] has gone far beyond me, and scared me not a little." In his place, Adams said, "I should have gone to bed and stayed there." Hay was pleased by his friend's recantation. The president was "no tenderfoot" he told Adams in his reply, adding with great satisfaction no doubt: "many among the noble and the pure have had occasion to change their minds about [McKinley]." Alfred Thayer Mahan confided to Lodge that the president's handling of foreign affairs during the war crisis had given him "a higher opinion of his decisiveness of character that I have before entertained." McKinley's private secretary, George Cortelyou, in July 1898, called the president "the strong man of the Cabinet, the dominating force." Yet, he observed, McKinley led with "such gentleness and graciousness in dealing with men that some of his victories have been won apparently without struggle."[10]

Though the revisionists have been persuasive, the substance of the newer

interpretations has failed to supplant some of the more persistent and color-
ful myths that surround McKinley's decision to take the Philippines.[11] The
story cited most often comes from statements he made to a delegation of
Methodist clergymen in November 1899. The president insisted that he did
not want the islands initially. "[T]hey came to us as a gift from the gods," he
said. "I did not know what to do with them."[12] McKinley told his visitors
that he gave no thought to the consequences when he ordered Dewey to
attack the Spanish fleet, except the threat it posed to the coasts of Oregon
and California. When he realized, in his words, "that the Philippines had
dropped into our laps," the president sought advice from both Democrats
and Republicans on the question of their disposition. According to the story,
still uncertain after these political deliberations, McKinley turned to prayer.
"And one night late," the president confided to his fellow Methodists, "it
came to me this way . . . : (1) That we could not give them back to Spain—
that would be cowardly and dishonorable; (2) that we could not turn them
over to France or Germany—our commercial rivals in the Orient—that
would be bad business and discreditable; (3) that we could not leave them to
themselves—they were unfit for self-government—and they would soon
have anarchy and misrule over there worse than Spain's was; and (4) that
there was nothing left for us to do but take them all, and to educate the
Filipinos, and uplift and civilize and Christianize them, and by God's grace
do the very best we could by them, as our fellow-men for whom Christ had
died. And then I went to bed, and went to sleep, and slept soundly, and the
next morning I sent for the chief engineer of the War Department (our map
maker), and I told him to put the Philippines on the map of the United
States [pointing to the large map on the wall of his office], and there they are,
and there they will stay while I am President!"[13] This account is both suspect
and revealing. On the former point, as Akira Iriye has noted, if the story is to
be believed, the decision to annex the Philippines had little to do with
national interests.[14] On the latter, we see a president on his knees in search of
divine guidance, but just as important, when he comes to a decision he is
alone.

To understand how McKinley arrived at his decision, it is important to
acknowledge both the circumstances that confronted him and how each
narrowed his options regarding the islands' disposition. Military victories
gave the United States the islands; after that, possession all but determined
the president's course of action. In the beginning he wanted no more than a
fraction of the islands—Manila or perhaps Luzon, the largest island in the

archipelago—for a naval base, but geography, strategy, and the threats that other great powers represented made that impossible. His only choices, then, were between taking all the islands or none. Politics and public opinion excited by fervor for the war narrowed McKinley's options even further: taking nothing was not an option, for the president and other Republicans feared that voters would punish them severely at the polls. He had to demand them all, a decision he arrived at, it seems, with no small amount of regret. "If old Dewey had just sailed away when he smashed the Spanish fleet," he said to a friend, "what a lot of trouble he would have saved us."[15]

Dewey's attack on the Spanish fleet in Manila Harbor set into motion what followed. The attack was part of a war plan, the Kimball Plan, devised two years before McKinley's election. Once the war began, the president acted within the framework of the plan, sending troops despite being warned by an adviser, Oscar Strauss, that the result would be "nothing but entanglement and embarrassment." Strauss told the president that once American soldiers landed in the Philippines, "we will not be able afterwards to withdraw . . . without turning over the islands to anarchy and slaughter."[16] McKinley would come to a similar conclusion only after the flaws and blind spots of the Kimball plan had enveloped him.

Once the military was fully engaged in the Philippines, on land and sea, the administration found itself, unexpectedly it seems, at the epicenter of an international struggle over position in East Asia. The great powers of Europe, Russia, and Japan were in a predatory competition for commercial and strategic advantage in pursuit of the vast and legendary China market. Where the European nations had little interest in the disposition of Cuba and Hawaii, East Asia was another matter entirely. Spain's defeat and retreat threatened to upset the equilibrium that sustained peace and order in the region. Tensions escalated over which nation or nations would gain and lose in the reorganization of power that was certain to follow. All involved understood that the United States held the key.

Britain's and Japan's interests were secure in the status quo antebellum. Both were quick to advise the United States to keep the Philippines. Britain was working toward a rapprochement with the Americans, but more important, its leaders were loath to see its principal naval rival, Germany, benefit from the chaos they were convinced would erupt if the United States withdrew. Japan's counsel arose from similar apprehensions that its main rival, Russia, might gain some advantage if the United States retreated or partitioned the islands. Spanish power collapsed so quickly and utterly that Britain and Japan were convinced that it could no longer maintain stability, peace, and order in the Philippines if the islands were returned. Furthermore, both nations were also convinced that an independent Philippines led by a native government would not be able to maintain itself for long. They predicted that internal corruption, dissent, and disorder would lead to the islands' seizure by some predator nation (or nations). The result would be a general, multilateral war.

Rumblings from abroad seemed to substantiate these fears. John Hay, the American ambassador to England at the start of the war, cabled Washington, D.C., with intelligence that Germany was maneuvering for "a few coaling stations." The French ambassador, Jules Jusseraud, told Hay that it was the opinion of his government that the islands should not be returned to Spain. Jusseraud predicted that "they will probably be fought over by England and Germany" and insisted that the United States would "do well to keep out of the quarrel."[17] The *New York Times* reported France's attempt to negotiate with Spain to purchase the entire chain as well as German, Russian, and Japanese military and diplomatic movements.[18] Reports from American diplomats abroad and alarming dispatches from Dewey—the best information available to the president at the time—all indicated that a fierce and probably violent scramble would erupt between the great powers over the Philippines if the United States withdrew.

Brilliant victories had important consequences on the domestic front that combined with international pressures to influence McKinley's decision. Public response to America's military success was overwhelming and thoroughly favorable. Many observers seemed to understand from a very early time in the war that the public would not tolerate giving up completely what had been won so dramatically. In his essay "Cuba, the Philippines, and Manifest Destiny," Richard Hofstadter remarked that it is not an easy thing to persuade a people or a government, at a high pitch of war enthusiasm, to abandon a gain already well in hand.[19] This would be especially true of a society deeply affected by Protestant and Calvinist doctrines and therefore inclined to read its smashing military successes as a sign of divine favor and moral righteousness. Albert K. Weinberg observed that as soon as Dewey's victory made the Philippines a likely prize, many felt that it would be barbarous either to return the Filipinos back to Spanish oppression or to abandon them.[20] Feelings of intense and sometimes irrational hostility toward the Spanish fed and amplified these instincts. An anonymous writer in the

Atlantic denounced Spain as "the most backward nation in Europe" and
contended that at the bottom of the conflict between the United States and
Spain lay "an irreconcilable difference of civilizations . . . deeper than the
differences between any other two 'Christian' civilizations that are brought
together anywhere in the world."[21] "Common sense tells us to keep what has
cost us so much to wrest from an unworthy foe," said the *Baltimore Ameri-*
can on 11 June 1898, and "back of that is the solid, irresistible sentiment of the
people." George Hobart of the *Baltimore News* called on the nation to hold
on to the islands following Manila, after Dewey "[m]ade [his] point an' won
[his] fight." His poem continued:

> Doctah Dewey, doan' yo' care,
> Hol' dem Philippines?
> Let that German ge' man swear,
> Hol' dem Philippines!
>
> Reckon dat yo' saw dem first,
> Jus' yo' say to Weinerwurst:
> "Come en' take dem if yo' durst!"
> Hol' dem Philippines.[22]

A similar feeling moved another writer, Andrew Jackson Andrews, to imagine "an international conversation between the queen of Spain and Uncle
Sam": "The Queen—Can't you return me the Philippines without further
fuss? / Uncle Sam—Not at all, Madam, for they belong to U.S."[23]

Mr. Dooley articulated what the less-knowledgeable but patriotic American
felt at the time. "I know what I'd do if I was Mack [McKinley]," said Hennessy. "I'd hist a flag over th' Ph'lippeens, an' I'd take in th' lot iv them."
Dooley asked Hennessy: "If yer son Packy was to ask ye where th' Ph'lippeens
is, cud ye give him anny good idea whether they was in Rooshia or jus' west
iv th' tracks?" "Mebbe I cudden't," Hennessy replied, "butt I'm f'r takin'
thim anyhow."[24] A correspondent told Secretary of the Navy John Davis
Long that handing the islands back to Spanish "misgovernment seems . . .
little more consistent with our duty . . . [than] in the War of the Rebellion,
the sending back into slavery of the negroes who came into our lines and
even those who fought as soldiers under our own flag."[25] Even those not so

inclined toward imperialism found the tide hard to resist. One antiexpansionist senator confessed that he would "as soon turn a redeemed soul over
to the devil as give the Philippines back to Spain."[26]

McKinley, too, believed that returning the Philippines to a defeated power
would be immoral and inconsistent with the goal of liberating oppressed
peoples from Spanish brutality. In light of public sentiment for the war,
handing back the archipelago would be utterly foolish from the standpoint
of politics. Whitelaw Reid understood the "difficulties and dangers" that
were connected to taking the islands, problems that the public did not
understand. (Reid himself was ambivalent. "I haven't in the least undertaken
to shut the people's eyes to the difficulties and dangers of the Philippines
business," he told John Hay, "but I don't see how we can honorably give
them back to Spain, or do anything with them but try to make the best of
what Dewey flung into our arms.") Reid thought that the people's naïveté or
misunderstanding presented a great problem for those who wanted the
islands as well as for those who were opposed to taking them. He wrote in
August that "the American people are in no mood to give up Manila or
Luzon, and . . . many are inclined to hold on to this whole archipelago, while
others, who don't want it, are much perplexed by the moral and physical
difficulties of giving it up."[27]

Public spirit and sentiment, though strong, did not indicate a specific
policy, but from the standpoint of domestic politics it did close off several
options: the president could not retire from the islands completely, give
them back to Spain, or abandon them and allow them to fall into the orbit of
a rival power. Elections were coming in the fall of 1898, and such decisions
would have sabotaged the Republican Party in the House and Senate campaigns. Some feared the repercussions that a poor or unpopular decision
might have on the 1900 campaigns. Party politics, together with the accrual
of other factors and forces, demanded that McKinley hold on to some part
of the archipelago—enough territory to maintain honor in the eyes of the
public and avoid entirely even the appearance of capitulation to Spain, a
nation that the press and many politicians had gone to great lengths to
demonize.

Lodge, as one of the leading men in the Republican Party, felt these
pressures most acutely. As already noted, he did not want the entire chain,
only a naval base in Manila: "enough to give us a foothold for trade."[28] As a
nationalist, the senator wanted America to have access to East Asian markets, but other considerations that affected his thinking are worth note.

Race, no doubt, was among them. The racial sentiments he articulated in his remarks on the Hawaiian cable resolution and again in the article "Our Blundering Foreign Policy" were factors in this instance as well. The Filipinos would have been no more compatible with American institutions than were the native Hawaiians or the peoples of South and Central America he had spoken of just a few years earlier. And as with other hot places Lodge considered to be unacceptable acquisitions, the climate of the Philippines would not have been hospitable to Anglo-Saxons. He also weighed the political and military difficulties, questions involving nation building and defense inherent in taking all the islands, as well as the perils the Republican Party would confront domestically if the president decided to take nothing at all. Lodge therefore searched for a pragmatic course, a secure middle ground.

Rumors that the cabinet was divided on the Philippines and may have been preparing to give the entire chain of islands back to Spain spread through the capital during the summer of 1898. Lodge was dismayed, and his fears were fed by L. A. Coolidge, a correspondent from the Boston Journal, who told the senator on 27 July that the administration was "getting ready to give up the Philippines—if it can. That seems to be the undertone of everything that comes from the inside." Secretary of State William Rufus Day, he said, "is not only against retaining anything more than a coaling station but he has taken pains to ask some of his newspaper friends to try to work up a sentiment in the press which will prepare men's minds for the surrender of the islands when it comes to terms of peace." Coolidge reported that he had warned Day "that there was no sentiment in New England which a Republican administration could convince in favor of the abandonment of the Philippines," but doubted that the point made any impression on Day. He was more concerned with McKinley, who Coolidge cast as the timid, wavering man "waiting to see what public sentiment is, but he hopes it will be against taking the Philippines." Coolidge told Lodge: "I think it is important that the President . . . know right away what people are thinking about this thing. He is too apt to get the opinion of some people who don't really know what's going on." Coolidge, from the information he was able to gather from the "inside," arrived at a conclusion that must have startled the senator: "If terms were to be named today I believe the Philippines would be given back to Spain."[29]

Three days later Lodge sent a private handwritten note to the president; its purpose was "to say a single word as to the Philippines." The senator, who did not want to appear presumptuous in this instance, maintained that he had no intention of telling the president what to do with the islands as he did not consider it his place. Lodge wrote, he said, only to inform the president on "one point on which I find practical unanimity everywhere, even among those opposed to annexation, and that is that we must not and cannot without grave discredit return them to Spain. Should we do so," Lodge speculated, "the Democrats, both annexationists and anti-annexationists would unite in attacking us and would establish an issue difficult if not impossible to meet. They would say 'You went to war to free the Cubans [and] you have also freed the Philippine people. Now you hand them back to a tyranny far worse than that of Cuba and turn over to Spanish . . . cruelty men you have aided and encouraged to fight.' To this attack," he concluded grimly, "I see no defense." Loath to close on a note so pessimistic, Lodge told McKinley that "the general sentiment among the people is . . . in favor of holding them." Republican newspapers were similarly inclined. According to Lodge, both constituencies reasoned that the islands should not be returned to Spain. The United States freed them so Americans "alone should decide their fate."[30]

In this instance Lodge was a messenger delivering public opinion to the president, whose wartime duties had isolated him from and—the senator feared—deafened him to the vox populi. A second point that can be drawn from the Lodge note pertains to the arguments he used to try to move McKinley. There is no hint of social Darwinism, racial mission, or uplift ideology. There is only partisanship and political calculation. Even the gesture toward humanitarianism is weighed in relation to the needs of the Republican Party. This factor was most critical, in an election year. The Republicans were anxious to maintain their hold on the national government and hoped that the war spirit would carry them to victory in the fall. (In the spring the Republicans' attitude was reflected in the comment of a midwestern partisan: "As a rule whatever arouses patriotism is good for us." On election day the Democrats gained fifty seats in the House of Representatives. The Republicans lost nineteen seats in the House but retained a twenty-two-vote advantage. They added six seats in the Senate.)[31] Lodge understood what would, what would not, and what should influence the president and used his knowledge to help McKinley make a decision consistent with the best interests of the Republican Party.

By the time Lodge drafted his note, postwar Philippine policy had been in the making for three months. From the start American diplomats and strat-

Senator Henry Cabot Lodge
(Library of Congress, Prints and Photographs Division
[LC-US262-68226])

egists expressed the desire to take away nothing less than a coaling station. In both May and June 1898, in response to British inquiries into peace terms, the president expressed a desire to keep very little. According to a cable sent on 3 June, McKinley would agree to end the war on the condition that Spain evacuated itself from Cuba and surrendered Puerto Rico and an island in the Ladrones (now the Marianas), probably Guam, to the United States. Spain would keep the Philippines, except, the cable read, "[that] a port and necessary appurtenances, to be selected by, the United States, shall be ceded to the United States."[32] The president so far wanted very little. His request for bases, and only bases, was consistent with the policy of noncolonial commercial expansion practiced in the Caribbean.

On 23 July the president consulted his cabinet regarding the disposition of the Philippines and found it split. On the matter of the United States retaining a naval base and coaling station, they all agreed. The cabinet parted ways, however, over the question of whether the administration should demand more or return the entire archipelago (except for the American base) to Spain. Three wanted only enough for a base, and the remaining three proposed seizing them all, citing evangelical opportunities. McKinley listened intently but decided that before taking any action he would request more information from Dewey, who was still in the field, and other experts. In the meantime, the president wanted to keep every option open. He even went so far as to suppress a draft of a peace protocol that would have required Spain to cede only enough territory for a naval base. When asked by the secretary of state why he put down this motion, McKinley replied: "I was afraid it would be carried!"[33]

The war ended when representatives of the United States and Spain signed a peace protocol on 12 August. Hours later in the Philippines, American forces overwhelmed the Spanish garrison in Manila. The surrender ended Spain's control of the islands. Over the next several weeks the president received regular dispatches on the unstable political situation in the islands. Strategists also advised McKinley on his remaining options. Dewey responded to the president's inquiry about the defensibility of several of the archipelago's islands: he would keep Luzon, the largest island, because of its position in relation to the other islands and its deepwater ports.[34]

The vital question at this time was not how the United States could justify keeping the Philippines but rather how it could take what it wanted—Luzon—and then dispose of the remaining islands peacefully. McKinley told his commissioners before their departure for Paris that the nation's aim in their forthcoming negotiations "should be directed to lasting results and to the achievement of the common good under the demands of civilization, rather than on ambitious designs." Spain had to be removed from the Caribbean, he said, because its continued presence was incompatible "with the assurance of permanent peace on and near our own territory."[35]

The Philippines involved a more difficult and unprecedented set of decisions; their disposition did not involve the Monroe Doctrine or defending the nation's shoreline. The archipelago "stand[s] upon a different basis," McKinley told his commissioners. He said that although the United States had harbored no "thought of complete or even partial acquisition" before the war, "the presence and success of our arms at Manila imposes upon us obligations which we can not disregard." Humanitarianism coexisted comfortably with commerce in the president's mind. The Philippines presented "commercial opportunity to which American statesmanship can not be indifferent." It was, he said, "just to use every legitimate means for the enlargement of American trade," but he included a telling caveat: "this new opening *depends less on large territorial possession* than upon an adequate commercial basis and . . . broad and equal privileges."[36] On this basis McKinley declared that the United States "cannot accept less than the cession of full right and sovereignty of the island of Luzon."[37] In little more than a month, then, President McKinley had moved from a position where all he wanted was just enough territory to build a naval base to demanding full political and military control over the largest island in the Philippines. Over the next several weeks McKinley received the evidence and advice that led him to order the annexation of the whole chain. The steps can be summarized briefly.

Though advice came to the president though many sources, historians generally suspect that the pivotal influence came from General Francis V. Greene. Greene, who had recently returned from the Philippines, visited the White House five times between 27 September and 1 October and presented McKinley with five options: "1st to return them to Spain; 2nd to turn them over to the [Filipino] Insurgents; 3rd to turn them over to some foreign nation; 4th to occupy and administer them jointly with one or more foreign nations; 5th to hold and administer them ourselves."[38] Every option but the last would be found unacceptable: the first, because the president believed that giving the Philippines back to a defeated power was immoral, inconsistent with the nation's efforts to liberate peoples oppressed by Spanish tyranny, and to do so would create terrible political repercussions at home; the second, because besides doubting their capacity for self-government, he believed that granting the Filipinos the independence they had fought for since 1896 would be like tossing a "golden apple of discord" among the rival great powers; the third McKinley dismissed as "bad business," an option no better than giving them to Spain; the fourth, because recent history—the collapse in 1888 of a tripartite protectorate arrangement over Samoa between the United States, Germany, and Great Britain which nearly resulted in a war—seemed to prove the fragility and perilous awkwardness of such a policy. In Paris, the American peace commission listened to similar compelling testimony from experts and strategists. The closeness and interdependence of the islands came up repeatedly as a possible encouragement to foreign intervention if the United States did not take them all.[39] Keeping and administering the Philippines became, to McKinley's reckoning, the least perilous choice strategically and militarily, commercially, and, looking forward to the elections of 1898 and 1900, politically.[40]

By the time he left Washington, D.C., in October 1898 on a campaign tour through the Midwest, McKinley had almost certainly decided to annex the entire chain. All the facts, maps, statistics, and counsel had come together in his mind and moved it toward a final decision. The president needed no more information that could be regarded as vital with the possible exception of public opinion. Some historians believe that McKinley, still unsure about what to do, took the tour to measure the public's feelings on the war and empire. They say that the enthusiastic applause his speeches received emboldened him to take all the islands. Others believe that the president had already decided to take the entire archipelago before he set one foot on the campaign trail and that he used his speeches to prepare the people for what was to come.

I prefer a third possibility. McKinley did not undertake his trip to discover the public's feelings, of which he was already aware. The president's understanding of the public's sentiment—his wariness of a reprisal at the polls if he took nothing—had already influenced his decision to take the islands.[41] It is also doubtful that his relatively brief tour constituted a serious effort to "lead" public opinion on such a complicated and controversial issue as imperialism. The content of his speeches are much too vague to offer strong support to an argument that insists otherwise. The tour was most likely meant to revitalize the nationalistic war spirit—which had had time to fade since the hostilities ended—in order to influence Congress. In other words, McKinley may very well have been working to pressure and manipulate the

Senate into ratifying his treaty by demonstrating, months after the end of the war, the extent to which he, a wartime president who had led his nation in a historic and epoch-making triumph, still commanded the overwhelming support and adulation of the people. Rather than measuring, following, or leading public opinion, McKinley was wielding public sentiment, first as the carrot to maintain party unity and keep wavering Republicans loyal, and then as the stick against congressional adversaries in both parties, pushing them, indirectly yet forcefully, to ratify his treaty.

Whatever McKinley's true motives were, it is clear that as his tour pressed on through Iowa, Nebraska, Illinois, and Ohio, his speeches became less cautious and reserved, but hardly more substantive and informative. The first speeches, delivered on 11 October, emphasized national unity and tradition; all were conservative, unsurprising, safe. They were received, according to the record, with generally warm applause. By the tour's end ten days later, a less restrained McKinley spoke in triumphant tones about the flag, duty, unity, and destiny. Audiences responded to the later speeches with excited cheers, jubilant shouts, and applause, but under close scrutiny their content was still hardly remarkable.[42] The people, it seems, most of them already admirers of the president, were reacting to sentiment rather than reason: his words were more akin to Henry V's blaring exhortations, steeling his worn, weary, and fearfully outnumbered men right before the battle of Agincourt, than Franklin Roosevelt's edifying and measured fireside chats. The substance of the reasoned discussions that McKinley had engaged in over the previous weeks with Republican and Democratic politicians, foreign diplomats, and military advisers is missing from these speeches. His intention it seems was to raise emotion, rally sentiment, not to inform. Thus the speeches ignored the complex and difficult: issues of strategy and defense, domestic politics, and the nation's daunting role in maintaining peace and order in East Asia. Some looked into McKinley's rhetoric, trying to discern his true purpose. Henry Adams told his confidant Elizabeth Cameron that the administration would most likely have to make some "trade" with Congress over this policy but then suggested that McKinley might still get his way: to Adams's reckoning, the president was "easily first in genius for manipulation." McKinley, he said, "is just the President for us in our present condition."[43] Others, more skeptical and suspicious, criticized the speeches, knowing that they had avoided the hard issues surrounding this new departure for the nation. Andrew Carnegie, grumbling into the ear of John Hay, wrote: "When a jelly-fish wishes to conceal its whereabouts it does so by ebullitions of blubber—this is what people say the President did on his winter tour."[44]

On 25 October the peace commissioners cabled the state department, outlining the differences of opinion among them regarding the Philippines question. At the same time, they requested instructions on how to proceed with the Spanish. Each member believed in the commercial advantages of keeping the islands, and by this time each commissioner understood that remaining there in any permanent capacity meant keeping the entire archipelago. Only one was determined to abandon the Philippines, convinced that keeping them would be contrary to the spirit of "a great, powerful, and Christian nation."[45] However deeply felt, objections like this would have no more influence on the president.

The next day, John Hay, who had been recalled from England and installed as secretary of state, cabled Paris to inform the commission of McKinley's final decision. Hay said that since their departure, information had come to the president that convinced him that "the cession of Luzon alone, leaving the rest of the islands subject to Spanish rule, or to be the subject of future contention, can not be justified on political, commercial, or humanitarian grounds. The cession," he said, "must be of the whole archipelago or none. The latter is wholly inadmissible and the former must therefore be required." Hay assured the commission that the president felt the full weight of the decision, that he was "deeply sensible of the grave responsibilities it will impose." However controversial the decision turned out to be, McKinley believed that he had made the correct one because, Hay wrote, the option of taking the whole Philippine chain would "entail less trouble than any other, and best serve the interests of the people involved, for whose welfare we can not escape responsibility."[46]

The treaty ending the war with Spain was signed on 10 December 1898. It granted the United States a vast, bi-oceanic empire with virtual control over the Caribbean and important insular possessions in the Pacific. Articles 1 and 2 required Spain to relinquish Cuba, cede Puerto Rico, "other islands . . . under Spanish sovereignty in the West Indies," and Guam to the United States. Cuba's liberation was ostensibly the nation's primary goal when it declared war; the Teller Amendment, an attachment to the war's first appropriations bill, precluded any postwar claims on that island. The remaining acquisitions under articles 1 and 2 were minor in terms of territorial extension, though vital to America's future interests, commercial and strategic, within its own hemisphere and in the Pacific.

Article 3 was easily the most profound of the treaty's provisions. In it, Spain surrendered the entire Philippine archipelago to the United States in exchange for twenty million dollars. When compared with the other possessions identified in the treaty, the Philippines presented the most unique and formidable problems. Unlike the Caribbean islands or Hawaii, the Philippines were too distant and unfamiliar for the administration to justify taking them on the grounds of historic interest or national defense. The United States had no history of colonizing or administering extracontinental territory, and the Constitution offered no explicit guidance in the matter. That document recognized only the states already in the Union and territories on their way to becoming states. Distance was the most obvious obstacle to statehood, but the islands' racial composition made their formal incorporation, by the standards of the time, utterly impossible. Their population was estimated to number about ten million individuals belonging to three distinct races: the Negrito, the Indonesian, and the Malayan. From these ethnological groups, eighty-four separate tribes were identified. Of these eighty-four, only eight were regarded as "civilized." Each of these issues would reemerge in the Senate's debates, but the race question would dominate.

The fundamental question of this chapter remains: what effect did race and racism have on McKinley's decision to annex the Philippines? The simplest answer would be that their effect was ambiguous and peripheral. McKinley is a troublesome character to any narrative that connects domestic racism and colonial imperialism. No one can doubt that the decision to take the Philippines belonged to the president, not Roosevelt, Lodge, Mahan, or anyone else easily marked as a racial determinist or social Darwinist. The main factors in that decision were weighed toward its military, strategic, and political elements.

We cannot read over the president's shoulder to discern his mind on this question, which also complicates the historian's task. He left no writings, books, letters, or speeches that help the scholar very much. Outwardly, McKinley was a moderate, generally unmoved by issues of race. In *The Racial Attitudes of American Presidents*, George Sinkler went a step further, suggesting that McKinley was, by temperament, timid on things racial when political contingencies were involved. A cartoon titled "Civilization Begins at Home" by *New York World* illustrator Charles Bush shows McKinley staring intensely at a map of the Philippines. The map draws an outline of the islands, which is otherwise blank, without any indication that they are populated. Also, there is no indication that they lie anywhere near Asia. Next

"Civilization Begins at Home," by Charles Bush, *New York World*.
President McKinley ponders the fate of the Philippines while ignoring
Justice and racial strife at home.

to the president stands Justice. Holding her sword and scales in one hand,
she pulls back a curtain with the other to reveal African Americans being
terrorized in the South: hunted, chased, shot, and lynched. The president is
depicted as being so consumed by his mission in East Asia that he is blind to
the racial terror going on at home. It is not clear whether he ignores all this
purposefully.[47]

The president accepted the prejudices and racist structures of the time as a
fundamental part of the nation's social order. Although (for political reasons) McKinley showed more sensitivity and concern toward the plight of
African Americans than the Bush cartoon indicated, he considered the Chinese "a primitive people," and there can be little doubt that a sense of the
superiority of western civilization coursed through his feeling that the

United States was obligated to uplift the Philippines. This sentiment collided, apparently, with a competing idea. In July 1898, William Laffan, an advisor and friend of Henry Cabot Lodge, told the senator that in private McKinley worried about "the question of race, climate, etc.," and that these thoughts left the president hesitant, "doubtful . . . about our keeping the whole group."[48] Race and uplift do not appear to have provided a motive for the president; not, at least, until his famous meeting with the Christian ministers the following year. In the course of making such a pivotal choice in the fall and winter of 1898, race engendered in the president's mind little, other than doubt and hesitation.

Others were not able to set aside race or the obstacles rooted in the racial social order so easily. Racism continued to be the great obstacle to empire. In "Distant Possessions—the Parting of the Ways," the iconic industrialist and anti-imperialist Andrew Carnegie spoke to the foundational assumptions of racial nationalism when he asked: "Is the Republic to remain one homogeneous whole, one united people, or to become a scattered and disjointed aggregate of widely separated and alien races?" Hannis Taylor, a former minister to Spain, attacked the matter more subtly and legalistically, but his objections were otherwise identical to Carnegie's: "The question is, whether under our less flexible Constitution we can govern colonies effectively without running the risk incident to the admission of distant and alien peoples to full citizenship." The editors of The Nation concurred. Acknowledging the troublesome fact that possession determined action, that the emotionalism of the war spirit had overtaken the public's logic, the journal sought an antidote: to appeal to the racial fears of its constituents. "We do not now discuss the wisdom or folly of annexing this archipelago. We simply point out that its acquisition would mean the incorporation into our system of an immense group of islands on the other side of the globe, occupied by eight millions of people of various races, that are for the most part either savage or but half-civilized; which the most ardent advocate of the policy admits can never become States of the Union."[49]

Two weeks later The Nation again bound together the racial and political consequences of annexation. Since 1860, it said, referring to the former slaves, the United States had assumed "the most onerous responsibilities" that had ever befallen a nation. "To the negroes we made the necessary gift of the suffrage, but not another thing" because, it declared, "we know well that their ignorance and barbarism threaten our future." The editorial concluded by mocking the concept of the "white man's burden" with a gruesome image: "The sole thing that we do with alacrity for the negro is to burn him alive when he does very wrong. But it will not be so easy to burn the Tagals and other races. We shall not have men enough to lynch decently in 1,200 islands, if that be our national mode of reclaiming the erring."[50]

In a speech titled "Our Foreign Policy," Carl Schurz revived the old yet still powerful arguments he had made thirty years earlier fighting President Grant. Speaking at Saratoga Springs in August 1898, the grizzled patriot told his audience that annexation would lead to one of two outcomes, both dangerous and obnoxious: the Philippines would become states of the Union equal to every other state, or they would have to be governed outside of the Constitution as subject provinces. The fate of the islands—the sand, rock, and soil, that is—did not concern Schurz. Their inhabitants represented the real danger to the republic. As a backward race, Schurz argued, the Filipinos were hardly fit to govern themselves. Would his audience, he asked, tolerate alien colonies "govern[ing] the whole Union by participating in the making of its laws and in the election of Presidents?" This was unthinkable. The islands were ungovernable because savages, he said, made up the far larger fraction of inhabitants of the Philippines ("a large mass of . . . barbarous Asiatics, descendants of Spaniards, mixtures of Asiatics and Spanish blood"), greatly outnumbering the "very few persons of northern races."[51]

The imperialists had already worked to remove race from the debate, insisting that the mass of alleged savages that frightened anti-imperialist alarmists such as Schurz was, in actuality, small and insignificant: it hardly represented a danger to democratic institutions at home. The old radical in Schurz would not let his rivals snatch from him his most effective weapon. He said that at first glance—being so far away and relatively few in number, compared with the entire population of the United States—the Filipinos might not appear to be "much of a force." But he insisted that they would exercise "a good deal of force" come election time, "when political parties run close, and when the passage of an important law, the determination of a general policy of Government or even the election of a President may depend, as they often have done, on a few votes." He demanded that his audience weigh and ponder a time when "such votes . . . come from a population which, in language, in traditions, habits and customs, in political, social, and even moral notions are utterly unlike our people and can, under the tropical sun at least, never be assimilated. It will be a good deal of a force," he warned, "when party politicians begin to bargain and traffic with them to win their support." Acquisitions, he continued, of Puerto Rico, the Dominican Republic, Haiti, and Cuba would grant those future states "a political force five times as great in the Senate and nearly as great in the Electoral College as that of the State of New York." In a later speech, Schurz posed this question to the young men of the University of Chicago: "what would the nation do since the letter and spirit of the Constitution would demand that these territories be organized into States?" The nation would make them into states, he concluded ominously, and "[t]hey would govern us."

In this speech the essence of Schurz's anti-imperialism was revealed. It is significant, as well, because he was fully capable of saying what a formidable segment of the people—whose wariness, skepticism, or hostility to empire was articulated in a deep, unsettling, churning sensation rather than in words—could not. To Schurz, annexation had to be opposed because, when it moved off the continent, it inverted some of the most vital elements of America's expansionist tradition: it placed savagery before civilization and the darker races before the white. Annexation, in this instance, would work to the detriment rather than for the unique benefit of whites.

Samuel Gompers joined in the debate in order to amplify "the view which the organized wage-earners of our country hold regarding" empire. As the leader of the American Federation of Labor, Gompers claimed to speak for all the nation's workers, not just members of his union or only the organized (he said: "I believe that it can not be successfully disputed that the expressions of the organized labor movement fairly represent the interests, and often the unexpressed convictions of the toiling masses of our country. If the organized wage-earners do not represent the views and convictions of the wage-earners of our country as wage-earners, who pray, can speak for them by authority?"). It was the workers, Gompers explained, who fought the wars, mourned "wounded and suffering brothers," and willingly bore "the necessary burdens of taxation, to maintain the glory of our arms, as well as to secure the achievements of peace." They built the nation, he said, and "the glory of each additional star to the flag" filled their "hearts with ecstasy." But he warned that labor was vigilant, aware and protective of its interests, and opposed to policies that would undermine them. Imperialism, Gompers declared, was labor's enemy.[52]

Hawaii's annexation had hurt American workers, he contended, because it bound the United States to an economy dependent on contract labor: the fifty thousand Chinese, Japanese, Portuguese, and "South Sea Islanders" there, said Gompers, were "practically slave laborers." Hawaii's absorption lent legitimacy to contract labor and brought down workers' wages and status at home. It is important to be explicit about what this labor leader was doing. Speaking for the working classes, he denounced a system that he and millions of American workers opposed on economic, moral, and ideological grounds. By binding these "gut issues" with imperialism, Gompers took foreign relations—a matter that was a vague, distant, and abstract thing to the vast majority of Americans—and made it clear, immediate, and tangible.

To confirm his point with his constituencies, Gompers resorted to racism. Defeating Philippine annexation was tantamount, he said, to "saving American labor from the evil influence of close and open competition of millions of semi-barbaric laborers." Appropriating some of the imperialists' rhetoric, Gompers maintained that it was the country's "duty" and "manifest destiny" to make the United States into "a vast workshop," raise the condition of its workers to "the most exalted standard of life," and reach for "the highest pinnacle of national glory and human progress." But to do this, he asked, was it necessary to acquire the Philippines, "with their semi-savage population"? Gompers's answer was a simple and emphatic no.[53]

Gompers knew that the events of 1898 were not unprecedented. Imperialism, or what he called "the government and domination of the many by the few," had occurred before in the nation's history. "We have ruled savages against their will in the process of uprooting the Indian tribes," he said. Significantly, surveying it through a racial optic, the leader of the American Federation of Labor did not condemn the expansionism of the past because it was consistent with the nation's grandest traditions: because, he said, it was "reasonably certain that their places would soon be taken *by a settled white population.*" That rationale simply did not apply in 1898. "In the Philippines," Gompers argued, "with its 7,000,000 or 8,000,000 in an area less than half that of the State of Texas, no such change can ever take place." Like many others at this time, then—Lodge, Bryce, Schurz, imperialists, anti-imperialists, and neutrals—Gompers stopped at the barriers dictated by climate, race, history, and tradition. He embraced inherited belief in white racial limitations: that hot places were hostile to members of his race and discriminated against his constituents. "The climate," he declared, "forbids forever manual labor by Americans, as it does the planting of American families, to live and flourish form one generation to another." To be acceptable, Gompers, like many other Americans, believed that expansion must benefit whites, particularly white workers.[54]

Americans would accept empire under certain conditions: if it was accidental (or swaddled so as to take on the appearance of an accident) rather than by design, for example. At least as important, so long as expansion did not hurt whites, deprive them of moral or material comforts, or diminish the sphere of white privilege in the established racial social order, the people would prove to be accepting. One reason for this can be traced back to the moderation and conservatism of the leading imperialists, men who wanted territory but only in small amounts, many of whom had already proven themselves to be staunch defenders of the prevailing racial order. Henry Cabot Lodge was a representative figure in this regard. He was a founding member of the Immigration Restriction League, thus his expansionism was tempered by a devout interest in defending cultural hegemony and native white labor. Another imperialist of this stripe was John Tyler Morgan, a Democrat and senator from Alabama. Two months before the end of the war, Morgan's meditation "What Shall We Do with the Conquered Islands?" appeared in the *North American Review*. In it, he expressed hope that Cuba might at some undetermined time in the future join "the union of American states." The glimmer of potential the senator recognized in the Cuban people was not indigenous but came from an Americanness and whiteness he thought he detected in them. This, according to Morgan, came from their "close contact with our free, constitutional government" and the fact that "many of their leading men have been educated in our schools." From these intimate contacts, he asserted, the Cubans had "acquired the capacity for just and enlightened self-government." Puerto Rico was disqualified in Morgan's mind given that its population could not "increase in so limited an area to the strength that is essential to independent statehood."[55] Since Puerto Rico is, geographically, larger in size than two states already in the Union, Rhode Island and Delaware, we can only speculate on what the senator meant by this statement.

Of the three conquered islands, the Philippines presented what Morgan saw as "the greatest difficulty." Here, again, the population was the crucial obstacle. Morgan, a prominent expansionist, wanted only small patches of territory: "certain bays and harbors" for military outposts and coaling stations "and places of refuge for our warships and other national vessels."[56] Morgan, like the vanguard of imperialism, wanted only naval stations and only as much territory as was necessary for that purpose. He had no desire to annex the people inhabiting any of these territories because he believed them to be members of incongruent races, alien to American democracy.

It is interesting to note, however, that Morgan spoke of the Filipinos in very gentle and favorable terms, especially compared with the way the anti-imperialists spoke of them. He likened the Filipinos to the Japanese with regard to their "mental endowments, and in physical stature and strength." Their "gentle disposition" reminded Morgan of the Hawaiians, "to whom," he wrote, "they bear a strong racial resemblance." He never called them savage or backward. Morgan never explicitly denied their capacity to become a "free and self-governing people," calling it an open question that could be answered "through the friendly offices" of either the United States or some other "just and liberal government." All this aside, it was clear that Morgan could not accept the Filipinos as fellow citizens, any more than he would welcome the groups he compared them with. Again, racism marked the borders of territorial expansion for a prominent imperialist: this one a southerner and dedicated white supremacist. Morgan wanted bases, but nothing more if it could be avoided. The "United States is an American power," he said, "with high national duties that are, in every sense, American." The Philippines, unlike Cuba, were too far away, "not within the sphere of American political influence." They were in no way American, and again, unlike Cuba, they gave, to the senator's reckoning, no indication that they could ever become American.

The great obstacle was the United States' inability to settle, occupy, and establish cultural hegemony. The entrenched culture of East Asia was in several crucial ways the opposite of the American order, Morgan wrote: "All American States are Christian, and, in nearly all of them, the political relations between the Church and the State, so that religion is free and untrammeled," he said. In the "Eastern Hemisphere," he insisted, "the reverse condition has always been a source of discord that is apparently uneradicable." Morgan concluded from this that "[u]ntil this impediment is removed, which cannot be done by mere political agencies, a republic like ours will find a barrier to the annexation of European or Asiatic countries, which we could not surmount without danger to our government." The islands of the Philippines "are Asiatic," said Morgan, "and should remain Asiatic."[57] Morgan's imperialism was tightly circumscribed and narrowed by racial belief, not widened or extended. He clearly recognized white racial limitations and the limits of white supremacy as a crusading ideology.

The debates over the annexation of the Philippines began almost a month before the treaty reached the Senate when on 6 December, George Vest of Missouri introduced Senate Resolution 191. It stated that under the Constitution "no power is given to the Federal Government to acquire territory to be held and governed permanently as colonies. The colonial system of European nations cannot be established under our present Constitution," it said, "but all territory acquired by the Government, except such small amounts as may be necessary for coaling stations, correction of boundaries, and similar governmental purposes, must be acquired with the purpose of ultimately organizing such territories into States suitable for admission into the Union."[58]

Vest presented the resolution, he said, only to determine "the powers of Congress in regard to the acquisition and government of new territory," not to discuss the treaty being negotiated at that moment in Paris. Its content indicates other purposes: to create the grounds on which strict interpreters of the Constitution and others opposed to annexation could compromise with the imperialists, and to acquire just enough territory to suit purposes that were strictly American, thus avoiding the objections that would be raised at home against colonial governance and the burdens of ruling over "inferior" races. This imperialist resolution devised a scheme in which the nation's demands could be satisfied without violating the Constitution and without mention of benevolent assimilation or a "white man's burden"—in other words, without unnecessarily exciting the race issue.

Four days after the resolution's announcement in the Senate, American and Spanish diplomats signed the Treaty of Paris, ending the war. All the treaty's provisions were made public, reproduced in newspapers and journals throughout the country. Overnight, in all parts of the nation, they became the subject of conversation and debate. The deliberations over the Vest resolution were set on a new trajectory by the appearance of article 3: altered from a debate on "the powers of Congress in regard to the acquisition and government of new territory" to one over citizenship. Would annexation confer citizenship rights—the right to work, earn, and vote—to the inhabitants of America's new possessions? To Vest's mind the answer was yes. On 12 December he said: "the fundamental idea of our American institutions is citizenship to all within the jurisdiction of the Government," the only exception being Native Americans. "With that single exception," he said, "all of the people of the United States within its jurisdiction are to be citizens." Vest did not know if this would affect the adult population of the Philippines immediately, but he was certain that under the Fourteenth Amendment "all children born within our jurisdiction, no matter what the condition of the parents as to citizenship, are made citizens of the United States." Furthermore, Vest asserted that under the Fifteenth Amendment "all

citizens shall be entitled to the right of suffrage" and that it was "unquestionably the intention of the framers of this amendment and of the States
which adopted it that American citizenship should apply to all the inhabitants of our common country."[59] The citizenship provisions of the Constitution put race at the center of this debate for Vest and turned the senator, and
many others no doubt, against empire.

On 19 December, Republican senator Orville Platt attacked Vest's arguments. A staunch party man and imperialist, Platt insisted that the resolution wrongly intended to circumscribe expansion, "the law of our national
growth . . . the great law of our racial development."[60] The error, he said,
came from Vest's flawed reading of the Constitution: a reading hostile to the
imperialists' cause because it both threatened to overthrow tradition and fix
people of color at the center of their project. Platt was bound by party
interest to defend the administration, the treaty, article 3, and the annexation of the whole archipelago, along with its inhabitants. His tactic, like
those of imperialists before, was to camouflage the race issue and do his best
to remove it from the debate.

"Where is it in the Constitution," he asked, "that the territory acquired by
conquest must be held by the United States for the purpose of admitting
States?" To persuade his colleagues of his rightness and the shortsightedness
of his rival's assertion, Platt asked them to consider "an extreme case" in
which the "imperative interests of the United States demand at some future
time that we shall have some territory on the coast of Africa and we take it by
conquest, and we acquire dominion over savages and barbarians. Where is
the clause in the Constitution, or the implied obligation in the Constitution,
that we admit it as a State in the Union?"[61] Pointing to the canal bill that had
been put forward by Senator Morgan, Platt demanded to know "what clause
in the Constitution . . . says we must organize a State along the canal and
make the people who are there citizens of the United States, with all the
rights pertaining to citizens who live in the States?" His conclusion was
simple and direct: "No[t] one."[62]

Platt admonished his fellow senators, Republicans and Democrats, who
"fear that in throwing around those who may acquire citizenship in our new
possessions . . . great harm either to them ourselves [will be done], and from
that moment the end of republican government will begin." He connected
this "fear" to Vest's contention that the Fifteenth Amendment guaranteed
each citizen the vote. This, said Platt, was "without foundation." The cit-

izen's right to vote was invested in the state in which he voted, not by the authority of the United States. Furthermore, he asserted, citizenship did not confer voting rights. "Women are citizens; they do not vote," Platt declared. "Minors are citizens; they do not vote." To Platt's reckoning, citizenship conferred no right to vote and the Fifteenth Amendment granted no right of voting upon the citizen.[63] His conclusion was as simple as his argument's motive: race, contained and kept apart from citizenship, should be no obstacle to empire.

Senator Henry Teller supported Platt's arguments. "We do not . . . allow everybody to participate in the affairs of government. We exclude the alien, we exclude the ignorant and vicious, we exclude women and infants—rightfully." Teller reasoned that "the interests of the few must give way to the interests of the great mass; because it might be dangerous to the body politic to allow a certain class to participate in the affairs of government. The disabilities that exist must be disabilities that render them unfit and unsuitable for the discharge of political duties. . . . [A]s they are now, nobody wants to take them into the body politics. Nobody wants to make Cuba or Porto Rico or the Philippines States of the Union."[64]

On 6 January, the day the Treaty of Paris was formally introduced, Senator Donelson Caffrey of Louisiana picked up the argument begun by Vest. His contention, rooted assumptions of race and nationalism, was that the American government was "inhibited from acquiring territory for the purpose of incorporating it and its people into the Union" without their consent; that if the territory in question was acceptable in "its condition, character, soil, climate, and population," it must be governed by Congress with the ultimate intent of making it a state; that if, however, the people of a territory were "incapable of self-government," the United States "can not incorporate them into the Union nor hold them as dependencies to be governed despotically by Congress." To close any loophole, Caffrey said, "[t]hat even if capable of self-government and they give their consent, but are inhabitants of a distant country beyond the sea and of a dissimilar race, with different laws, religions, customs, manners, traditions, and habits, it is impolitic, unwise, and dangerous to incorporate them into the Union." To close, the senator repeated the mainstay of anti-imperialist objection: that whenever America acquired territory in full sovereignty, the inhabitants of that territory became citizens of the United States. The Filipinos' carnal nature and depravity was reason enough to reject annexation. "[I]f such a people are unfit and in all human probability never will be fit for the glorious privileges, franchises, and functions of an American citizen, we ought not in that case to even think of incorporating them into the United States."[65]

On 11 January another resolution was introduced which was designed to secure annexation in the Senate by removing the Filipinos, and race, from the debate. The Bacon resolution, introduced by Augustus Bacon of Georgia, said that in demanding and receiving the distant islands, the nation in no way intended to "secure and maintain dominion" over them "as part of the territory of the United States"—this was meant to dispense with the controversial question of statehood—"or," it added significantly, "incorporate the inhabitants thereof as citizens of the United States."[66]

The imperialists' attempts to defuse race and cover it over, though pursued with ingenuity and deliberateness, failed to silence racist counterattacks from their rivals. Two days after the Bacon resolution's first hearing, Senator John McLaurin of South Carolina dragged race back into the debate. McLaurin, who claimed to be "peculiarly qualified to speak upon . . . the incorporation of a mongrel and semi-barbarous population into our body politic," declared that the South's history was "pregnant with lessons of wisdom for our guidance in the Philippine matter." His speech was not concerned with applying these lessons to policy formation; rather, the senator's motives were domestic and bluntly partisan: bludgeoning the treaty's supporters and Republicans with accusations of hypocrisy. "It is passing strange," he said, "that Senators who favored universal suffrage and the full enfranchisement of the negro should now advocate imperialism." McLaurin had found "a glaring inconsistency in these positions," he said. If the expansionists and Republicans were "sincere in their views as to the Philippines," he taunted, "they should propose an amendment to the Constitution which will put the inferior races in this country and the inhabitants of the Philippines upon an equality as to their civil and political rights, and thus forever settle the vexed race and suffrage questions in this country as well as the outlying territories."[67]

Pleased with this line of argument, McLaurin pushed further. How could the treaty's supporters justify a policy "embracing races so nearly akin to the negro"—a policy that denied the Filipinos the rights of citizenship and representation—which differed "so radically from the policy adopted as to that race in the South"? There could be only one answer, "and that is that they substantially admit, in light of a third of a century's experience, that universal suffrage is a monumental failure."[68] The senator mocked his rivals, saying: "It is indeed comforting to hear some of those who in the past criticized us, now that the question is brought home, completely justify our methods in providing a scheme of colonial government." For if the Philippines were annexed, he said, Congress "would contain about one-seventh Japanese, Malays, Chinese, or whatever mixture they have out there. We would have representatives with a voice in directing the affairs of this country from another continent, speaking another language, different in race, religion, and civilization—a people with whom we have nothing in common. For me," McLaurin confessed, "I can not tolerate the thought. . . . Our people will never consent for the people of that far-off land to ever have a voice in the affairs of our country."[69]

McLaurin's fellow senator and South Carolinian, Ben Tillman, adopted his junior colleague's thesis; he also accused the treaty's mostly Republican supporters of base hypocrisy. On 20 January, Knute Nelson of Minnesota reassured skeptical and wavering politicians of the annexationists' promise: that acquisition of a territory would not automatically confer citizenship rights on its inhabitants; that only the land mattered, to the exclusion of the people. This policy was justified, Nelson said, on the grounds that the Filipinos were unassimilable and incapable of self-government. Tillman was outraged and called on Nelson to explain why he "and others who are now contending for a different policy in Hawaii and the Philippines gave the slaves of the South not only self-government, but they forced on the white man of the South, at the point of the bayonet, the rule and domination of those ex-slaves. Why the difference?" he demanded to know. "Why the change? Do you not acknowledge that you were wrong in 1868?" Tillman's furious racial, partisan, and sectionalist baiting failed to draw Nelson into a fight. The "Negro question" was part of "the dreary past," said Nelson, who asserted that it was not at all relevant to the matter at hand. He answered Tillman timidly, assuring him that the expansionists had no intention of making "your load or your burden heavier."[70]

Senator George Frisbie Hoar of Massachusetts broke with his party over the Philippines. He agreed with Nelson's observations regarding suffrage— that "[t]he matter . . . is not necessarily incident of citizenship"—but balked when he considered, through the eyes of his working-class constituents, other rights that accompanied citizenship. If the islands were annexed, Hoar inquired, "[w]ill not these people have a right to go anywhere in the United States and take up residence and get work; and when they are there—speaking of voting in our territory—will they not have the right to become voters without regard to their race, color, or previous condition?"[71] When Nelson told his fellow Republican that this would not occur if the Philippines were annexed, Hoar was incredulous. The Minnesotan turned on his colleague and asked why, if the question of Filipino citizenship was so perilous in his mind, did Hoar, with "no conscientious scruples on the subject," vote in favor of the annexation of Hawaii "where over 95 per cent of the people were of inferior races." Hoar's response is remarkable for both its politics and the racial sensibilities it contains: he expected, he said, that within fifty years those islands would be filled with Americans, "a Northern and largely New England population."[72]

Of those who spoke in favor of annexation and the treaty, Henry Cabot Lodge presented testimony that is especially significant because of his reputation as a leading imperialist and his place in the historical literature. Beyond this, his remarks deserve special attention for two reasons. They stand out as a well-articulated example of the protreaty position, particularly how it was defined by political exigency, reason, and moderation rather than the single-minded pursuit of markets and romantic sentiment. Also, Lodge's speech of 24 January 1899 demonstrates that his thoughts on race and expansion had not changed considerably since the publication of "Our Blundering Foreign Policy" almost four years earlier.

Lodge believed and stated unequivocally that under the Constitution the United States indeed had the power to "acquire territory" and "to hold it and govern it." To the senator's mind, however, this question was peripheral. The main question, the one "demanding actual and immediate decision," he insisted, "is whether the treaty with Spain shall be ratified or not." Lodge observed that the Philippine question was the only one to arouse an opposition; "therefore," he said, "[i]t is the sole point upon which I desire to touch."[73]

His points were clear and concise. The United States had smashed Spanish power in the islands. The Paris treaty simply acknowledged an established and irrefutable fact: the Philippines "belonged" to the United States. The senator especially praised the treaty's vagaries: "It is wisely and skillfully drawn," because it committed the United States "to no policy, to no course of action whatever." The Philippines would fall under American control, but the treaty was mute on matters of governance. This pleased the senator greatly. It meant that ratification would give the nation "full power" over the archipelago, leaving it "absolutely free to do with those islands as we please."

Lodge wanted the Philippines, but to get them, he would not be dragged into a debate on the Filipinos. He would not tumble into a race trap or provoke the opposition with calls for benevolent assimilation or pleas to take up the "white man's burden." His strategy was to state fact and avoid controversy. Thus, Lodge covered over race with promises that whatever their condition, the annexation of those islands would never upset the domestic social order, particularly the privileges of white citizenship. During the previous fall's campaign, Lodge had told his Massachusetts constituents that he "could never assent to hand those islands back to Spain." At the same time, he wanted "no subject races and no vassal States." He believed that the nation had a solemn obligation to the Filipinos: to "protect them from the rapacity of other nations" and to give them "an opportunity for freedom, for peace, and for self-government." The references to duty are hardly surprising coming from a man, and pointed at an electorate, raised on New England's traditions of reform and uplift. Yet at the same time these themes camouflaged the stickier matters that touched race.

Lodge made critical distinctions. He effectively separated wanting to rescue the islands from the Filipinos, whom he did not want—only independent self-government free from any dependence on, any political connection to, the United States. "I believe," Lodge told his senate Colleagues, "that we shall have the wisdom not to attempt to incorporate those islands with our body politic, or make their inhabitants part of our citizenship, or set their labor alongside of ours and within our tariff to compete in any industry with American workingmen." His strongest arguments for ratification focused on bringing the war to an end and a return to normalcy. "I want to get this country out of war and back to peace," he said. "I want to take the disposition and control of the Philippines out of the hands of the war power and place them where they belong, in the hands of the Congress and of the President." In the final days before the Senate voted on the Treaty of Paris, Lodge wanted to assure the American people beyond a doubt that imperialism would never undermine their material interests or topple the pillars of the racial social order.

The Senate's debates continued along these lines until February. In the meantime, the Senate Foreign Relations Committee recommended that the treaty be ratified without amendment and marked 6 February as the date the final vote would be taken. In the final hours, as the tenor of the debates became more strident and coarse, two more resolutions were presented. Both sought to help annexation and imperialism by nullifying the racial objections. The Allen resolution, the initiative of William V. Allen of Nebraska, sought to "place the inhabitants of the Philippine Islands and Puerto Rico on exactly the same position as respects their relations to the United States as the inhabitants of Cuba" under the Teller Amendment: excluded from citizenship. The McEnery Resolution, submitted by Samuel McEnery of Louisiana, contained even stronger exclusionary language. It declared that ratification was "not intended to incorporate the inhabitants of said islands into citizenship of the United States." Neither would it "permanently annex the islands as an integral part of the territory of the United States"; once a viable independent government had been established, a final disposition would occur "as will best promote the interests of the citizens of the United States and the inhabitants of said islands."[74] The same day that this resolution appeared, 6 February, the Treaty of Paris was ratified by a 57 to 27 vote. It passed by only the narrowest margin: a single vote more than the required two-thirds majority.

Many forces were at work at the eleventh hour to attract the last few necessary votes. Nelson Aldrich of Rhode Island politicked hard among his fellow senators, distributing bribes and favor trading in exchange for several critical "yeas." Samuel McEnery and John McLaurin were won over with promises of patronage. George Gray, a Democrat, a member of the peace commission, and its lone opponent of annexation during the treaty's negotiation, also reversed course and voted for the treaty. Shortly after casting this vote, President McKinley rewarded him with a federal judgeship. While some were rewarded, Ben Tillman observed that many senators, rather than acting freely or according to principle and conscience, were pressured to cast favorable votes. William Jennings Bryan, to the surprise of many, called for annexation and used his influence on Senate Democrats and Populists.[75] The outbreak of fighting between American forces and Filipino nationalists just two days before the final vote may have aided the treaty as well. A vote for annexation could be interpreted as patriotic, a vote against, as hostile to American soldiers fighting in jungles on the other side of the world, which was bad politics.

What is clear, however, is that the crusading impulses and rhetoric that many historians have focused on, in particular the racial justifications, taken all together, were still not enough to assure the annexation of the Philippines against the weight and inertia of history. In its aftermath, Lodge called the treaty fight one of the most difficult he had ever faced: "We were down in the engine room and did not get the flowers, but we did make the ship move." The success of the imperialists in 1898 came about through tough partisan politics, the keeping of strict party discipline through controversy, and no small amount of mischief, bribery, backroom bargaining, and corruption: common practices in this era whose impact, unfortunately, is not acknowledged often enough.[76]

With the treaty ratified, the Senate turned to the task of clarifying, by resolution, its long-range policy toward the Philippines. Senators Hoar and Bacon, both anti-imperialists, attempted to amend the McEnery resolution. Hoar's amendment was tabled and Bacon's, which would have granted the Philippines independence immediately after the establishment of a stable, indigenous government, was defeated by a tie-breaking vote cast by Vice President Garret Hobart. Unamended, the McEnery resolution was adopted by a 26 to 22 vote. The resolution was approved, in part, because its vague wording would not impede what the administration ultimately wanted most: a free hand in the Philippines. It did, however, explicitly prohibit Filipino citizenship, the fundamental point on which imperialists and anti-imperialists thoroughly agreed.

Epilogue

Every war is ironic, said Paul Fussell, and every war constitutes an irony of situation because its means are so melodramatically disproportionate to its presumed ends.[1] The Spanish-American War, being no exception, began with the selfless declaration on the part of the United States that it fought not for its own aggrandizement or territory but to free Cuba and its people from foreign tyranny. At the war's end, however, America had seized a new empire reaching from the Caribbean to the Pacific and governance over more than ten million people. Another great irony was that after the events of 1898, the territorial phase of American imperialism came to a startling and abrupt close. Imperialists abandoned annexation, a tradition reaching back to the first days of the nation's independence, as a viable policy option.

The trajectory of this retreat (much like the expansionist rush) was marked like a meteor trail by Theodore Roosevelt, in whom reckless, muscular aggressiveness gave way, with his rise from peripheral offices to a position of real life-and-death responsibility, to a more mature vision of the world and its entanglements and dangers. Less than a decade after fighting (with politicos at home and with guns against the Spanish in Cuba) to win the new American empire, President Roosevelt, disenchanted, dismissed the Philippines as a "white elephant," a conspicuous point of weakness in its security, a dangerous burden to the nation. The part of the president's mind cordoned off to matters of naval strategy realized, in the face of a rising Japanese presence, that those islands had become a point of vulnerability for the United States just as they had once been for Spain. Once the arch imperialist of the 1890s, in the new century Roosevelt wanted to grant the Philippines their independence, once a viable government could be established there.

The Caribbean provides the more impressive example of this reversal and the practical abandonment of annexation. In 1907, confronted with local disorders in Haiti and the Dominican Republic and a serious threat of a foreign invasion to collect unpaid debts led by Germany, an adviser suggested that Roosevelt could settle the matter pretty quickly, simply by annexing both countries. Roosevelt's terse, instinctive reply is famous: he was no more interested in annexing Hispaniola "than a gorged boa constrictor would be to swallow a porcupine wrong-end-to." To his reckoning, he and the nation had gobbled too much already. The prospect of taking one more island and its dark populace was cast as a gruesome, painful impossibility.

How do we account for this change in attitude and belief in what was possible, even desirable, after 1900? Very recent history had shown that annexation was achievable. Precedence, the apparent consent of the people, the military accoutrements of power, the motives and impulses—economic, political, cultural, and missionary—that made territorial imperialism a practical, even attractive policy option were each in place. Reforms in the military and diplomatic corp initiated by Elihu Root, as well as an accelerated naval program, only improved the apparatus that won the empire of 1898. Arguably, the nation was better prepared to extend its territorial empire than it had ever been.

More significant still, race was no longer an obstacle, at least not in law. In the Insular Cases the Supreme Court determined that the Constitution, specifically the Bill of Rights, did not follow the flag, extending automatically to the inhabitants of distant places. In short, the court gave the president and Congress a free hand to carry out a grand expansionist project: to seize and annex distant places, to govern their populations as they saw fit. Unless Congress explicitly did so, annexation would not grant U.S. citizenship to the hypothetical subject peoples. More than removing the dismal obstacles of race and racism, this should have been interpreted as a positive encouragement to empire, but history shows that it was not.

The retreat from annexation in the new century had several causes. Popular support for government activism in foreign affairs waned precipitously after the war with Spain. The public's traditional indifference to world affairs returned—Roosevelt once complained that the "bulk of our people are curiously ignorant of military and naval matters, and full of ignorant self-

confidence, which is, I hope, the only quality they share with the Chinese"[2]—
coupled with a cold disillusion with the alleged glories of empire. Three
years of war in the Philippines was a shameful and bloody affair, awful in all
its details. The costs were terrible: 200,000 American soldiers were sent
halfway around the world, and over 4,000 died to crush the First Philippine
Republic. Filipino casualties were staggering: between fifteen and twenty
thousand soldiers were killed in combat, and hundreds of thousands of
civilians died from war-related injury, famine, and disease. Although the
casualties were far fewer, the ferocious guerilla war between Britain and the
South African Boers (1899–1902) underscored the disaffection Americans
felt toward global imperialism. Kipling's "The White Man's Burden" expressed this disillusion particularly well:

> Take up the White Man's burden—
>   The savage wars of peace—
> Fill full the mouth of Famine,
>   And bid the sickness cease;
> And when your goal is nearest
>   (The end for others sought)
> Watch sloth and heathen folly
>   Bring all your hope to nought.

And further along:

> Take up the White Man's burden—
>   Ye dare not stoop to less—
> Nor call too loud to Freedom
>   To cloak your weariness.
> By all ye will or whisper,
>   By all ye leave or do,
> The silent sullen peoples
>   Shall weigh your God and you.

Again, Roosevelt, who had always been suspicious of the public's twitchy
will and temerity, was a keen observer. He confided to a close friend in 1904:
"I appreciate . . . the full . . . difficulty of committing oneself to a course of
action in reliance upon the proposed action of any free people which is not
accustomed to carrying out with iron will a long-continued course in for-

eign policy." Experience had utterly convinced the president that it would be "well nigh impossible" for the United States to "engage with another [country] to carry out any policy, save one which had become part of the inherited tradition of the country, like the Monroe Doctrine." If he bound the nation to some sort of entangling alliance, regardless of necessity or desirability, Roosevelt said, his reward would be "reckon[ing] with a possible overthrow in Congress [and] the temper of the people."[3]

Race and racism, then, were not the only reasons for the abandonment of annexation, but both are fundamental to understanding it. The Insular Cases may have solved the political and legal questions of alien, nonwhite citizenship that unsettled imperialists and made many anti-imperialists, but the fanatical emotionalism and the social and cultural dilemmas that race excited remained. The war in the Philippines, together with the pre- and postwar fairs and expositions that celebrated America's political, cultural, and white racial supremacy, reaffirmed the image of the savage, barbaric, heathen occupiers of the world's torrid zones and waste places. This would have occurred at the same time that domestic race relations solidified around Jim Crow, the Mississippi Plan, and *Plessy v. Ferguson*: policies of separation, segregation, disfranchisement, immigration restriction, and exclusion. Here, even the most hopeful image of racial conciliation, in which black and white Americans were "separate as the fingers," arose from a premise of separate and unequal station.

Just as important, and perhaps more, was the persistence of notions of white racial limitations. Africa and Asia had been, or were in the process of being, mapped and divided among the great powers. America was a latecomer to the race for empire. There were few desirable places left to take in the aftermath of European expansion and, to the American mind, even fewer places suitable for whites to go. The possessions taken in 1898 were too distant, too tropical, and too thick with indigenous peoples to displace them as Native Americans had been displaced. Beliefs about race and climate still prohibited white settlement and occupation, removing a powerful and traditional incentive to expand and annex territory. In addition to the disincentives to move, there were countless reasons to stay. The frontier "closed" in 1890, according to popular belief, but there was still room to develop the nation from within. The economic downturn of the 1890s gave way to a grand recovery. Although the boom-bust cycles would go on, few Americans believed that emigration was a solution: history and faith told them that good times would return. Besides, where would they go?

The great departure in American foreign relations often cited in this period crystallized when policymakers learned that the benefits of empire could be had without the entanglements attached to race. The strategies they devised in response to their encounters with nonwhite peoples reveal the presence of this understanding. When Roosevelt (following his famous boast) took the Canal Zone, for example, not all of Panama was taken, despite the support for doing so. The Americans took only enough territory on either side of the canal to build it and to suit its defense and other purposes: it was as if the policymakers and strategists were bound by the Vest resolution. The Americans surveyed, occupied, built, and fortified that part of a distant, alien, tropical country they needed and avoided annexing the people around it. This was not an accident.

A brief survey of policies characteristic of the period reveals other examples that, taken together, form a pattern demonstrating similar intent. The Open Door Notes (1899–1900) gave the United States a point of entry into China, intent on expanding commerce, yet free from the traps of territorial control. The Foraker Act of 1900 established a frame of governance over Puerto Rico which excluded statehood and citizenship. The Platt Amendment of 1903 provided the United States with the authority to intervene in Cuba to maintain peace, order, and the island's independence. At the same time, the United States took possession of Guantánamo Bay for use as a naval station, extending the apparatus of empire in the Caribbean. The Roosevelt Corollary (1904) proclaimed that when "chronic wrongdoing" by a weak or bankrupt nation in the Western Hemisphere might incite "intervention by some civilized nation," the United States had the right to exercise "international police power." Americans used the corollary to occupy Cuba from 1906 to 1909 and then to take over Santo Domingo's customhouses and pay its foreign creditors, thus avoiding German intervention and, perhaps, Roosevelt's sitting down to a meal of prickly porcupine. His corollary would be used to justify interventions in the Caribbean and Central America for three decades.

A few years after the war with Spain ended, a new policy direction, absent annexation, was firmly in place. The United States had the best of both worlds: hegemony in its hemisphere without the more daunting or politically hazardous responsibilities over their "new caught sullen peoples, half Devil and half child."

Notes

ABBREVIATIONS

CSP   Carl Schurz Papers, Library of Congress, Washington, D.C.

FRUS   U.S. Department of State, *Papers Relating to the Foreign Relations of the United States* (Washington, D.C.: Government Printing Office, 1870–1916)

GBCP   George B. Cortelyou Papers, Library of Congress, Washington, D.C.

GCP   Grover Cleveland Papers, Library of Congress, Washington, D.C.

HCLP   Henry Cabot Lodge Papers, Massachusetts Historical Society, Boston, Mass.

HFP   Hamilton Fish Papers, Library of Congress, Washington, D.C.

JDLP   John Davis Long Papers, Massachusetts Historical Society, Boston, Mass.

NPBP   Nathaniel Prentiss Banks Papers, Library of Congress, Washington, D.C.

SDP   Sanford Dole Papers, Hawaiian Historical Society, Honolulu, Hawaii

WGP   Walter Q. Gresham Papers, Library of Congress, Washington, D.C.

PREFACE

1 Freehling, "Founding Fathers and Slavery," 83.

2 Marx, "Eighteenth Brumaire of Louis Bonaparte," in *Social Theory*, 42; Roberts, *Penguin History of Europe*, 1.

3 Williamson, *Rage for Order*, viii.

CHAPTER ONE

1   A very fine and incisive summary of more recent literature on late-nineteenth-century U.S. imperialism can be found in Hoganson, *Fighting for American Manhood*, 209–14.

2   Painter, *Standing at Armageddon*, 150, 151; Dawley, *Struggles for Justice*, 50, 51.

3   Hunt, *Ideology and U.S. Foreign Policy*, 80, 81; Campbell, *Transformation of American Foreign Relations*, 149. Campbell did not support this observation with argument and evidence but instead described it as "a reasonable guess."

4   Fry, "Phases of Empire," 265. See also Hays, *Response to Industrialism*, 208–15; Weston, *Racism in U.S. Imperialism*, 11–12; Rosenberg, *Spreading the American Dream*, 42; and Woodward, *Origins of the New South*, 324–26, and *Strange Career of Jim Crow*, 72–73.

5   Gatewood, *Black Americans and the White Man's Burden*, ix–x; Rydell, *All the World's a Fair*, 104, 105–53.

6   Jacobson, *Barbarian Virtues*, 221–65.

7   Gaines, "Black Americans' Racial Uplift Ideology," 433–55.

8   See, for example, Weston, *Racism in U.S. Imperialism*, 11–12; and Hoganson, *Fighting for American Manhood*, 214. For examples of how this narrative is repeated in highly regarded and best-selling college-level textbooks, see Brinkley, *American History*, 691–714; Murrin, *Liberty, Equality, Power*, 746–75; Norton, *A People and a Nation*, 691–714; and Woods, *America Interpreted*, 621–48.

9   Crapol, "Coming to Terms with Empire," 597.

10 LaFeber, *Cambridge History of American Foreign Relations*, 2:162.

11 Merk, *Manifest Destiny*, 237–47.

12 Field, "American Imperialism," 664–68, 669, 674.

13 Ferrell, *American Diplomacy*, 365.

14 In *Social Darwinism and American Thought*, Richard Hofstadter wrote: "It would . . . be easy to exaggerate the significance of Darwin for race theory and militarism" in the United States. By the 1890s, Americans, he said, were a people "long familiar with Indian warfare on the frontier and the pro-slavery arguments of Southern politicians and publicists had been thoroughly grounded in notions of racial superiority" (171, 172).

15 Lasch, "Anti-Imperialists, the Philippines, and the Inequality of Man," 71.

16 Franklin, *From Slavery to Freedom*, 425.

17 Litwack, *North of Slavery*, vii.

18 Tocqueville, *Democracy in America*, 1:359–60.

19 Fredrickson, *Black Image in the White Mind*, 304, 305.

20 Takaki, *Strangers from a Different Shore*, 114.

21 Daniels, *Politics of Prejudice*, 17; Daniels and Graham, *Debating American Immigration*, 8.

22 Breen and Innes, *"Myne Owne Ground,"* 31.

23 See, for example, Jordan, *White Man's Burden*, vii; Fredrickson, *White Supremacy*, xii; and Wellman, *Portraits of White Racism*, 3. Alexander Saxton used racism very effectively in *Rise and Fall of the White Republic*, 14–15.

24 Fredrickson, *Racism*, 6.

25 Fields, "Slavery, Race and Ideology in the United States of America," 95–118; Higginbotham, "African American Women's History and the Meta-Language of Race," 4.

26 Fredrickson, *Racism*, 5.

27 Rydell, *Reason Why the Colored American Is Not in the World's Columbian Exposition*, 65, 67, 76, 80.

28 Du Bois, *Souls of Black Folk*, 364.

29 The problems of white supremacy are described in Horne, "Race from Power."

30 Sparks, *Works of Benjamin Franklin*, 2:320.

31 Donald, *Lincoln*, 222.

32 Benton, *Thirty Years' View*, 2:474.

33 Malone, *Jefferson the President*, 349–50.

34 Knudson, "The Jefferson Years," 214.

35 Schroeder, *Mr. Polk's War*, 123.

36 Cralle, *Works of John C. Calhoun*, 4:397.

37 Ibid., 410.

38 Ibid., 411, 412.

39 Bancroft, "Seward's Ideas of Territorial Expansion," 83.

40 Weinberg, *Manifest Destiny*, 168.

41 Gossett, *Race*, 6.

42 Emerson, *Selected Essays*, 364, 370; Tocqueville, *Democracy in America*, 1:431.

43 Tocqueville, *Democracy in America*, 1:369.

CHAPTER TWO

1 Quotations here and in the following paragraph from Fiske, *American Political Ideas*, 101, 102.

2 Pletcher, "Rhetoric and Results," 93–105.

3 Adams, "Session," 57.

4 LaFeber, *Cambridge History of American Foreign Relations*, 7; Beisner, *From the Old Diplomacy to the New*, 27.

5 Bancroft, "Seward's Ideas of Territorial Expansion," 144.

6 George Bancroft, *Life of William H. Seward*, 470; LaFeber, *New Empire*, 24.

7 Beisner, *From the Old Diplomacy to the New*, 45.

8 Seward to Z. S. Spaulding, 5 July 1868, in *FRUS*, 1894, app. 2, 144. Charles Sumner

concurred with this observation, writing in a letter dated 30 May 1868: "We are now on the eve of a Presidential election, and already 'economy' has become a battle cry. With this is mingled an opposition toward Mr. Seward's s[c]hemes of foreign acquisition. . . . I doubt if any diplomatic [a]ction can prevail at this time" (Palmer, *Selected Letters of Charles Sumner*, 2:249).

9 Weinberg, *Manifest Destiny*, 224.

10 Leonard Curry, *Blueprint for Modern America*.

11 This acknowledges a familiar historical convention in which the Civil War functions as an interpretive centerpoint in the history of the United States, a tradition adopted by historians of American foreign relations as well. See, for example, LaFeber, *New Empire*, and *Cambridge History of American Foreign Relations*; Beisner, *From the Old Diplomacy to the New*; Campbell, *Transformation of American Foreign Relations*; and Plesur, *America's Outward Thrust*.

12 A brilliant summary of Agassiz's theories can be found in Stephen Jay Gould, *Mismeasure of Man*, 74–82.

13 Ibid., 75.

14 Agassiz to Sumner, 6 April 1867, Charles Sumner Papers, Library of Congress, Washington, D.C., series 1, reel 38.

15 Ernest R. May, *American Imperialism*, 99.

16 *New York Herald*, 2 April 1867.

17 Nevins and Thomas, *Diary of George Templeton Strong*, 129.

18 *New York Herald*, 1 April 1867.

19 *New York Tribune*, 1 April 1867.

20 Armstrong, *E. L. Godkin and American Foreign Policy*, 105.

21 *New York Herald*, 1 April 1867.

22 Weinberg, *Manifest Destiny*, 230.

23 LaFeber, *Cambridge History of American Foreign Relations*, 2:11.

24 Armstrong, *E. L. Godkin and American Foreign Policy*, 105.

25 Palmer, *Selected Letters of Charles Sumner*, 2:430.

26 Banks to Mary Theodosia Banks, 9 March 1869, NPBP, container 5.

27 Quoted in Holt, *Treaties Defeated by the Senate*, 107.

28 Tansill, *United States and Santo Domingo*, 343–50.

29 Nevins, *Hamilton Fish*, 1:254–55.

30 Tansill, *United States and Santo Domingo*, 350.

31 Moya Pons, *Dominican Republic*, 225–26.

32 Ibid., 227.

33 *Congressional Globe*, 40th Cong. 3d sess., 317–19, 333–40.

34 Eric Foner, *Reconstruction*, 494.

35 Fish to Babcock, 13 July 1869, Senate Executive Document 17, 41st Cong., 3d sess., 79.

36 McFeely, *Grant*, 297.

37 Ibid., 298.

38 Ibid., 297–98.

39 Fish to Sumner, 12 December 1869, Charles Sumner Papers, Library of Congress, Washington, D.C.

40 Nevins, *Hamilton Fish*, 1:271.

41 Ibid., 269.

42 Ibid., 264.

43 Ibid., 271; Hesseltine, *Ulysses S. Grant*, 198; Charles Francis Adams, *Lee at Appomattox*, 130.

44 Nevins, *Hamilton Fish*, 1:268.

45 Senate Executive Document 17, 98.

46 *New York Herald*, 22 December 1869. News of the treaty began to appear in the press soon after it was signed in November 1869.

47 *Nation*, 13 January 1870.

48 21 December 1869, HFP, container 311, reel 1.

49 Simon, *Papers of Ulysses S. Grant*, 20:74–76.

50 Ibid., 74, 75.

51 Ibid., 75.

52 Ibid., 76.

53 Ibid., 75, 76.

54 Ibid., 74.

55 Ibid., 74–75.

56 Jefferson's apprehensions may appear both ironic and hypocritical given the results of recent scientific studies of DNA which appear to confirm that he fathered five children by his slave Sally Hemings; such would not be the case, however. Had Jefferson been less of a gentleman or bold enough to speak of sexuality in a more forthright manner, he might have said that he was not fearful of the slave "staining the blood of his master" so much as he was afraid that the slave would "stain the blood" of his master's wife and daughter.

57 Donald, *Lincoln*, 166–67.

58 Gideon Welles, *Diary of Gideon Welles*, 1:150–53; McPherson, *Ordeal by Fire*, 43–44; Lincoln, *Speeches and Writings*, 355.

59 Gillette, *Retreat from Reconstruction*, 7.

60 Eric Foner, *Reconstruction*, 313.

61 Gillette, *Retreat from Reconstruction*, 9, 10.

62 McFeely, *Grant*, 259, 278–79, 283.

63 Ibid., 315.

64 Nevins, *Hamilton Fish*, 1:313.

65 Ibid., 262.

66 *London Spectator*, 29 January 1870; *Littell's Living Age*, 104:634–36.

67 The best account of this meeting appears in Donald, *Charles Sumner*, 434–38.

68   Ibid., 436.

69   Ibid.

70   Nevins, *Hamilton Fish*, 1:317; Hesseltine, *Ulysses S. Grant*, 202; Pierce, *Sumner*, 440.

71   *New York Tribune*, 18 March 1870.

72   Ibid., 20 March 1870.

73   "Annexation in the West Indies—the President and Congress," *New York Herald*, 24 March 1870.

74   *New York Tribune*, 23 March 1870.

75   Hamilton to Fish, 20 March 1870, HFP, Correspondence of Hamilton Fish, 68.

76   Adams, "Session," 58.

77   Henry Adams, *Education of Henry Adams*, 221.

78   Beisner, *Twelve against Empire*, 19.

79   Schurz, *Reminiscences*, 3:307–9.

80   Grant to Fish, 22 March 1870, HFP.

81   *New York Tribune*, 25 March 1870.

82   *New York Herald*, 25 March 1870; *New York Tribune*, 28 March 1870.

83   Donald, *Charles Sumner*, 442.

84   *New York Herald*, 26 March 1870.

85   *New York Herald*, 28 March 1870.

86   Douglass, *Life and Times*, 1029.

87   Storey, *Charles Sumner*, 328; Pierce, *Sumner*, 4:441.

88   Donald, *Charles Sumner*, 442–43.

89   Ibid., 443.

90   *New York Times*, 26 March 1870.

91   *New York Herald*, 26 March 1870.

92   Ibid.; emphasis added.

93   Detailed accounts of Schurz's speech appear in the *New York Times*, *New York Herald*, and *New York Tribune*, 29 March 1870; Feuss, *Carl Schurz*, 164–65.

94   Schurz to W. M. Grosvenor, 31 March 1870, CSP.

95   *New York Times*, *New York Tribune*, and *New York Herald*, 29 March 1870.

96   Davis to Fish, 26 and 27 March 1870, HFP, Correspondence, vol. 68; Schurz, *Reminiscences*, 2:403.

97   *New York Herald*, 13 May 1870.

98   Ibid.

99   San Domingo File, CSP.

100   14 May 1870, HFP.

101   21 May 1870, HFP.

102   Davis to Fish, 15 May 1870, HFP, Correspondence, vol. 69.

103   Nevins, *Hamilton Fish*, 1:325.

104   Richardson, *Messages and Papers*, 9:4015–17.

105   13 June 1870, HFP, container 311, reel 1.

106   Ibid., 17 June 1870.

107   Campbell, *Transformation of American Foreign Relations*, 38.

108   Nathaniel Banks to Mary Theodosia Banks, 1 July 1870, NPBP.

109   Charles Richard Williams, *Diary and Letters of Rutherford Birchard Hayes*, 5:110.

110   Richardson, *Messages and Papers*, 9:4053, 4054.

111   *Congressional Globe*, 41st Cong., 3d sess., 53.

112   Ibid., 191.

113   Ibid., 226; Sumner, *Works*, 18:262–99. A useful analysis of the speech appears in Donald, *Charles Sumner*, 470–73.

114   *Congressional Globe*, 41st Cong., 3d sess., 414, 416, 431.

115   Charles Richard Williams, *Diary and Letters of Rutherford Birchard Hayes*, 5:135.

116   Simon, *Papers of Ulysses S. Grant*, 21:149; Gail Hamilton, *Biography of James G. Blaine*, 248.

117   *Congressional Globe*, 41st Cong., 3d sess., app.: 26, 29, 30.

118   Cox to Schurz, 21 February 1871, CSP.

119   Simon, *Papers of Ulysses S. Grant*, 21:238.

120   Ibid., 285.

121   Ibid., 294.

122   Richardson, *Messages and Papers*, 9:4366, 4367.

123   *New York Herald*, 24 July 1878.

124   Ulysses Grant, *Personal Memoirs*, 550.

125   Jesse R. Grant, *In the Days of My Father*, 138.

126   Ibid., 138.

CHAPTER THREE

1   Stevens, *American Expansion in Hawaii*, 217.

2   *FRUS*, 1894, app. 2, 207–8.

3   "Queen Liliuokalani's Protest against the Actions of Minister Stevens in Hawaii Sent by Special Messenger to Secretary of State John W. Foster," 18 January 1893, GCP, series 2, reel 2.

4   Ferrell, *American Diplomacy*, 329.

5   Takaki, *Strangers from a Different Shore*, 111.

6   Ibid. In 1888 the prohibition was broadened to include "all persons of the Chinese race," exempting Chinese officials, teachers, students, tourists, and merchants.

7   Osborne, *"Empire Can Wait,"* 2; Pratt, *Expansionists of 1898*, 119; Stevens, *American Expansion in Hawaii*, 232–34. All the terms brought to the negotiations by Hawaii's delegation appear in *FRUS*, 1894, app. 2, 235–36.

8   Pratt, *Expansionists of 1898*, 118–20; Devine, *John W. Foster*, 66–67; Baker, "Benjamin Harrison and Hawaiian Annexation," 295–316.

9   *FRUS*, 1894, app. 2, 201.

10   Ibid., 202–5.

11   "Poll of Congress regarding Hawaii," *New York Herald*, 6 February 1893.

12   Foster, *Diplomatic Memoirs*, 1:168.

13   Gresham, *Life of Walter Quintin Gresham*, 2:744.

14   Richardson, *Messages and Papers*, 8:5825.

15   Nevins, *Grover Cleveland*, 552.

16   Foster, *Diplomatic Memoirs*, 2:168.

17   Calhoun, *Gilded Age Cato*, 146.

18   18 January 1893, GCP, series 2, reel 2.

19   Gresham to Blount, 11 March 1893, *FRUS*, 1894, app. 2, 467–68, 1185–87; Pratt, *Expansionists of 1898*, 124.

20   *FRUS*, 1894, app. 2, 42.

21   Kuykendall, *Hawaiian Kingdom*, 192.

22   Seager, *And Tyler Too*, 185.

23   Charles Francis Adams, *Memoirs of John Quincy Adams*, 274–75.

24   Kuykendall, *Hawaiian Kingdom*, 192, 193.

25   *FRUS*, 1894, app. 2, 43.

26   Ibid., 42.

27   Ibid., 39.

28   Kuykendall, *Hawaiian Kingdom*, 193; Charles Francis Adams, *Memoirs of John Quincy Adams*, 275.

29   *FRUS*, 1894, app. 2, 39.

30   A survey of the various figures appears in Stannard, *Before the Horror*, 3–31.

31   Beechert, *Working in Hawaii*, 20.

32   Rufus Anderson, *Hawaiian Islands*, 272.

33   Ibid., 272.

34   Ibid., 273–74.

35   Twain, *Mark Twain's Speeches*, 7–20.

36   Bird, *Six Months in the Sandwich Islands*, 176.

37   Ibid., 177.

38   Kuykendall, *Hawaiian Kingdom*, 75, 76.

39   Beechert, *Working in Hawaii*, 61.

40   Comly to Evarts, 5 July 1880, *FRUS*, 1882, 614–15.

41   Blaine to Lowell, 23 April 1881, in Tyler, *Foreign Policy of James G. Blaine*, 195.

42   Ibid., 195–96.

43   *FRUS*, 1882, 623–27.

44   Ibid., 627–28.

45 Blaine to Comly, 19 November 1881, in *FRUS*, 1894, app. 2, 1155–56; Stevens, *American Expansion in Hawaii*, 157.

46 Comly to Blaine, 14 February 1881, in *FRUS*, 1882, 620.

47 Blaine to Comly, 1 December 1881, in Blaine, *Political Discussions*, 395; *FRUS*, 1894, app. 2, 1159–60.

48 Quotations here and in the following two paragraphs from *FRUS*, 1894, app. 2, 1161.

49 Ibid., 1162. The suggestion that Blaine had African Americans in mind to be the ideal replacements for the Chinese is only implied since the statement ends here and is not picked up again.

50 Blaine, *Political Discussions*, 222.

51 Tansill, *Foreign Policy of Thomas F. Bayard*, 127–28.

52 Conroy, *Japanese Frontier in Hawaii*, 127–28; Daniels, *Politics of Prejudice*, 3–4.

53 Daniels, *Politics of Prejudice*, 5; Montgomery, *Imperialist Japan*, 156–57.

54 Stevens to Foster, 20 November 1892, in *FRUS*, 1894, app. 2, 377.

55 Ibid., 381.

56 Ibid.

57 Cleveland to Schurz, 19 March 1893, CSP; George Bancroft, *Schurz*, 5:133–34.

58 *FRUS*, 1894, app. 2, 88–102.

59 *Congressional Globe*, 32d Cong., 1st sess., app. 1084.

60 Marcy to Gregg, 4 April 1854, *FRUS*, 1894, app. 2, 121.

61 Ibid., 127.

62 Ibid., 128.

63 Marcy to Gregg, 31 January 1855, in ibid., 133.

64 Kuykendall, *Hawaiian Kingdom*, 410.

65 Robert E. May, *Southern Dream of a Caribbean Empire*, 40–76.

66 Richardson, *Messages and Papers*, 6:2731–32.

67 Ibid., 133.

68 Gara, *Presidency of Franklin Pierce*, 147; Nichols, *Franklin Pierce*, 393–99; Barrett, "William Learned Marcy," 6.

69 A brief account can be found in Holt, *Treaties Defeated by the Senate*, 90.

70 Patterson, "The United States and Hawaiian Reciprocity," 14–26; *FRUS*, 1894, app. 2, 19.

71 Quoted in Foster, *American Diplomacy in the Orient*, 367; Foster, *Century of American Diplomacy*, 435.

72 Hinsdale, *Works of James Abram Garfield*, 2:320; *Congressional Record*, 44th Cong., 1st sess., 2273.

73 Hinsdale, *Works of James Abram Garfield*, 2:322.

74 *The Nation* 57 (9 February 1893).

75 A survey of newspapers appears in the *New York Times*, 2 February 1893.

76   A survey of newspaper opinion appears in the *New York Herald*, 8 February 1893.

77   *New York Herald*, 2 February 1893.

78   *New York Evening Post*, 16 February 1893.

79   "Why Should We Annex Hawaii?" *New York Herald*, 23 February 1893.

80   Carl Schurz, "The Annexation Policy," *Harper's Weekly*, March 1893.

81   Schurz to Cleveland, 11 March 1893, CSP, reel 52.

82   Carl Schurz, "Manifest Destiny," *Harper's Weekly*, October 1893.

83   Ibid., 739.

84   Ibid., 741.

85   Ibid., 742.

86   Schurz to Gresham, 24 September 1893, WGP, vol. 41; Gresham to Schurz, 6 October 1893, WGP, vol. 41.

87   Bishop, "Her Majesty 'Lily-of-the-Sky,' " 227–33.

88   Ibid., 227, 228.

89   Quotations here and in the following two paragraphs are from the *New York Evening Post*, 8 February 1893.

90   Pratt, "Hawaiian Revolution," 275.

91   Queen Liliuokalani, *Hawaii's Story by Hawaii's Queen*, 239, 241.

92   *New York Herald*, 16 February 1893.

93   *New York Times*, 31 January 1893.

94   "Senator Morgan's Views," *New York Times*, 3 February 1893.

95   *Southern Workman*, 22 February 1893; Harlan, *Booker T. Washington*, 58–59.

96   *New York Evening Post*, 3 February 1893.

97   *Southern Workman*, 22 February 1893.

98   Wilson to Gresham, 24 July 1893, WGP, vol. 40.

99   Calhoun, *Gilded Age Cato*, 148.

100   Ibid.

101   Gresham, *Life of Walter Quintin Gresham*, 837.

102   Ibid., 754.

103   Willis to Gresham, 16 November 1893, in *FRUS*, 1894, app. 2, 1241–43. Liliuokalani's version of this meeting, written years later, appears in *Hawaii's Story by Hawaii's Queen*, 246–51. Here the Queen appears more moderate. She cited the authority of the law making treason a capital crime but wrote that she "would be more inclined to punish them by banishment, and confiscation of their property to the government." She said, however, that she would consult with her advisers "before deciding on any definite action."

104   Dole to Willis, 23 December 1893, in *FRUS*, 1894, 1282, 1276.

105   *FRUS* 1894, app. 2, 458.

106   Welch, *Presidencies of Grover Cleveland*, 173; *FRUS*, 1894, app. 2, 445.

107   Morton to Gresham, 17 November 1893, WGP, vol. 41. Morton went on to say that taking Hawaii would lead to the acquisition of Cuba, "which commands

the entrance to the Gulf of Mexico." "[H]uman nature being what it is," he wrote, "it is reasonably certain that the United States would be embarked upon a career of stupendous conquest of which no man could see the end." Other notes supporting Gresham appear throughout this volume of the Gresham Papers.

108   Calhoun, *Gilded Age Cato*, 37.

109   Ibid., 155.

CHAPTER FOUR

1   Blisk to Dole, 21 December 1893, SDP.

2   Dole to Mrs. Mills, 12 January 1894, SDP.

3   Charles Fletcher Dole to Sanford Dole, 21 April [?] 1893, SDP. Further along Dole wrote that imperialism had quite altered his politics: "The fact is I have been [moving] towards the Democratic side of late . . . on the ground that if [unreadable] for wisdom put on the brakes for a while at least." C. F. Dole had arrived at an unpleasant conclusion: that the Republicans had gone too far with "expansion and centralization."

4   Armstrong to Dole, 4 November 1893, SDP. The sections of the Mississippi constitution Armstrong enclosed were 241, 242, 244, and 249 of article 12, the literacy clause which required that potential voters should be able to read and understand the state constitution "or he shall be able to understand the same when read to him, or give a reasonable interpretation thereof." Armstrong also enclosed "a statement of the Monroe Doctrine" and stated: "Although our islands are non-contiguous, still we have intimate commercial relations with the Pacific States, and belong to the American hemisphere, so that it does not seem an unwarrantable stretch to extend the protection of the Monroe Doctrine to us."

5   Albert Willis to Walter Gresham, 24 March 1894, *FRUS*, 1894, app. 2, 1316.

6   *The Nation* 59 (26 July 1894); Pratt, *Expansionists of 1898*, 190–91.

7   Madden, "Letters of Sanford B. Dole and John W. Burgess," 71–72.

8   Burgess to Dole, 13 April 1894, in ibid., 73.

9   Ibid., 74.

10   Dole to Burgess, 18 December 1894, ibid., 75.

11   Stevens, *American Expansion in Hawaii*, 271, 272; Rowland, "Establishment of the Republic of Hawaii," 201–20.

12   *FRUS*, 1894, app. 2, 1325.

13   Healy, *U.S. Expansionism*, 53.

14   Richardson, *Messages and Papers*, 9:559, 560.

15   *Congressional Record*, 53d Cong., 3d sess., 1167.

16   2 March 1895, in ibid., 3076–77.

17   Quotations here and in next paragraph in Ibid., 3077.

18   This is especially significant since the prevailing narrative often cites the "missionary impulse" and the missionaries themselves as two of the main agents behind the imperial movement of the 1890s.

19   Ibid., 3079.

20   Ibid., 3080.

21   Ibid., 3079, 3080.

22   Ibid., 3080.

23   Ibid., 3082.

24   Ibid., 3080.

25   Israel, "The 'Old Empire,'" 95; Painter, *Standing at Armageddon*, 150; Healy, *U.S. Expansionism*, 57; Pratt, *Expansionists of 1898*, 204; Grenville and Young, *Politics, Strategy, and American Diplomacy*, 201.

26   Christopher Lasch argued that there were few substantive differences between the imperialists and anti-imperialists on matters of race. See his "Anti-Imperialists, the Philippines, and the Inequality of Man," 319–31. George Fredrickson disagreed, stating that there was a difference: "an examination of what was actually said on the subject of race by the imperialists and by anti-imperialists suggests that competitive racism did not, in fact, harmonize readily with the new expansionist ideology." See Fredrickson, *Black Image in the White Mind*, 305.

27   Pratt, *Expansionists of 1898*, 206–8; Dulles, *America's Rise to World Power*, 30–36; Zimmerman, *First Great Triumph*, 149–53; Painter, *Standing at Armageddon*, 149–52.

28   Lodge, "Our Blundering Foreign Policy," 8, 9.

29   Ibid., 12.

30   Ibid., 16.

31   Ibid., 14.

32   Ibid., 16.

33   Ibid., 17.

34   Ibid.

35   Cooley, "Grave Obstacles to Hawaiian Annexation," 395.

36   Ibid.

37   Ibid., 399.

38   Bryce, "Policy of Annexation for America," 388.

39   Ibid., 388, 390.

40   Ibid., 389.

41   Ibid., 389, 390.

42   Ibid., 392.

43   Porter and Johnson, *National Party Platforms*, 94, 95.

44   Foster, *Diplomatic Memoirs*, 2:169.

45   Henry Wayne Morgan, *William McKinley and His America*, 292.

46   Lewis L. Gould, *Presidency of William McKinley*, 48.

47   Fuess, *Carl Schurz, Reformer*, 349.

48   Pratt, *Expansionists of 1898*, 216.

49   Foster, *Diplomatic Memoirs*, 2:172; Devine, "John W. Foster," 29–50.

50   Senate Report no. 681, 55th Cong., 2d sess., 66.

51   Ibid., 75.

52   Ibid., 75, 76.

53   William Morgan, "Anti-Japanese Origins of the Hawaiian Annexation Treaty," 23–44.

54   Stevens, *American Expansion in Hawaii*, 284.

55   *Address*, 1.

56   Ibid., 5.

57   Ibid., 5, 6; emphasis added.

58   Ibid., 6.

59   Ibid., 6–7.

60   Ibid., 7.

61   Thurston, *Handbook*.

62   Ibid., 3.

63   Ibid., 6.

64   Ibid., 7–8.

65   Ibid.

66   Ibid.

67   Ibid.

68   Ibid.

69   *Public Opinion*, 24 June 1897, 771–73.

70   Ibid., 1 July 1897, 5, 6.

71   "Should Hawaii Be Annexed?," 216.

72   Appel, "American Labor and the Annexation of Hawaii," quotations found on pages 4 and 6.

73   Richardson, *Messages and Papers*, 10:38, 39.

74   Ibid., 39.

75   Stevens, *American Expansion in Hawaii*, 293.

76   Senate Report no. 681, 55th Cong., 2d sess.

77   Ibid., 27–31.

78   Ibid., 10.

79   Ibid.

80   Ibid., 11.

81   Ibid.

82   Ibid., 12, 13.

83   Ibid., 15.

84   Ernest May, *Imperial Democracy*, 243.

85   Robinson, *Thomas B. Reed*, 366–67.

86   *Congressional Record*, 55th Cong., 2d sess., 5772.

87   Ibid., 6344.

88   Ibid., 5778, 5788.

89   Ibid., 6144.

90   Ibid., 6141.

91   Ibid., 6357.

92   Ibid., 614.

93   Ibid., 617.

94   Ibid., 5783.

95   Ibid., 5773, 5774.

96   Ibid., 5773.

97   Ibid., 5774.

98   Ibid., 5786.

99   Ibid., 5785, 5786.

100 Hoar, *Autobiography*, 2:306, 307, 308.

101 *Congressional Record*, 55th Cong., 2d sess., 5775.

102 Ibid., 5774, 5775.

103 Ibid., 5778.

104 Ibid., 5896.

105 Ibid., 5775.

106 Ibid., 5787.

107 Ibid., 5789, 5883, 6260.

108 *American Monthly Review of Reviews* 18 (August 1898):124.

109 Campbell, *Transformation of American Foreign Relations*, 294.

110 Damon, *Sanford Ballard Dole and His Hawaii*, 332.

111 Allen, *Sanford Ballard Dole*, 222.

112 "Hawaii Annexed," *Public Opinion*, 14 July 1898, 41.

113 Ernest May, *Imperial Democracy*, 243.

114 Nevins, *Letters of Grover Cleveland*, 502.

115 "Hawaii Annexed," 41.

116 Ibid.

117 Fry, *John Tyler Morgan*, 154–97.

CHAPTER FIVE

1   Mahan to Lodge, 27 July 1898, in Seager and Maguire, *Letters and Papers of Alfred Thayer Mahan*, 2:569; Grenville and Young, *Politics, Strategy, and American Diplomacy*, 291–94; Healy, *U.S. Expansionism*, 60; Ernest May, *Imperial Democracy*, 245.

2   Seager and Maguire, *Letters and Papers of Alfred Thayer Mahan*, 2:619.

3   Healy, *U.S. Expansionism*, 60.

4   A survey of newspaper opinion from the first weeks of the war appears in *Public Opinion*, 12 May 1898.

5   Stoler, *George Marshall*, 12.

6   Reed to Lodge, 7 October 1897, HCLP, General Correspondence, box 10.

7   Ibid.

8   Pratt, *Expansionists of 1898*, 327; Fry, "William McKinley and the Coming of the Spanish-American War," 77–97; Ephraim Smith, "William McKinley's Enduring Legacy," 205–49.

9   Olcott, *Life of William McKinley*, 2:55–56; Grenville and Young, *Politics, Strategy, and American Diplomacy*, 239–40.

10 Adams to Hay, 5 May 1898, in Samuels, *Letters of Henry Adams*, 2:582; Hay to Adams, 9 May 1898, in ibid., 3:136; Mahan to Lodge, 27 July 1898, in Seager and Maguire, *Letters and Papers of Alfred Thayer Mahan*, 2:569; Fry, "William McKinley and the Coming of the Spanish-American War," 79.

11 See, for example, Schulzinger, *American Diplomacy in the Twentieth Century*, 18. Schulzinger stated that the Philippines were taken "because President McKinley thought he heard God's voice." See also Pratt, *Expansionists of 1898*, 334–35; Dulles, *Imperial Years*, 163; May, *Imperial Democracy*, 252–53; Cashman, *America in the Gilded Age*, 321–22; and Painter, *Standing at Armageddon*, 147.

12 Olcott, *Life of William McKinley*, 2:110.

13 Ibid., 110–11.

14 Iriye, "Imperialism and Sincerity," 119–25.

15 Kohlsaat, *From McKinley to Harding*, 68.

16 May, *Imperial Democracy*, 246.

17 Hay to McKinley, 13 June 1898, GBCP, box 56.

18 For reports of German landings in the Philippines, see the *New York Times*, 23 June 1898, 29 June 1898, 30 June 1898, and 19 July 1898. On Germany's intention to acquire some part of the archipelago, see *New York Times*, 12 May 1898. On France's attempt to purchase the Philippines and Germany's protest, see *New York Times*, 29 May 1898. Europe's jealousy is reported in the *Times* on 15 May and 17 May 1898. Japan's views of the war are described in the *Times* on 17 May and 19 May 1898. Russia's posture is reported on in the *New York Times* on 21 May 1898. See also Gould, *Spanish-American War and President McKinley*, 82; Trask, *War with Spain*, 377–78; and Pratt, *Expansionists of 1898*, 333.

19 Hofstadter, *Paranoid Style of American Politics*, 167.

20 Weinberg, *Manifest Destiny*, 189.

21 "The War with Spain and After," *Literary Digest*, 11 June 1898, 695.

22 *War Poems of 1898*, compiled by the California Club, 122–23.

23 Andrews to John Davis Long, 29 July 1898, JDLP, General Correspondence, box 43.

24 Dunne, *Mr. Dooley in Peace and in War*, 43.

25 Thomas Talbot to Long, 30 July 1898, in JDLP, General Correspondence, box 43.

26 Olcott, *Life of William McKinley*, 2:62.

27 Cortissoz, *Life of Whitelaw Reid*, 2:255; Contosta and Hawthorne, *Rise to World Power*, 43.

28 Lodge to "James," 15 August 1898, HCLP, General Correspondence, box 13. In a letter contained in the folder marked "Unidentified," Lodge wrote: "The close of the war, as you say, opens up some very grave problems. The administration is evidently hesitating as to how much it shall hold in the Philippines, but I trust they will retain enough there to give us a foothold for trade. I do not think we ought to part with Manila, which is really the great prize, and which we have fairly won."

29 Coolidge to Lodge, 27 July 1898, HCLP, General Correspondence, box 13.

30 Lodge to McKinley, 30 July 1898, GBCP, box 56.

31 Lewis Gould, *Presidency of William McKinley*, 129, 137.

32 Gould, *Spanish-American War and President McKinley*, 63.

33 Ibid.; Henry Morgan, *William McKinley and His America*, 397.

34 "Papers Relating to the Treaty with Spain," Senate Document no. 148, 56th Cong., 2d sess., 16, 17.

35 *FRUS*, 1898, 907; Senate Document no. 148, 6.

36 *FRUS*, 1898, 907; Senate Document no. 148, 7; emphasis added.

37 *FRUS*, 1898, 908; Senate Document no. 148, 8.

38 Ephraim Smith, " 'A Question from Which We Could Not Escape,' " 371–72.

39 *FRUS*, 1898, 918–22, 925–27; Senate Document no. 148, 18–21, 24–26.

40 The most reliable piece of evidence documenting McKinley's thinking and reasoning comes from the record of an interview that took place in the White House on 19 November 1898. It read in part: "On the question of the Philippines the President said that he had given the subject most careful and conscientious and profound consideration and that he was unable to arrive at any other conclusion than that we must keep all the islands; that we could not give them back to Spain, for the very reasons which justified the war that would be impossible; that we could not give them or dispose of them to any European power for we should have a war on our hands in fifteen minutes, and furthermore why should that be done; the only reason would be to escape responsibility for our own acts and that we could not do; our duty and destiny demanded that we undertake our own responsibilities and the people should not be alarmed or anxious about their ability to fulfill their obligations." McKinley was also greatly impressed by the peculiar geography of the Philippines and the strategic issues that demanded he take more than he would have preferred: "He [the president] spoke of the peculiar formation of the islands which were often separated only by a narrow strip of water and consequently if only one of the islands were kept and the rest

returned, which was one of the possible alternatives proposed, we should then have a hostile territory, over which we had no control, literally within a stones [*sic*] throw of us and that seemed in itself, apart from other considerations of which there were many, to be sufficient to prevent that disposition of them." Ephraim Smith, " 'A Question from Which We Could Not Escape,' " 369.

41 In this light, Lodge's letter gains significance. The president not only received information on the public mind but also appears to have sought it out for himself. The magazine *Public Opinion* reported that after the war broke out the president would sit "hour after hour listening to this or that man, gauging the rise and fall of public opinion." The magazine added proudly: "President Mc-Kinley has been a subscriber for PUBLIC OPINION since November 1892. The last renewal of his subscription was received on November 26, 1897." The announcement would appear to be merely self-serving if not for the precise dates given for the president's long-standing subscription. *Public Opinion*, 14 July 1898, 40.

42 McKinley, *Speeches and Addresses of William McKinley*, 84–154.

43 Samuels, *Letters of Henry Adams*, 2:622.

44 Carnegie to Hay, 24 November 1898, John Hay Papers, Library of Congress, Washington, D.C., reel 6.

45 *FRUS*, 1898, 935.

46 Ibid.

47 Sinkler, *Racial Attitudes of American Presidents*, 369; Lewis Gould, *Presidency of William McKinley*, 28, 29.

48 Lewis Gould, *Presidency of William McKinley*, 101.

49 Carnegie, "Distant Possessions," 239–48; *North American Review* 167 (November 1898): 619–24; *The Nation*, 3 November 1898, 323.

50 *The Nation*, 3 November 1898, 362.

51 Quotations here and in paragraph below from Bancroft, *Schurz*, 5:480–81, 483, 484, 6:1–9.

52 "The Future Foreign Policy of the United States," *American Federationist* 5 (September 1898): 136–40.

53 Ibid., 138.

54 Ibid., 139.

55 John Morgan, "What Shall We Do with the Conquered Islands?" 641–49.

56 Ibid., 643, 644.

57 Ibid., 642, 643, 644, 647.

58 *Congressional Record*, 55th Cong., 3d sess., 20, 92.

59 Ibid., 94.

60 Ibid.

61 Ibid., 291.

62 Ibid., 291–92.

63 Ibid., 295.

64 Ibid., 326, 327.

65 Ibid., 436.

66 Ibid., 561.

67 Ibid., 639.

68 Ibid.

69 Ibid., 639, 640.

70 Ibid., 837.

71 Ibid.

72 Ibid., 837–38.

73 Quotations here and in the following three paragraphs are from Ibid., 959.

74 Ibid., 1479.

75 Colletta, *William Jennings Bryan*, 236.

76 Pettigrew, *Imperial Washington*, 192.

EPILOGUE

1 Fussell, *The Great War and Modern Memory*, 7.

2 Morison, *The Letters of Theodore Roosevelt*, 1:637.

3 Gwynn, *Letters and Friendships of Sir Cecil Spring Rice*, 1:442–43.

Bibliography

MANUSCRIPT COLLECTIONS

Boston, Mass.
   Massachusetts Historical Society
      Charles Francis Adams Jr. Papers
      George Frisbie Hoar Papers
      Henry Cabot Lodge Papers
      John Davis Long Papers
      Moorefield Storey Papers

Cambridge, Mass.
   Houghton Library, Harvard University
      Charles Sumner Papers

Honolulu, Hawaii
   Hawaiian Historical Society
      Sanford Dole Papers

Washington, D.C.
   Library of Congress
      Nelson W. Aldrich Papers
      American Colonization Society Papers
      American Federation of Labor Papers
      Chester A. Arthur Papers
      Nathaniel P. Banks Papers

Albert J. Beveridge Papers
Benjamin Butler Papers
Simon Cameron Papers
Grover Cleveland Papers
George B. Cortelyou Papers
Hamilton Fish Papers
John W. Foster Papers
Ulysses S. Grant Papers
Horace Greeley Papers
Walter Q. Gresham Papers
Benjamin Harrison Papers
Rutherford B. Hayes Papers
Andrew Johnson Papers
William McKinley Papers
Justin Morrill Papers
Richard Olney Papers
Whitelaw Reid Papers
Theodore Roosevelt Papers
Elihu Root Papers
Carl Schurz Papers
William Henry Seward Papers
Elihu Washburn Papers

NEWSPAPERS AND MAGAZINES

American Monthly Review of Reviews
Atlantic Monthly
Century Magazine
DeBow's Review
Forum
Harper's Weekly
Lippincott's Magazine
Literary Digest
Littell's Living Age
London Spectator
The Nation
New National Era
New York Evening Post
New York Herald
New York Sun

New York Times
New York Tribune
North American Review
Public Opinion
Southern Workman
Workingman's Advocate

PUBLISHED SOURCES

Abrahamson, James L. *America Arms for a New Century: The Making of a Great Military Power*. New York: Free Press, 1981.

Adams, Charles Francis, ed. *Memoirs of John Quincy Adams*. Vol. 11. Philadelphia: J. B. Lippincott and Company, 1876.

Adams, Charles Francis, Jr. *Lee at Appomattox and Other Papers*. Boston: Houghton Mifflin, 1902.

Adams, Henry. *The Education of Henry Adams*. New York: Oxford University Press, 1999.

——. "The Session." *North American Review* 61 (1870): 54–67.

An Address by the Hawaiian Branches of the Sons of the American Revolution, Sons of Veterans, and the Grand Army of the Republic to Their Compatriots in America Concerning the Annexation of Hawaii. Washington, D.C.: Gibson Brothers, 1897.

Albright, Robert Edwin. "Politics and Public Opinion in the Western Statehood Movement of the 1880s." *Pacific Historical Review* 3 (September 1934): 296–306.

Ali, Mehmed. "Ho'ohui'aina Pala K Mai'a: Remembering Annexation One Hundred Years Ago." *Hawaiian Journal of History* 32 (1998): 141–54.

Allen, Helena G. *Sanford Ballard Dole: Hawaii's Only President, 1844–1926*. Glendale: Arthur H. Clark Company, 1988.

Anderson, Eric, and Alfred A. Moss Jr. *The Facts of Reconstruction: Essays in Honor of John Hope Franklin*. Baton Rouge: Louisiana State University Press, 1991.

Anderson, Rufus. *The Hawaiian Islands: Their Progress and Condition under Missionary Labors*. Boston: Gould and Lincoln, 1865.

——. *History of the Sandwich Islands Mission*. Boston: Congregational Publications Society, 1870.

Appel, John C. "American Labor and the Annexation of Hawaii." *Pacific Historical Review* 23 (February 1954): 1–18.

Archdeacon, Thomas J. *Becoming American: An Ethnic History*. New York: Free Press, 1983.

Archibald, Douglas. "Why Not Annex Hawaii?" *English Illustrated Magazine* 17 (April 1897): 499–502.

Armstrong, William M. *E. L. Godkin and American Foreign Policy, 1865–1900*. New York: Bookman Associates, 1957.

Bailey, Thomas. "America's Emergence as a World Power: The Myth and the Verity." *Pacific Historical Review* 30 (February 1961): 1–16.

———. "Japan's Protest against the Annexation of Hawaii." *Journal of Modern History* 3 (March 1931): 46–61.

———. "Why the United States Purchased Alaska." *Pacific Historical Review* 3 (March 1934): 39–49.

Baker, George W., Jr. "Benjamin Harrison and Hawaiian Annexation: A Re-Interpretation." *Pacific Historical Review* 33 (August 1964): 295–316.

Bancroft, Frederic. *The Life of William H. Seward*. New York: Harper and Brothers, 1900.

———. "Seward's Ideas of Territorial Expansion." *North American Review* 167 (July 1898): 79–89.

Bancroft, George, ed. *Speeches, Correspondence, and Political Papers of Carl Schurz*. 6 vols. New York: G. P. Putnam's Sons, 1913.

Barrows, Chester Leonard. *William M. Evarts: Lawyer, Diplomat, Statesman*. Chapel Hill: University of North Carolina Press, 1941.

Beechert, Edward W. *Working in Hawaii: A Labor History*. Honolulu: University of Hawaii Press, 1985.

Beisner, Robert L. *From the Old Diplomacy to the New*. Arlington Heights: Harlan Davidson, 1986.

———. "Thirty Years before Manila: E. L. Godkin, Carl Schurz, and Anti-Imperialism in the Gilded Age." *Historian* 30 (August 1968): 561–77.

———. *Twelve against Empire: The Anti-Imperialists, 1898–1900*. New York: McGraw-Hill, 1968.

Bellwood, Peter. *The Polynesians: Prehistory of an Island People*. London: Thames and Hudson, 1987.

Bemis, Samuel Flagg, ed. *The American Secretaries of State and Their Diplomacy*. Vols. 8 and 9. New York: Alfred A. Knopf, 1928.

Benedict, Michael Les. "Preserving the Constitution: The Conservative Basis of Racial Reconstruction." *Journal of American History* 61 (June 1974): 65–90.

Bingham, Hiram. *A Residence of Twenty-One Years in the Sandwich Islands*. Canandaigua: H. D. Goodwin, 1848.

Bird, Isabella. *Six Months in the Sandwich Islands*. London: John Murray, 1881.

Bishop, Sereno E. "Her Majesty 'Lily-of-the-Sky,' Queen of the Sandwich Islands." *Review of Reviews* 4 (September 1892): 227–33.

Blaine, James G. *Political Discussions: Legislative, Diplomatic, and Popular, 1856–1886*. Norwich: Henry Bill Publishing Company, 1887.

———. *Twenty Years in Congress*. Norwich: Henry Bill, 1884.

Bliss, William R. *Paradise in the Pacific: A Book of Travel, Adventure, and Facts in the Sandwich Islands*. New York: Sheldon and Company, 1873.

Bradley, Harold W. *The American Frontier in Hawaii: The Pioneers, 1789–1843*. Stanford: Stanford University Press, 1942.

Breen, T. H., and Stephen Innes. *"Myne Owne Ground": Race and Freedom on Virginia's Eastern Shore, 1640–1676*. New York: Oxford University Press, 1980.

Bryan, William Jennings. *The Memoirs of William Jennings Bryan*. Philadelphia: United Publishers of America, 1925.

Bryce, James. *The American Commonwealth*. Chicago: Charles H. Sergel and Company, 1891.

———. "The Policy of Annexation for America." *Forum* 24 (December 1897): 388–94.

Buck, Paul H. *The Road to Reunion, 1865–1900*. Boston: Little, Brown and Company, 1937.

Budnick, Richard. *Stolen Kingdom: An American Conspiracy*. Honolulu: Aloha Press, 1992.

Bulmer, Martin, and John Solomos, eds. *Racism*. New York: Oxford University Press, 1999.

Bundy, William P., ed. *Two Hundred Years of American Foreign Policy*. New York: New York University Press, 1977.

Burgess, John W. "The Decision of the Supreme Court in the Insular Cases." *Political Science Quarterly* 16 (1901): 478–88.

Calhoun, Charles W. *Gilded Age Cato: The Life of Walter Q. Gresham*. Louisville: University Press of Kentucky, 1988.

———. "Morality and Spite: Walter Q. Gresham and U.S. Relations with Hawaii." *Pacific Historical Review* 52 (August 1983): 292–311.

Cambiera, Alan. *Quisueya la Bella: The Dominican Republic in Historical and Cultural Perspective*. Armonk: M. E. Sharpe, 1997.

Campbell, Charles S. *The Transformation of American Foreign Relations, 1865–1900*. New York: Harper and Row, 1976.

Carnegie, Andrew. "Distant Possession—the Parting of the Ways." *North American Review* 167 (August 1898): 239–48.

Carter, Charles L. *The Hawaiian Question: An Open Letter to Secretary Gresham, by Ex-Commissioner Charles L. Carter*. Honolulu: Star Publishing, 1893.

Cashman, Sean Dennis. *America in the Gilded Age*. New York: New York University Press, 1993.

Castel, Albert. *The Presidency of Andrew Johnson*. Lawrence: Regents Press of Kansas, 1979.

Castle, Alfred L. "Advice for Hawaii: The Dole-Burgess Letters." *Hawaiian Journal of History* 15 (1981): 24–30.

———. "Tentative Empire: Walter Q. Gresham, U.S. Foreign Policy, and Hawai'i, 1893–1895." *Hawaiian Journal of History* 29 (1995): 83–96.

Challener, Richard D. *Admirals, Generals, and American Foreign Policy, 1898–1914.* Princeton: Princeton University Press, 1973.

Chapin, James B. "Hamilton Fish and American Expansionism." In *Makers of American Diplomacy from Benjamin Franklin to Henry Kissinger*, edited by Frank J. Merli and Theodore Wilson, 223–51. New York: Charles Scribner's Sons, 1974.

Clark, Dan E. "Manifest Destiny and the Pacific." *Pacific Historical Review* 1 (March 1932): 1–17.

Cohen, Bernard C. *The Press and Foreign Policy*. Princeton: Princeton University Press, 1963.

——. *The Public's Impact on Foreign Policy*. New York: Little, Brown, and Company, 1973.

Colletta, Paolo E. *William Jennings Bryan: Political Evangelist, 1860–1908*. Lincoln: University of Nebraska Press, 1964.

Commanger, Henry Steele. *The American Mind: An Interpretation of American Thought and Character since the 1880s*. New Haven: Yale University Press, 1950.

Conroy, Hilary. *The Japanese Frontier in Hawaii, 1868–1898*. Berkeley: University of California Press, 1953.

Contosta, David N., and Jessica R. Hawthorne, eds. *Rise to World Power: Selected Letters of Whitelaw Reid, 1895–1912*. Philadelphia: American Philosophical Society, 1986.

Cooley, Thomas. "Grave Obstacles to Hawaiian Annexation." *Forum* 15 (June 1893): 389–406.

Coolidge, Louis A. *Ulysses S. Grant*. Boston: Houghton Mifflin Company, 1917.

Cortissoz, Royal. *The Life of Whitelaw Reid*. 2 vols. New York: Charles Scribner's Sons, 1921.

Corwin, Richard. *The President: Office and Powers, 1787–1948*. New York: New York University Press, 1948.

Cox, John H., and Lawanda Cox. "Negro Suffrage and Republican Politics: The Problem of Motivation in Reconstruction Historiography." *Journal of Southern History* 33 (August 1967): 303–30.

——. *Politics, Principle, and Prejudice, 1865–1876: Dilemma of Reconstruction America*. New York: Free Press of Glencoe, 1963.

Craft, Mable. *Hawaii Nei*. San Francisco: William Doxey, 1899.

Cralle, Richard K., ed. *The Works of John C. Calhoun*. New York: D. Appleton and Company, 1883.

Crapol, Edward. *America for Americans: Economic Nationalism and Anglophobia in the Late Nineteenth Century*. Westport: Greenwood Press, 1973.

——. "Coming to Terms with Empire: The Historiography of Late-Nineteenth Century American Foreign Relations." *Diplomatic History* 16 (Fall 1992): 273–397.

——, ed. *Women and American Foreign Policy: Lobbyists, Critics, and Insiders*. Wilmington: Scholarly Resources, 1992.

Crosby, Alfred W. *Ecological Imperialism: The Biological Expansion of Europe, 900–1900*. Cambridge: Cambridge University Press, 1986.

Crowley, Herbert. *The Promise of American Life*. New York: Macmillan Company, 1909.

Curry, Leonard. *Blueprint for Modern America: Non-Military Legislation of the First Civil War Congress*. Nashville: Vanderbilt University Press, 1968.

Curry, Richard O., ed. *Radicalism, Racism, and Party Alignment: The Border States during Reconstruction*. Baltimore: Johns Hopkins University Press, 1969.

Damon, Ethel M. *Sanford Ballard Dole and His Hawaii*. Palo Alto: Pacific Books, 1957.

Daniels, Roger. *The Politics of Prejudice: The Anti-Japanese Movement in California and the Struggle for Japanese Exclusion*. Berkeley: University of California Press, 1977.

Daniels, Roger, and Otis L. Graham, eds. *Debating American Immigration, 1882–Present*. Lanham: Rowman and Littlefield Publishers, 2001.

Davis, Gavan. *Shoal of Time: A History of the Hawaiian Islands*. Honolulu: University of Hawaii Press, 1968.

DeConde, Alexander, and Armin Rappaport, eds. *Essays Diplomatic and Undiplomatic of Thomas A. Bailey*. New York: Appleton-Century-Crofts, 1969.

Degler, Carl N. "Black and White Together: Bi-Racial Politics in the South." *Virginia Quarterly Review* 47 (Summer 1971): 421–444.

Dennis, Alfred M. P. *Adventures in American Diplomacy, 1896–1906*. New York: E. P. Dutton and Company, 1928.

DeSantis, Vincent. "President Hayes Southern Policy." *Journal of Southern History* 21 (November 1955): 476–94.

Devine, Michael J. *John W. Foster: Politics and Diplomacy in the Imperial Era, 1873–1917*. Athens: Ohio University Press, 1981.

——. "John W. Foster and the Struggle for the Annexation of Hawaii." *Pacific Historical Review* 46 (February 1977): 29–50.

Doenecke, Justus D. *The Presidencies of James A. Garfield and Chester A. Arthur*. Lawrence: Regents Press of Kansas, 1981.

Donald, David. *Charles Sumner and the Rights of Man*. New York: Alfred A. Knopf, 1970.

——. *Lincoln*. New York: Simon and Schuster, 1995.

Douglass, Frederick. *Life and Times of Frederick Douglass*. In *Douglass: Autobiographies*. New York: Library of America, 1994.

Dozer, Donald. "Anti-Expansionism during the Johnson Administration." *Pacific Historical Review* 12 (September 1943): 253–75.

Duara, Prasenjit. *Rescuing History from the Nation*. Chicago: University of Chicago Press, 1995.

Du Bois, William Edward Burghardt. *Black Reconstruction in America, 1860–1880*. New York: Atheneum, 1992.

Dulles, Foster Rhea. *America's Rise to World Power, 1898–1954*. New York: Harper and Row, 1954.

——. *The Imperial Years*. New York: Thomas Y. Crowell Company, 1956.

——. *Prelude to World Power: American Diplomatic History, 1860–1900*. New York: Macmillan, 1965.

Dunne, Finley Peter. *Mr. Dooley at His Best*. New York: Charles Scribner's Sons, 1938.

——. *Mr. Dooley in Peace and in War*. Boston: Small, Maynard, and Company, 1899.

Dyer, Brainerd. "The Persistence of the Idea of Negro Colonization." *Pacific Historical Review* 12 (March 1943): 53–65.

——. "Robert J. Walker on Acquiring Greenland and Iceland." *Mississippi Valley Historical Review* 27 (September 1940): 263–66.

Dyer, Thomas G. *Theodore Roosevelt and the Idea of Race*. Baton Rouge: Louisiana State University Press, 1980.

Ellis, William. *The American Mission in the Sandwich Islands*. Honolulu: H. M. Whitney, 1866.

Faulkner, Harold U. *Politics, Reform, and Expansion: 1890–1900*. New York: Harper and Row, 1959.

Ferrell, Robert. *American Diplomacy*. New York: W. W. Norton, 1969.

Field, James A., Jr. "American Imperialism: The Worst Chapter in Almost Any Book." *American Historical Review* 83 (June 1978): 644–83.

——. "Novus Ordo Seclorum." *Diplomatic History* 13 (Winter 1989): 113–22.

Fishel, Leslie H. "The Negro in Northern Politics, 1870–1900." *Mississippi Valley Historical Review* 42 (December 1955): 466–89.

——. "Northern Prejudice and Negro Suffrage, 1865–1870." *Journal of Negro History* 39 (January 1954): 8–26.

Fiske, John. *American Political Ideas from the Standpoint of Universal History*. New York: Harper and Brothers, 1885.

Foner, Eric. *Politics and Ideology in the Age of the Civil War*. New York: Oxford University Press, 1980.

——. *Reconstruction: America's Unfinished Revolution, 1863–1877*. New York: Harper and Row, 1988.

Foner, Philip. *Frederick Douglass*. New York: Citadel Press, 1964.

——. *The Spanish-Cuban-American War and the Birth of American Imperialism, 1895–1902*. New York: Monthly Review Press, 1972.

——, ed. *The Life and Writings of Frederick Douglass*. Vol. 4. New York: International Publishers, 1964.

——. *The Life and Writings of Frederick Douglass*. Vol. 5. New York: International Publishers, 1975.

Foster, John W. *American Diplomacy in the Orient*. Boston: Houghton Mifflin, 1904.

——. *A Century of American Diplomacy*. Boston: Houghton, Mifflin and Company, 1900.

——. *Diplomatic Memoirs*. 2 vols. Boston: Houghton Mifflin, 1909.

Fredrickson, George. *The Arrogance of Race: Historical Perspectives on Slavery, Racism, and Social Inequality*. Middletown: Wesleyan University Press, 1988.

——. *The Black Image in the White Mind: The Debate on Afro-American Character and Destiny, 1817–1914*. New York: Harper and Row, 1971.

——. *Racism: A Short History*. Princeton: Princeton University Press, 2002.

Freehling, William. "The Founding Fathers and Slavery." *American Historical Review* 77 (February 1972): 81–93.

Fry, Joseph A. *John Tyler Morgan and the Search for Southern Autonomy*. Knoxville: University of Tennessee Press, 1992.

——. "William McKinley and the Coming of the Spanish-American War: A Study in the Besmirching of an Historical Image." *Diplomatic History* 3 (Winter 1979): 77–97.

Fuess, Claude. *Carl Schurz: Reformer*. New York: Kennikat Press, 1963.

Fussell, Paul. *The Great War and Modern Memory*. New York: Oxford University Press, 2000.

Gaines, Kevin K. "Black Americans' Racial Uplift Ideology as 'Civilizing Mission': Pauline E. Hopkins on Race and Imperialism." In *Cultures of United States Imperialism*, edited by Amy Kaplan and Donald E. Pease, 433–55. Durham: Duke University Press, 1993.

——. *Uplifting the Race: Black Leadership, Politics, and Culture in the Twentieth Century*. Chapel Hill: University of North Carolina Press, 1996.

Gara, Larry. *The Presidency of Franklin Pierce*. Lawrence: University Press of Kansas, 1991.

Garraty, John A. *Henry Cabot Lodge: A Biography*. New York: Alfred A. Knopf, 1953.

——. *The New Commonwealth, 1877–1890*. New York: Harper and Row, 1968.

Gatewood, Willard. *Black Americans and the White Man's Burden, 1898–1903*. Urbana: University of Illinois Press, 1975.

Gillette, William. *Retreat from Reconstruction, 1869–1879*. Baton Rouge: Louisiana State University Press, 1979.

Gossett, Thomas F. *Race: This History of an Idea in America*. New York: Oxford University Press, 1987.

Gould, Lewis L. *The Presidency of William McKinley*. Lawrence: University of Kansas Press, 1980.

——. *The Spanish-American War and President McKinley*. Lawrence: University Press of Kansas, 1982.

Gould, Stephen Jay. *The Mismeasure of Man*. New York: W. W. Norton, 1996.

Graebner, Norman A. *Empire on the Pacific: A Study in American Continental Expansion*. Claremont: Regina Books, 1983.

——. *Foundations of American Foreign Policy: A Realist Appraisal from Franklin to McKinley*. Wilmington: Scholarly Resources, 1985.

Grant, Jesse R. *In the Days of My Father General Grant*. New York: Harper and Brothers, 1925.

Grant, Ulysses. *Personal Memoirs*. New York: Library of America, 1990.

Grenville, J. A. S., and George Berkeley Young. *Politics, Strategy, and American Diplomacy: Studies in Foreign Policy*. New Haven: Yale University Press, 1966.

Gresham, Matilda. *Life of Walter Quintin Gresham, 1832–1895*. 2 vols. Chicago: Rand McNally and Company, 1919.

Gwynn, Stephen. *The Letters and Friendships of Sir Cecil Spring Rice*. Boston: Houghton Mifflin Company, 1929.

Haines, Gerald K., and J. Samuel Walker. *American Foreign Relations: A Historiographical Review*. Westport: Greenwood Press, 1981.

Hamilton, Gail. *Biography of James G. Blaine*. Norwich: Henry Bill Publishing Company, 1895.

Hamilton, Michael P. *American Character and Foreign Policy*. Grand Rapids: William B. Eerdmans Publishing Company, 1986.

Handlin, Oscar. *Race and Nationality in American Life*. New York: Doubleday, 1957.

Harlan, Louis. *Booker T. Washington: The Making of a Black Leader, 1856–1901*. New York: Oxford University Press, 1972.

——. "Booker T. Washington and the White Man's Burden." *American Historical Review* 71 (January 1966): 441–67.

Hays, Samuel P. *The Response to Industrialism, 1885–1914*. Chicago: University of Chicago Press, 1957.

Head, Morrell. "Business Attitudes towards European Immigration, 1880–1900." *Journal of Economic History* 44 (Summer 1953): 291–304.

Heald, Morrell, and Lawrence S. Kaplan. *Culture and Diplomacy*. Westport: Greenwood Press, 1977.

Healy, David. *U.S. Expansionism: The Expansionist Urge in the 1890s*. Madison: University of Wisconsin Press, 1970.

Hellwig, David J. "Building a Black Nation: The Role of Immigrants in the Thought and Rhetoric of Booker T. Washington." *Mississippi Quarterly* 31 (Fall 1978): 529–50.

Hesseltine, William B. *Ulysses S. Grant: Politician*. New York: Dodd, Mead and Company, 1935.

Hinsdale, Burke A., ed. *The Works of James Abram Garfield*. 2 vols. Boston: James R. Osgood and Company, 1883.

Hirschfeld, Charles. "Brooks Adams and American Nationalism." *American Historical Review* 69 (January 1964): 371–92.

Hirshon, Stanley P. *Farewell to the Bloody Shirt: Northern Republicans and the Southern Negro, 1877–1893*. Bloomington: Indiana University Press, 1962.

Hoar, George Frisbie. *Autobiography of Seventy Years*. 2 vols. London: Bickers and Son, 1904.

Hobsbawm, Eric. *The Age of Capital, 1848–1875*. New York: Vintage Books, 1987.
——. *The Age of Empire, 1875–1914*. New York: Vintage Books, 1987.
Hofstadter, Richard. *Social Darwinism in American Thought*. Boston: Beacon Press, 1992.
——. *The Paranoid Style of American Politics and Other Essays*. Chicago: University of Chicago Press, 1964.
Hoganson, Kristin. *Fighting for American Manhood*. New Haven: Yale University Press, 1998.
Holbo, Paul S. "Presidential Leadership in Foreign Affairs: William McKinley and the Turpie-Foraker Amendment." *American Historical Review* 72 (July 1967): 1321–35.
——. *Tarnished Expansion: The Alaska Scandal, the Press, and Congress, 1867–1871*. Knoxville: University of Tennessee Press, 1983.
Holt, W. Stull. *Treaties Defeated by the Senate: A Study in the Struggle between President and Senate over the Conduct of Foreign Relations*. Baltimore: Johns Hopkins University Press, 1933.
Horne, Gerald. "Race from Power: U.S. Foreign Policy and the General Crisis of 'White Supremacy.'" *Diplomatic History* 23 (Summer 1999): 437–61.
Horsman, Reginald. *Race and Manifest Destiny*. Cambridge: Harvard University Press, 1981.
Ignatiev, Noel. *How the Irish Became White*. New York: Routledge, 1995.
Iriye, Akira. *Across the Pacific: An Inner History of American–East Asian Relations*. New York: Harcourt, Brace and World, 1967.
——. "Imperialism and Sincerity." *Reviews in American History* 1 (March 1973): 119–25.
Israel, Jerry. "The Old Empire." *Reviews in American History* 10 (March 1981): 95–99.
Jensen, Ronald J. *The Alaska Purchase and Russian-American Relations*. Seattle: University of Washington Press, 1975.
Josephson, Matthew. *The Politicos: 1865–1896*. New York: Harcourt, Brace and Company, 1938.
Kaczorowski, Robert J. "To Begin the Nation Anew: Congress, Citizenship, and Civil Rights after the Civil War." *American Historical Review* 92 (February 1987): 45–68.
Keller, Morton. *Affairs of State: Public Life in Late Nineteenth Century America*. Cambridge: Harvard University Press, Belknap Press, 1977.
Kennan, George F. *American Diplomacy*. Chicago: University of Chicago Press, 1984.
Keyssar, Alexander. *The Right to Vote: The Contested History of Democracy in the United States*. New York: Basic Books, 2000.
Kleppner, Paul. *Who Voted? The Dynamics of Electoral Turnout, 1870–1980*. New York: Praeger Publishers, 1982.
Knight, Franklin W., and Colin Palmer, eds. *The Modern Caribbean*. Chapel Hill: University of North Carolina Press, 1989.

Kohlsaat, H. H. *From McKinley to Harding: Personal Recollections of Our Presidents*. New York: Charles Scribner's Sons, 1923.

Koht, Halvdan. "The Origins of Seward's Plan to Purchase the Danish West Indies." *American Historical Review* 50 (July 1945): 762–67.

Kuykendall, Ralph S. *Hawaii: A History from Polynesian Kingdom to American Commonwealth*. New York: Prentice Hall, 1948.

——. *The Hawaiian Kingdom, 1778–1854: Foundation and Transformation*. Honolulu: University of Hawaii Press, 1938.

——. *The Hawaiian Kingdom, 1854–1874: Twenty Critical Years*. Honolulu: University of Hawaii Press, 1953.

Kuykendall, Ralph, and A. Grove Day. *Hawaii: A History*. New York: Prentice Hall, 1948.

LaFeber, Walter. "The Background of Cleveland's Venezuelan Policy: A Reinterpretation." *American Historical Review* 66 (July 1961): 947–67.

——. *The Cambridge History of American Foreign Relations*. Vol. 2, *The American Search for Opportunity, 1865–1913*. Cambridge: Cambridge University Press, 1993.

——. *The New Empire: An Interpretation of American Expansion, 1860–1898*. Ithaca: Cornell University Press, 1963.

Lander, Ernest McPherson, Jr. *Reluctant Imperialists: Calhoun, the South Carolinians, and the Mexican War*. Baton Rouge: Louisiana State University Press, 1980.

Langer, William L. "A Critique of Imperialism." *Foreign Affairs* 14 (October 1935): 102–19.

Lasch, Christopher. "The Anti-Imperialists, the Philippines, and the Inequality of Man." *Journal of Southern History* 24 (August 1954): 319–31.

Learned, H. Barrett. "William Learned Marcy." In *American Secretaries of State and Their Diplomacy*, edited by Samuel Flagg Bemis, 6:144–294. New York: Alfred A. Knopf, 1928.

Lemert, Charles, ed. *Social Theory*. Boulder: Westview Press, 1999.

Lewis, Elsie M. "The Political Mind of the Negro, 1865–1900." *Journal of Southern History* 21 (May 1955): 189–202.

Lewis, Gordon K. *Puerto Rico: Freedom and Power in the Caribbean*. New York: M. R. Press, 1963.

Liliuokalani. *Hawaii's Story by Hawaii's Queen*. Rutland: Charles Tuttle and Company, 1964.

Lincoln, Abraham. *Speeches and Writings, 1859–1865*. New York: Library of America, 1989.

Livermore, Seward. "American Strategy and Diplomacy in the South Pacific." *Pacific Historical Review* 12 (March 1943): 33–51.

Lodge, Henry Cabot. *Certain Accepted Heroes and Other Essays in Literature and Politics*. New York: Harper and Brothers, 1897.

——. "Our Blundering Foreign Policy." *Forum* 19 (March 1895): 8–17.

Maclennan, Carol A. "Hawai'i Turns to Sugar: The Rise of Plantation Centers, 1860–1880." *Hawaiian Journal of History* 31 (1997): 97–126.

Madden, Henry Miller. "Letters of Sanford B. Dole and John Burgess." *Pacific Historical Review* 5 (March 1936): 71–78.

Malcomson, Scott L. *One Drop of Blood: The American Misadventure of Race*. New York: Farrar Straus Giroux, 2000.

Martinez-Fernandez, Luis. *Torn between Empires: Economy, Society, and Patterns of Political Thought in the Hispanic Caribbean, 1840–1878*. Atlanta: University of Georgia Press, 1994.

May, Ernest R. *American Imperialism: A Speculative Essay*. Chicago: Imprint Publications, 1991.

———. *Imperial Democracy: The Emergence of America as a Great Power*. Chicago: Imprint Publications, 1991.

May, Robert E. *The Southern Dream of a Caribbean Empire, 1854–1861*. Athens: University of Georgia Press, 1989.

Mayer, George H. *The Republican Party, 1854–1966*. New York: Oxford University Press, 1967.

McCormick, Richard. "The Party Period of Public Policy: An Exploratory Hypothesis." *Journal of American History* 66 (September 1979): 279–98.

McCormick, Thomas. "Insular Imperialism and the Open Door: The China Market and the Spanish-American War." *Pacific Historical Review* 32 (May 1963): 155–68.

McFeely, William S. *Grant*. New York: W. W. Norton, 1981.

McKinley, William. *The Speeches and Addresses of William McKinley, from March 1, 1897, to May 30, 1900*. New York: Doubleday and McClure, 1900.

McPherson, James M. *The Abolitionist Legacy: From Reconstruction to the NAACP*. Princeton: Princeton University Press, 1975.

———. "Grant or Greely? The Abolitionist Dilemma in the Election of 1872." *American Historical Review* 71 (October 1965): 43–61.

———. *Ordeal by Fire: The Civil War and Reconstruction*. New York: McGraw-Hill, 1992.

———. *The Struggle for Equality: Abolitionists and the Negro in the Civil War and Reconstruction*. Princeton: Princeton University Press, 1964.

McWilliams, Tennant S. "James H. Blount, Paramount Defender of Hawaii." In *The New South Faces the World: Foreign Affairs and the Southern Sense of Self, 1877–1950*, edited by Tennant S. McWilliams, 16–46. Baton Rouge: Louisiana State University Press, 1988.

———. *The New South Faces the World: Foreign Affairs and the Southern Sense of Self, 1877–1950*. Baton Rouge: Louisiana State University Press, 1988.

Merk, Frederick. *Manifest Destiny and Mission in American History*. Cambridge: Harvard University Press, 1963.

Merrill, Horace Samuel. *Bourbon Leader: Grover Cleveland and the Democratic Party*. New York: Little, Brown, and Company, 1957.

Michaels, Walter Benn. "Anti-Imperial Americanism." In *Cultures of United States Imperialism*, edited by Amy Kaplan and Donald E. Pease, 365–91. Durham: Duke University Press, 1993.

Miller, Stuart Creighton. *Benevolent Assimilation: The American Conquest of the Philippines, 1899–1903*. New Haven: Yale University Press, 1982.

Mohr, James C., ed. *Radical Republicans in the North: State Politics during Reconstruction*. Baltimore: Johns Hopkins University Press, 1976.

Montejano, David. *Anglos and Mexicans in the Making of Texas, 1836–1986*. Austin: University of Texas Press, 1987.

Montgomery, Michael. *Imperialist Japan*. London: Christopher Helm, 1987.

Morgan, Henry Wayne. *From Hayes to McKinley: National Party Politics, 1877–1896*. Syracuse: Syracuse University Press, 1969.

——. *William McKinley and His America*. Syracuse: Syracuse University Press, 1963.

——. "William McKinley as a Political Leader." *Review of Politics* 28 (October 1966): 417–32.

Morgan, John T. "What Shall We Do with the Conquered Islands?" *North American Review* 166 (June 1898): 641–49.

Morgan, William Mitchell. "The Anti-Japanese Origins of the Hawaiian Annexation Treaty of 1897." *Diplomatic History* 6 (Winter 1982): 23–44.

Morison, Elting E., ed. *The Letters of Theodore Roosevelt*. 8 vols. Cambridge: Harvard University Press, 1951–54.

Morison, Samuel Eliot, Frederick Merk, and Frank Freidel. *Dissent in Three American Wars*. Cambridge: Harvard University Press, 1970.

Moya Pons, Frank. *The Dominican Republic: A National History*. Princeton: Markus Weiner Publishers, 1998.

Muller, Dorothea R. "Josiah Strong and American Nationalism: A Reevaluation." *Journal of American History* 53 (December 1966): 487–503.

Nevins, Allan. *Grover Cleveland: A Study in Courage*. New York: Dodd, Mead, and Company, 1933.

——, ed. *Hamilton Fish: The Inner History of the Grant Administration*. 2 vols. New York: Frederick Ungar Publishing Company, 1936.

——. *The Letters of Grover Cleveland, 1850–1908*. Boston: Houghton Mifflin, 1933.

Nevins, Allan, and Milton Halsey Thomas, eds. *The Diary of George Templeton Strong: The Post-War Years, 1865–1875*. New York: Macmillan, 1952.

Nichols, Roy Franklin. *Franklin Pierce*. Philadelphia: University of Pennsylvania Press, 1931.

Ninkovich, Frank. "Interests and Discourse in Diplomatic History." *Diplomatic History* 13 (Spring 1989): 135–61.

Ogden, Rollo. *Life and Letters of Edward Lawrence Godkin*. 2 vols. New York: Macmillan, 1907.

Olcott, Charles Sumner. *The Life of William McKinley.* 2 vols. Boston: Houghton Mifflin, 1916.

Osborne, Thomas J. *"Empire Can Wait": American Opposition to Hawaiian Annexation, 1893–1898.* Kent: Kent State University Press, 1981.

———. "Trade or War? America's Annexation of Hawaii Reconsidered." *Pacific Historical Review* 50 (August 1981): 285–307.

Painter, Nell Irvin. *Standing at Armageddon: The United States, 1877–1919.* New York: W. W. Norton, 1987.

Palmer, Beverly Wilson, ed. *The Selected Letters of Charles Sumner.* 2 vols. Boston: Northeastern University Press, 1990.

Parmet, Robert D. *Labor and Immigration in Industrial America.* Boston: Twayne Publishers, 1981.

Patterson, John. "The United States and Hawaiian Reciprocity, 1867–1870." *Pacific Historical Review* 7 (February 1938): 14–26.

Paul, Rodman W. "The Origin of the Chinese Issue in California." *Mississippi Valley Historical Review* 25 (September 1938): 181–96.

Peabody, Andrew. *The Hawaiian Islands, as Developed by Missionary Labors.* Boston: Proprietors of the *Boston Review,* 1865.

Pearce, George F. "Assessing Public Opinion: Editorial Comment and the Annexation of Hawaii—a Case Study." *Pacific Historical Review* 43 (August 1974): 324–41.

Peffer, George Anthony. *If They Don't Bring Their Women Here: Chinese Female Immigration before Exclusion.* Urbana: University of Illinois Press, 1999.

Perez, Louis A., Jr. *Cuba between Empires, 1878–1902.* Pittsburgh: University of Pittsburgh Press, 1983.

———. *The War of 1898: The United States and Cuba in History and Historiography.* Chapel Hill: University of North Carolina Press, 1998.

Perkins, Bradford. *The Cambridge History of American Foreign Relations.* Vol. 1, *The Creation of the American Empire, 1776–1865.* New York: Cambridge University Press, 1993.

———. *The Great Rapprochement: England and the United States, 1895–1914.* New York: Atheneum, 1968.

Perkins, Dexter. *The Monroe Doctrine, 1867–1907.* Baltimore: Johns Hopkins University Press, 1937.

Perret, Geoffrey. *Ulysses S. Grant: Soldier and President.* New York: Random House, 1997.

Peterson, Norma Lois. *The Presidencies of William Henry Harrison and John Tyler.* Lawrence: University Press of Kansas, 1989.

Pettigrew, Richard. *Imperial Washington: The Story of American Public Life from 1870–1920.* Chicago: Arno Press, 1922.

Pierce, Edward L. *Memoir and Letters of Charles Sumner.* 4 vols. Boston: Roberts Brothers, 1893.

Pike, Fredrick B. *The United States and Latin America: Myths and Stereotypes of Civilization and Culture.* Austin: University of Texas Press, 1992.

Plesur, Milton. *America's Outward Thrust: Approaches to Foreign Affairs, 1865–1900.* DeKalb: Northern Illinois University Press, 1971.

Pletcher, David M. *The Awkward Years: American Foreign Relations under Garfield and Arthur.* Columbia: University of Missouri Press, 1962.

——. "Caribbean 'Empire': Planned or Improvised?" *Diplomatic History* 14 (Summer 1990): 447–59.

——. *The Diplomacy of Involvement: American Economic Expansion across the Pacific, 1784–1900.* Columbia: University of Missouri Press, 2001.

——. "Rhetoric and Results: A Pragmatic View of Economic Expansionism, 1865–1898." *Diplomatic History* 5 (Spring 1981): 93–105.

Porter, Kirk H., and Donald Bruce Johnson, eds. *National Party Platforms, 1840–1956.* Urbana: University of Illinois Press, 1956.

Pratt, Julius. *Expansionists of 1898: The Acquisition of Hawaii and the Spanish Islands.* Gloucester: Peter Smith, 1959.

——. "The Hawaiian Revolution: A Re-Interpretation." *Pacific Historical Review* 1 (September 1932): 273–94.

Richardson, Heather Cox. *The Death of Reconstruction.* Cambridge: Harvard University Press, 2001.

Richardson, James D. *A Compilation of the Messages and Papers of the Presidents.* 10 vols. New York: Bureau of National Literature, 1897.

Roberts, J. M. *The Penguin History of Europe.* New York: Penguin Books, 1996.

Robinson, William. *Thomas B. Reed, Parlimentarian.* New York: Dodd, Mead and Company, 1930.

Rodgers, Daniel T. *The Work Ethic in Industrial America, 1850–1920.* Chicago: University of Chicago Press, 1974.

Rodman, Selden. *Quisqueya: A History of the Dominican Republic.* Seattle: University of Washington Press, 1964.

Roediger, David. *Towards the Abolition of Whiteness.* New York: Verso, 1994.

Rostow, Eugene V. *Toward Managed Peace: The National Security Interests of the United States, 1759 to the Present.* New Haven: Yale University Press, 1993.

Rowland, Donald. "The Establishment of the Republic of Hawaii, 1893–1894." *Pacific Historical Review* 4 (September 1935): 201–20.

——. "Orientals and Suffrage in Hawaii." *Pacific Historical Review* 12 (March 1943): 11–21.

Russ, William Adam, Jr. *The Hawaiian Revolution, 1893–94.* Selinsgrove: Susquehanna University Press, 1959.

——. "The Role of Sugar in Hawaiian Annexation." *Pacific Historical Review* 12 (December 1943): 339–50.

Said, Edward. *Culture and Imperialism.* New York: Vintage Books, 1993.

Samuels, Ernest, ed. *The Letters of Henry Adams*. 6 vols. Cambridge: Harvard University Press, Belknap Press, 1982–88.

Saxton, Alexander. *The Indispensable Enemy: Labor and the Anti-Chinese Movement in California*. Berkeley: University of California Press.

——. *The Rise and Fall of the White Republic: Class Politics and Mass Culture in Nineteenth-Century America*. New York: Verso, 1990.

Schulzinger, Robert. *American Diplomacy in the 20th Century*. New York: Oxford University Press, 1994.

Schurz, Carl. *The Reminiscences of Carl Schurz*. 3 vols. New York: Doubleday, Page and Company, 1908.

Seager, Robert, II. *And Tyler Too: A Biography of John and Julia Gardiner Tyler*. New York: McGraw-Hill, 1963.

——. "Some Denominational Reactions to Chinese Immigration in California, 1856–1892." *Pacific Historical Review* 28 (February 1959): 49–66.

——. "Ten Years before Mahan: The Unofficial Case for the New Navy, 1880–1890." *Mississippi Valley Historical Review* 40 (December 1953): 491–512.

Seager, Robert, II, and Doris D. Maguire, eds. *Letters and Papers of Alfred Thayer Mahan*. 2 vols. Annapolis: Naval Institute Press, 1975.

Seward, Frederick W. *Reminiscences of a War-Time Statesman and Diplomat, 1830–1915*. New York: Putnam, 1916.

Shenton, James P. "Imperialism and Racism." In *Essays in American Historiography: Papers Presented in Honor of Allan Nevins*, edited by Donald Sheehan and Harold C. Syrett, 231–50. New York: Columbia University Press, 1960.

Shklar, Judith. *American Citizenship: The Quest for Inclusion*. Cambridge: Harvard University Press, 1991.

"Should Hawaii Be Annexed?" *American Federationist* 4 (November 1897): 215–17.

Silbey, Joel H. *The American Political Nation, 1838–1893*. Stanford: Stanford University Press, 1991.

Simon, John Y., ed. *The Papers of Ulysses S. Grant*. 26 vols. to date. Carbondale: Southern Illinois University Press, 1967–.

Sinkler, George. *The Racial Attitudes of American Presidents from Abraham Lincoln to Theodore Roosevelt*. Garden City: Anchor Books, 1972.

Smith, Ephraim K. " 'A Question from Which We Could Not Escape': William McKinley and the Decision to Acquire the Philippine Islands." *Diplomatic History* 9 (Fall 1985): 363–75.

——. "William McKinley's Enduring Legacy: The Historiographical Debate on the Taking of the Philippine Islands." In *Crucible of Empire: The Spanish-American War and Its Aftermath*, edited by James C. Bradford, 205–49. Annapolis: Naval Institute Press, 1993.

Smith, Jean Edward. *Grant*. New York: Simon and Schuster, 2001.

Smith, Theodore Clarke. "Expansion after the Civil War, 1865–1871." *Political Science Quarterly* 16 (1901): 412–36.

——. *The Life and Letters of James Abram Garfield*. 2 vols. New Haven: Yale University Press, 1925.

Socolofsky, Homer E., and Allan B. Spetter. *The Presidency of Benjamin Harrison*. Lawrence: University Press of Kansas, 1987.

Sons of the American Revolution. *An Address by the Hawaiian Branches of the Sons of the American Revolution, Sons of Veterans, and the Grand Army of the Republic to their Compatriots in America Concerning the Annexation of Hawaii*. Washington, D.C.: Gibson Brothers, 1897.

Spoehr, Luther W. "Sambo and the Heathen Chinee: Californians' Racial Stereotypes in the Late 1870s." *Pacific Historical Review* 42 (May 1973): 185–204.

Sprout, Harold, and Margaret Sprout. *The Rise of American Naval Power, 1776–1918*. Princeton: Princeton University Press, 1939.

Stampp, Kenneth. *The Era of Reconstruction, 1865–1877*. New York: Alfred A. Knopf, 1966.

Stannard, David E. *Before the Horror: The Population of Hawai'i on the Eve of Western Contact*. Honolulu: Social Science Research Institute, University of Hawaii, 1989.

Stanton, William. *The Leopard's Spots: Scientific Attitudes toward Race in America, 1815–59*. Chicago: University of Chicago Press, 1960.

Stevens, Sylvester. *American Expansion in Hawaii, 1842–1898*. Harrisburg: Archives Publishing Company, 1945.

Stoddard, Henry L. *As I Knew Them: Presidents and Politics from Grant to Coolidge*. New York: Harper and Row, 1927.

Stoler, Mark A. *George Marshall: Soldier-Statesman of the American Century*. Boston: Twayne Publishers, 1989.

Storey, Moorefield. *Charles Sumner*. Boston: Houghton Mifflin Company, 1900.

——. *Ebenezer Rockwell Hoar: A Memoir*. Boston: Houghton Mifflin Company, 1911.

Sumner, Charles. *Works*. Boston: Lee and Shepard, 1900.

Takaki, Ronald. *Strangers from a Different Shore: A History of Asian Americans*. New York: Penguin Books, 1989.

Tansill, Charles C. *The Foreign Policy of Thomas F. Bayard, 1855–1897*. New York: Fordham University Press, 1940.

——. *The Purchase of the Danish West Indies*. Baltimore: Johns Hopkins University Press, 1932.

——. *The United States and Santo Domingo, 1798–1873*. Gloucester: Peter Smith, 1967.

Tate, Marze. "Great Britain and the Sovereignty of Hawaii." *Pacific Historical Review* 31 (November 1962): 327–48.

——. *Hawaii: Reciprocity or Annexation*. East Lansing: Michigan State University Press, 1968.

Terrell, John. *Prehistory in the Pacific Islands: A Study of Variation in Language, Customs, and Human Biology*. Cambridge: Cambridge University Press, 1986.

Thurston, Lorrin. *A Handbook on the Annexation of Hawaii*. St. Joseph, Mich.: A. B. Morse, 1897.

Tompkins, E. Berkeley. *Anti-Imperialism in the United States: The Great Debate, 1890–1920*. Philadelphia: University of Pennsylvania Press, 1970.

Toppin, Edgar A. "The Negro Suffrage Issue in Postbellum Ohio Politics." *Journal of Human Relations* 11 (Winter 1963): 232–46.

Trachtenberg, Alan. *The Incorporation of America: Culture and Society in the Gilded Age*. New York: Hill and Wang, 1982.

Trask, David F. *The War with Spain in 1898*. New York: Macmillan Publishing Company, 1981.

Trefousse, Hans L. *Carl Schurz: A Biography*. Knoxville: University of Tennessee Press, 1982.

Turk, Richard W. *The Ambiguous Relationship: Theodore Roosevelt and Alfred Thayer Mahan*. New York: Greenwood Press, 1987.

Twain, Mark. *Mark Twain's Speeches*. New York: Harper and Brothers, 1910.

Tyler, Alice Felt. *The Foreign Policy of James G. Blaine*. Minneapolis: University of Minnesota Press, 1927.

U.S. Congress. *Congressional Globe*. 46 vols. Washington, D.C., 1834–73.

U.S. Department of State. *Papers Relating to the Foreign Relations of the United States*. Washington, D.C.: Government Printing Office, 1870–1946.

VanDeusen, John G. "The Exodus of 1879." *Journal of Negro History* 21 (April 1936): 111–29.

Varg, Paul A. *United States Foreign Relations, 1820–1860*. East Lansing: Michigan State University Press, 1979.

Villard, Oswald Garrison. *Fighting Years: Memoirs of a Liberal Editor*. New York: Harcourt Brace, 1939.

Volwiler, Albert T. *The Correspondence between Benjamin Harrison and James G. Blaine, 1882–1893*. Philadelphia: American Philosophical Society, 1940.

Walzer, Michael. *What It Means to Be an American*. New York: Marsilio Publishing, 1992.

Wang, Xi. *The Trial of Democracy: Black Suffrage and Northern Republicans, 1860–1910*. Athens: University of Georgia Press, 1997.

Weinberg, Albert K. *Manifest Destiny: A Study in Nationalist Expansionism in American History*. Baltimore: Johns Hopkins University Press, 1935.

Welch, Richard E. *George Frisbie Hoar and the Half-Breed Republicans*. Cambridge: Harvard University Press, 1971.

———. "Motives and Objectives of the Anti-Imperialists, 1898." *Mid-America* 51 (April 1969): 119–29.

———. *The Presidencies of Grover Cleveland*. Lawrence: University Press of Kansas, 1988.

———. *Response to Imperialism: The United States in the Philippine-American War, 1899–1902*. Chapel Hill: University of North Carolina Press, 1979.

Welles, Gideon. *The Diary of Gideon Welles.* 3 vols. Boston: Houghton Mifflin, 1911.

Welles, Sumner. *Naboth's Vineyard: The Dominican Republic, 1844–1924.* New York: Payson and Clarke Limited, 1928.

Werking, Richard H. "Senator Henry Cabot Lodge and the Philippines: A Note on American Territorial Expansion." *Pacific Historical Review* 43 (May 1973): 234–40.

Weston, Rubin. *Racism in U.S. Imperialism: The Influence of Racial Assumptions on American Foreign Policy, 1893–1946.* Columbia: University of South Carolina Press, 1972.

White, Leonard. *The Republican Era: A Study in Administrative History, 1869–1901.* New York: Free Press, 1965.

Whittaker, William George. "Samuel Gompers, Anti-Imperialist." *Pacific Historical Review* 38 (December 1969): 429–45.

Wiarda, Howard J. *The Dominican Republic: Nation in Transition.* New York: Frederick A. Praeger, 1969.

Widenor, William C. *Henry Cabot Lodge and the Search for an American Foreign Policy.* Berkeley: University of California Press, 1980.

Wiebe, Robert H. *The Search for Order, 1877–1920.* New York: Hill and Wang, 1967.

Williams, Charles Richard, ed. *Diary and Letters of Rutherford Birchard Hayes, 19th President of the United States.* 5 vols. Columbus: Ohio Archeological and Historical Society, 1922–26.

Williams, R. Hal. *Years of Decision: American Politics in the 1890s.* New York: John Wiley and Sons, 1978.

Williams, Walter A. "United States Policy and the Debate over Philippine Annexation: Implications for the Origins of American Imperialism." *Journal of American History* 66 (March 1980): 810–31.

Williams, William Appleman. "Brooks Adams and American Expansion." *New England Quarterly* 15 (June 1952): 217–32.

———. *The Tragedy of American Diplomacy.* New York: W. W. Norton and Company, 1988.

Williamson, Joel. *The Crucible of Race.* New York: Oxford University Press, 1984.

———. *A Rage for Order: Black-White Relations in the American South since Emancipation.* New York: Oxford University Press, 1986.

Wittke, Carl. "Carl Schurz and Rutherford B. Hayes." *Ohio Historical Quarterly* 65 (October 1956): 337–55.

Wong, K. Scott, and Sucheng Chan. *Claiming America: Constructing Chinese American Identities during the Exclusion Era.* Philadelphia: Temple University Press, 1998.

Woodward, C. Vann. *Origins of the New South, 1877–1913.* Baton Rouge: Louisiana State University Press, 1951.

———. "Seeds of Failure in Radical Race Policy." In *New Frontiers of the American Reconstruction*, edited by Harold M. Hyman, 125–47. Urbana: University of Illinois Press, 1966.

——. *The Strange Career of Jim Crow*. New York: Oxford University Press, 1974.

——. *Tom Watson: Agrarian Rebel*. New York: Oxford University Press, 1938.

Young, Marilyn Blatt. "American Expansion, 1870–1900: The Far East." In *Towards a New Past: Dissenting Essays in American History*, edited by Barton Bernstein, 176–201. New York: Pantheon Books, 1968.

Zimmerman, Warren. *First Great Triumph: How Five Americans Made Their Country a World Power*. New York: Farrar, Straus and Giroux, 2002.

Index

Adams, Charles Francis, 29
Adams, Henry, 28, 52, 53, 165, 177
Adams, John Quincy, 81, 83
African Americans, xiii, xiv, 8–9, 15–17, 45, 46, 48, 49, 70–72, 93
Agassiz, Louis, 31, 32, 57
Alaska, 7, 28, 32, 33, 44, 58
Aldrich, Nelson, 194
Alexander, DeAlva, 152, 154, 155
Alien and Sedition Acts, xiii
Allen, William V., 193
Allen resolution, 193–94
American Colonization Society, 19, 46
American Federation of Labor (AFL), 80, 141, 142, 183
American Protective Association, xii
Anderson, Rufus, 84, 85, 107
Anglo-Saxonism, xi, xii, 1, 2, 8, 127, 128, 164
Aristotle, 24, 57
Armstrong, Samuel Chapman, 109–10
Armstrong, W. D., 116
Armstrong, W. N., 118

Babcock, Orville, 37–38, 40, 41, 43, 58
Bacon, Augustus, 190, 195

Bacon resolution, 190
Baez, Buenaventura, 36–37
Bancroft, George, 48
Banks, Mary Theodosia, 33
Banks, Nathaniel, 33, 37, 61, 64
Barnett, Ferdinand, 16
Bell, John, 155
Benevolent assimilation, xi, xii, xvii, 1, 8, 24
Benton, Thomas Hart, 19
Beveridge, Albert, 3, 6
Bingham, Hiram, 107
Bird, Isabella, 86–87, 107
Bishop, Artemis, 85, 86
Bishop, Sereno, 106–7, 122
Blaine, James G., 24, 66–67, 89, 90, 97, 136; response to Asian immigration in Hawaii, 90–93; resists annexation of Hawaii, 93; race and annexation of Hawaii, 93–95
Bligh, William, 84
Blisk, Samuel, 115
Blount, James H., 79, 80, 110, 111, 113, 123
Bryan, William Jennings, 131, 164, 194
Bryce, James, 128–30, 184
Burgess, John W., 118, 119

Burlingame Treaty (1868), 10, 11
Bush, Charles, 179–80
Butler, Benjamin, 37
Butler, Matthew, 78

Caffrey, Donelson, 189–90
Calhoun, John C., 21–22
Camden, Johnson, 78
Cameron, Elizabeth, 177
Carlisle, John, 78, 96
Carnegie, Andrew, 177, 181
Carpenter, Matthew, 60
Cass, Lewis, 23
Cazneau, William, 35, 36, 38, 68
Chinese Exclusion Acts (1882, 1892), xvii, 11, 15, 25, 75, 76, 78, 106, 119, 133; as obstacles to annexation, 149, 151
Chipman, John, 78
Civil War, 20, 100
Clarke, Champ, 150, 155
Cleveland, Grover, 74, 78, 79, 96, 104, 110, 111, 112, 113, 115, 120, 125, 131, 132, 157
Comly, James, 89, 91, 92, 94
Cook, Captain James, 81, 82, 84
Cooley, Thomas, 127–28
Coolidge, L. A., 171
Cortelyou, George, 165
Cox, Jacob, 40, 67–68
Cuba, xi, 39, 44, 61, 99, 128, 129, 130, 145, 161, 164, 174, 186, 189, 194
Cushing, Caleb, 56, 99

Davis, Cushman, 134
Davis, Garrett, 56
Davis, Jefferson, 65, 99
Davis, John C. Bancroft, 60, 61, 62
Day, William Rufus, 133, 171
Dewey, Commodore George, 148, 149, 157, 160, 165, 167, 168, 169, 174
Dinsmore, Hugh, 149
Dixon, Captain George, 84

Dole, Anna Prentice, 156–57
Dole, Charles Fletcher, 116
Dole, Sanford, 110, 112, 115, 116, 117, 118, 119, 125, 134, 136, 144
Dominican Republic (Santo Domingo), xvi, 7, 29–45 passim, 49, 50, 55, 56, 58, 65, 68, 69, 71, 72, 197
Douglas, Stephen, 19
Douglass, Frederick, 16, 57
Du Bois, W. E. B., 16–17
Dunne, Peter Finley, 162

Emerson, Ralph Waldo, 24

Fabens, Joseph, 35, 36, 37, 38, 43, 61, 63, 68
Fish, Hamilton, 13, 38, 40, 52, 55, 60, 62, 63, 64, 97, 100; racial attitudes of, 39; impressions of Caribbean, 39–40; sees racism as obstacle to annexation, 48–49; proposes compromises in annexation treaty, 62
Fiske, John, 27, 31
Foraker Act, 200
Force Bill (Federal Elections Bill of 1890), xii
Foster, John W., 74, 75, 76, 79, 95, 96, 109, 111, 131, 132, 133
Franklin, Benjamin, xii, 18–19
Frye, William, 132

Gardiner, Julia, 81
Garfield, James A., 101–2, 126
George, Henry, 11
Gillett, Frederick, 152
Godkin, E. L., 32, 33, 125, 126
Gompers, Samuel, 80, 183; racial objections to annexation of Philippines, 184
Gorman, Arthur, 78
Grant, Jesse, 72
Grant, Ulysses S., xiv–xvii, 13, 33–35, 40,

41, 42, 51, 52, 60, 62, 64, 66, 103; on
imperialism, 42–43; justifies annexation of Dominican Republic, 43–47;
and race and annexation, 45–47;
silence on race, 47–50, 55; ends silence
on race and annexation, 69–72
Greeley, Horace, 32, 33
Greene, Francis V., 175
Gregg, David L., 98, 99
Gresham, Walter, 78, 79, 96, 105, 111, 112,
113, 114
Guam, xi, 7, 174

Haalilio, Prince Timoteo, 81, 83
Haiti, xiii, 36, 37, 41, 44, 49, 56, 65, 197
Hamilton, John C., 52
Hanna, Mark, 11
Harrison, Benjamin, 74, 76, 79
Hatch, Francis, 132, 134
Hawaii, xi, xvii, 3, 6, 7, 10, 11, 13, 29, 30,
74–84 passim, 98, 100, 102, 112, 114,
119, 120, 121, 128–45 passim, 149, 150,
151, 160, 191, 192; population decline
in, 84–88; labor crisis in, 88; Chinese
immigration to, 88, 91–92, 94–95;
Japanese immigration to, 88–89, 134;
Asian presence in, 94, 96, 103, 107, 116,
117, 118, 123, 124, 129, 133–51 passim,
155; Japanese seen as threat in, 95–96,
134–37, 145, 147, 152; 1896 racial and
ethnic profile in, 130
Hay, John, 11, 165, 168, 170, 177, 178
Hayes, Rutherford, 64, 66
Hippocrates, 24
Hitt, Robert, 152, 154, 155
Hoar, Ebenezer Rockwell, 63, 64
Hoar, George Frisbie, 13, 153, 158, 191,
194
Hobart, Garret, 195
Hobart, George, 169
Homestead Act, 31
Hughes, Langston, xvi, 1

Immigration Restriction League, xii,
119, 185
Imperialism, xi, 1, 2, 3, 5
Insular Cases, 197, 199

Jefferson, Thomas, 19, 21, 46, 131
Johnson, Andrew, 37, 43, 113
Jusseraud, Jules, 168

Kalahaua, King, 90
Kamehameha III, King, 81, 82, 97
Kamehameha IV, King, 88
Kearney, Dennis, 11
Kipling, Rudyard, xviii, 6, 198
Know-Nothing Party, xiii, 113
Ku Klux Klan, 47

Labor unions: on annexation of Hawaii,
141–43
Laffan, William, 181
Liliuokalani, Queen, 73, 74, 77, 79, 96,
106, 107, 108, 111, 112, 113, 115, 156, 157
Lincoln, Abraham, 19, 46
Lodge, Henry Cabot, 11, 24, 121, 122, 124,
125, 131, 164, 173, 184, 194; ideas on
expansion, 125–26; places racial limitations on expansion, 126–27; on
annexation of Philippines, 159–60,
170–71; writes McKinley on annexation of Philippines, 171–72; arguments for annexation in Senate, 192–
93
Long, John Davis, 169
Lowell, James Russell, 89

Madison, James, 18
Mahan, Alfred Thayer, 11, 125, 165, 179;
on annexation of Hawaii, 108; ambiv-
alence toward Philippines, 159, 162
Manifest destiny, xi, 2, 44, 100, 104, 105
Marcy, William, 98, 99, 100
Marshall, George Catlett, 162

Marx, Karl, xiv, xv
McBride, James, 97
McCorkle, J. W., 97
McCreary, James, 78
McDowell, Calvin, 15, 16
McEnery, Samuel, 194
McKinley, William, 3, 14, 131, 132, 135,
  141, 143, 144, 145, 148, 162, 163, 194;
  reputation among contemporaries
  and historians, 164–65; decision to
  annex Philippines, 165–76, 179; race
  and annexation decision, 179–81
McKinley Tariff, 74
McLaurin, John, 13, 190–91, 194
Mela, Pomponius, 24
Mexican War, 21, 42–43, 97; race and
  annexation in aftermath of, 21–24, 97
Mexico, 6, 23, 59, 74
Midway Islands, 7, 28
Mississippi Plan, xviii, 4, 24, 106, 116,
  119, 199
Monroe Doctrine, 44, 47, 63, 68, 130,
  148, 160, 161, 162, 175, 199
Moore, John Bassett, 159
Morgan, John Tyler, 78, 188; on annexa-
  tion of Hawaii, 109, 149; opposes
  annexation of Philippines, 158, 185–
  86
Morrill, Justin, 150
Morrill Land-Grant College Act, 31
Morton, Oliver, 58, 113
Moss, Thomas, 15, 16
Motley, John Lothrop, 64

Native Americans, xii, 8, 15, 18
Naturalization Act (1790), xiii, 19
Necker Island, 120
Nelson, Knute, 191, 192
Newlands, Francis, 148, 154, 155

Olney, Richard, 111, 157
Open Door Notes, 200

Pacific Railroad Act, 31
Penn, Irvine Garland, 16
Pettigrew, Richard, 121–24, 131, 156
Pierce, Charles, 154
Pierce, Edward L., 57
Pierce, Franklin, 99, 100
Philippines, xi, xvii, 3, 7, 10, 13, 14, 80,
  148–99 passim
Plato, 57
Platt, Orville, 188–89
Platt Amendment, 200
Plessy v. Ferguson (1895), 25, 199
Polk, James K., 99
Portuguese, 118, 123, 124; racially con-
  structed as "white," 139, 146, 154
Puerto Rico, xi, 35, 161, 174, 185, 194, 200

Race, xi, xiv, xv
Race ideology, xiv; critique of as analyt-
  ical term, 5–8, 11
Racialism, xiv
Racism, xi, xii; defined, xv; as analytical
  concept, 14–17
Reconstruction, xii, xvi
Reed, Thomas B., 148, 164
Reid, Whitelaw, 119–20, 170
Revels, Hiram, 58
Richards, William, 81, 83
Roach, William, 150
Roosevelt, Theodore, 11, 13, 125, 159, 162,
  165, 179, 196, 197, 198, 200
Roosevelt Corollary, 200
Root, Elihu, 197

St. Thomas, 28, 34, 39, 40, 42
Santo Domingo. See Dominican
  Republic
Schurz, Carl, 13, 24, 53, 54, 62, 63, 64, 65,
  67, 70, 96, 103, 111, 125, 126, 184;
  opposes annexation of Dominican
  Republic, 53–55, 59–60; racial objec-
  tions to annexation of Dominican

Republic, 59–60; on annexation of Hawaii, 104–5, 106; racial objections to annexation of Philippines, 182–83

Severence, Luther, 97

Seward, William Henry, 22, 24, 28, 29, 30, 33, 34, 35, 37, 39, 41, 97, 98, 100

Sewell, Harold, 156

Sherman, John, 133, 141

Sherman, William Tecumseh, 38

Smith, William, 132

Social Darwinism, xi, 1, 3, 8, 13, 24, 25, 125, 164, 172

Sons of the American Revolution, 135–37; claim Hawaii for Americans, 136; warn of invasion from Asia, 136–37; respond to objections to annexation of Hawaii, 137

Spain, xi

Spanish-American War, xi, 1

Stevens, John L., 73, 74, 75, 79, 111, 113; on Asian presence in Hawaii, 95–96

Stewart, Henry, 15, 16

Stewart, William, 62

Storey, Moorefield, 57

Strauss, Oscar, 167

Strong, George Templeton, 32

Strong, Josiah, 3, 6, 125

Sumner, Charles, 13, 14, 32, 33, 39, 50, 52, 53, 56, 60, 65, 70, 126; racial objections to annexation, 56–57, 65–66; opposes annexation of Dominican Republic, 56–58

Sumner, William Graham, 13

Supreme Court, xiii

Taney, Roger, 19

Taylor, Hannis, 181

Teller, Henry, 189

Teller Amendment, 164, 178, 194

Texas, 6

Thornton, Sir Edward, 49, 50, 51

Thurston, Lorrin, 111, 154; argues for "American-ness" of Hawaii, 137–38; on dangers of Asian presence in Hawaii, 138, 139, 140; on essential whiteness of Hawaii, 138–39, 140; constructs Portuguese population as "white," 139, 146

Tillman, Benjamin, 191, 194

Tocqueville, Alexis de, 9, 24–25

Twain, Mark, 43, 86, 107

Tyler, John, 81, 82–83, 97

Tyler Doctrine, 82–83, 84, 89, 148

Vest, George, 186, 187–88

Vest resolution, 186–87

Vietnam, 14

Washington, George, xiii, 18, 131

Webster, Daniel, 81, 82, 83, 97

Welles, Gideon, 46

White, Stephen, 150

White man's burden, xi, xii, xvii, 1, 2, 3, 4, 6, 8, 24, 25, 151, 164

"White Man's Burden" (Kipling poem), 6, 198

Whiteness: and nation building, xii–xiii; effects on expansion, 12, 17–25; circumscribes expansion, 24–25, 54, 55, 57, 60, 116, 126–27, 155–56; as justification for annexation of Hawaii, 108, 110, 137–38, 144, 145–46, 152–55; as reason not to annex Hawaii, 128–29, 150, 155–56; and Portuguese in Hawaii, 139, 145–46, 154; as reason not to annex Philippines, 158, 183, 184–85

Willis, Albert S., 112

Wilson, Bluford, 111

World's Columbian Exposition (1893), 16

While whites valued expansion
only if it benefited whites,
blacks supported expansion to
incorporate the darker races & open
space for Bl. Americans only?